THE SUGAR RAY ROBINSON STORY

THE SUGAR RAY ROBINSON STORY

BOXING'S COMEBACK KING

JOHN JARRETT

First published by Pitch Publishing, 2019

Pitch Publishing
A2 Yeoman Gate
Yeoman Way
Worthing
Sussex
BN13 3QZ
www.pitchpublishing.co.uk
info@pitchpublishing.co.uk

A CIP catalogue record is available for this book
from the British Library.

ISBN 978 1 78531 535 0

Typesetting and origination by Pitch Publishing

Printed and bound by TJ International, Cornwall

CONTENTS

1
IN THE BEGINNING

AILEY IS a city in Montgomery County, Georgia, USA. According to the US Census Bureau, the city has a total area of two square miles.

In the 1920 census, the population numbered 385. Under Notable Persons are the names of Hugh Peterson, lawyer, and Sugar Ray Robinson, boxer. Ailey's claim to be the birthplace of Robinson is somewhat tenuous at best. Of nine sources, three list Ailey as Robinson's birthplace and six Detroit. There are seven birthdates in 1921 and two in 1920.

In his 2007 book *Being Sugar Ray,* author Kenneth Shropshire wrote, 'When Sugar Ray was born 3 May 1921 [that is the most consistent birthdate cited] the Smith family already had two girls, but many of the details of his early life are speculative. We can't be sure when or where he was born. To some extent, that is the way Robinson chose to live his life. Spinning a yarn, holding back on details, telling the story the audience wanted to hear – that was part of his genesis legend. It is also possible that he simply did not know.

'In his autobiography [ghostwritten by Dave Anderson] he says that he travelled to Detroit from Ailey, Georgia in his mother's womb. That certainly makes for a more compelling account about where his life began. In fact, many traditional explanations have him born in Detroit. Robinson's birth certificate says that he was born in Ailey in 1921.'[1] Walker Smith had grown up on a farm just outside Dublin, Georgia. He married a local girl, Leila Hurst, who had worked on a farm, and together they raised cotton, corn and peanuts, and children. Marie was born in 1917, followed by Evelyn two years later. Leila's sister and her husband lived in Detroit and they wrote back telling of plenty of good paying jobs. That sounded good to Walker Smith and he decided to go to Detroit, get a job and send for Leila and the children when he had saved enough money. Working on a construction site, he was soon making $60 a week and was able to send for Leila and the girls to join him.

'Pop had rented the first floor of a wooden frame house on McComb Street in Detroit's Black Bottom section,' Robinson would recall. 'It was Black because we lived there, Bottom because that's where we were at. That's where I was born on 3 May 1921. No hospital for me. No doctor, either. I arrived in Mom's bed with a midwife officiating at my first weigh-in. Seven pounds, 12 ounces. When Pop got home that night, he had my name picked out. "Junior," he told Mom. "My first boy baby has got to be a junior." Walker Smith, Junior. No middle name. Pop always called me Junior. Nobody ever called me Walker.'[2]

Walker Smith worked hard and he played hard. A sharp dresser, he liked a drink or two and Leila would argue with him about spending money. Junior was almost six when his mother packed him and his sisters on a train headed back to Georgia, to her mother's farm at Glenwood. Pop wasn't with them because Leila hadn't told him they were leaving. She returned to Detroit, where she worked at a big hotel. About a year later, Leila was back in Georgia. She wanted a divorce but she had to have the children living with her, so she went back to her mother's farm, gathered up her brood and headed back to Detroit.

---

1 Kenneth Shropshire *Being Sugar Ray* 2007

2 Sugar Ray Robinson with Dave Anderson *Sugar Ray* 1969

Junior had loved being on the farm, but now he was back in the city, back in Black Bottom, and it still looked black. Leila had a new job as a seamstress and she worried about Junior getting into trouble with the street gangs. Actually, the kid had started hanging around the Brewster Centre, which pleased his mother and she would give him the 25 cents, the monthly dues, which she really couldn't afford. Walker Smith Jr was taking his first steps on the road to fame and fortune.

Located at 637 Brewster Street, between St Antoines and Hastings, the two-storey red-brick building was Detroit's first community centre for blacks, opening in October 1929. Every day the basement gym was jammed with young men skipping, sparring, hitting punch bags of all size and weight, watched by older men chewing unlit cigars, a dirty towel slung around their neck, shouting rough instructions to their favourite fighter. Becoming one of the favourites was a husky young fellow named Joe Louis Barrow. Joe was a particular favourite of Walker Smith Jr. Joe couldn't get rid of the kid. He would follow Joe to the gym, tagging along behind the big fellow, and if Joe let him carry his gym bag, Junior was walking ten feet tall. He broke his heart when Joe, at that time a 17-year-old middleweight, took a whipping in his first amateur fight from Johnny Miler, a more experienced light-heavyweight who dropped Joe seven times and took the decision. Joseph Louis Barrow would later become Joe Louis, possibly the greatest heavyweight champion of all time.

Shortly after that, in early 1932, Leila loaded her family on to a bus headed for New York City. In her handbag was a letter she had received, with the address of a three-room flat. 'Four-nineteen West Fifty-third Street, that's near Times Square,' she told the kids. After paying the rent, she had exactly 40 cents left in her purse. That same day, dusting the shelves in her new home, she found 35 cents. With the 40 she already had, it was enough for supper that first night in New York.

'Leila Smith had been a field hand in the South,' wrote Wil Haygood in his 2009 biography of Robinson. 'She did not have a fragile psyche: she was coarse and blunt and aggressive with her language. She argued with grocery store clerks over bills and she argued with rent collectors. When little Walker seemed to need a hug, he often received more tough words from his mother, stinging language about standing up, about pride. Economic miseries were everywhere. In 1932, millions of Americans were losing jobs by the month. Wages were down 40 per cent compared to just three years earlier. Impoverished children were especially vulnerable. Little Walker Smith, who always seemed to be hungry, took free lunches at the local Salvation Army – "hot dogs and beans," he would sadly remember.'[3]

Junior was 13 years old and weighed about 85 pounds when he hammered some kid called Shake. When his sister's boyfriend pulled him off, the other kid's blood was all over the sidewalk and Junior felt pretty good about himself. He felt better a couple of days later when a little guy named Benny Booksinger stopped him in the street and said he had heard about him fighting and would like him to box on one of his amateur bills for the Police Athletic League. Junior beat a boy called Harmon over three rounds and was ready to fight the kid's big brother when his mother stepped in and chased him home and chased Benny Booksinger off the street.

'But Benny liked what he saw of young Smitty and kept matching him on his cards around the city. He won most of them but a tough little Irish kid beat him over three rounds one night. Years later, Billy Graham would remind Junior of that fight. "You know who the kid was?" he asked the fighter who had become Sugar Ray Robinson. "I never saw him again," said Ray. "You're looking at him now," said Graham, who had become a top welterweight contender. "Before the fight all the kids thought you were Joe Louis's nephew, because you had known him from Detroit. I was scared stiff." "You didn't fight like it," said Robinson.[4]

3 Wil Haygood *Sweet Thunder: The Life and Times of Sugar Ray Robinson* 2009

4 Sugar Ray Robinson with Dave Anderson *Sugar Ray* 1969

When young Walker Smith Jr was a pupil at Cooper Junior High School, a boy in his class named Warren Jones, an amateur boxer, told him his uncle was a trainer at the Salem-Crescent gym, which was in the basement of the Salem Methodist Church at 129th Street and Seventh Avenue. Leila Smith and her family were now living in Harlem, and one thing she noticed in her new community was the number of churches. Now it looked as though the church was going to save her son from the dangers of this new concrete jungle. 'Now he found himself in a neighbourhood rough at the best of times and now battered by the Depression, a place that could gobble him up, but he wouldn't let it. That descent into a church basement offered a kind of clarity he had never felt before. The boy – whose independent mind seems to have sprung directly from his strong-willed mother – could not allow a moment's worth of fear down where the fists were flying. The officials explained to him what was expected of a member of the Salem-Crescent Athletic Club, the name the young pugilists fought under. He told his mother about Salem-Crescent and its vaunted boxing programme. He wanted to join and his enthusiasm filled Leila Smith with joy. He would fight, just as she had long told him to, just as she herself did whenever she had to. She delighted in knowing that her son would have authority figures watching over him and teaching him, a mission his own father had abandoned.'[5]

One of the figures watching over Junior was George Gainford, who was big in amateur boxing around New York City. Gainford was big anywhere, standing over 6ft tall and packing 250 pounds on that frame. Junior's friend, Warren Jones, took him to the Salem-Crescent gym one night and introduced him to his Uncle George. George was not impressed. 'Smitty,' he said, 'What do you weigh?' Smitty answered, 'Hundred and eleven.' 'And how old are you?' 'Fifteen last month.' 'I need another flyweight,' Gainford said. 'Come back tomorrow and I'll take a look at you.'

---

5 Wil Haygood *Sweet Thunder: The Life and Times of Sugar Ray Robinson* 2009

'But after seeing the kid work out, Gainford realised there was a spark in the boy that could be fanned into possible greatness. So the big-hearted coach dug down in his own pocket and came up with $25 which he handed to the boy for equipment. "Take this money, Junior, and get yourself trunks, shoes, socks and a pair of punching bag gloves. Report back here tomorrow. We're going to work."

'A week later, there was still no sign of the boy, who had taken the money and happily dashed away. Gainford was more than slightly put out. He went looking for his protégé, found him, and dragged him back to the gym. Stern questioning revealed that the kid had spent the money. Fortunately for the future champion, Gainford forgave him; but to punish him, he made Smitty work out in his underwear shorts for a few days before buying him the necessary equipment. He continued to make Junior work – and work hard. Gainford knew how to make a boxer out of promising raw material.'[6]

'At first he didn't look like much fighter,' Gainford recalled. 'All he did was hit and run, but he had one thing. He wanted to learn. He was the first kid in the gym and the last to leave.'

Gainford had a problem with Walker Smith Jr. As the weeks went by, he could see the improvement in the boy and it excited him, but in the back of his mind were the words of Leila Smith. She had come to the gym one night and told him in no uncertain terms was he to make a fighter out of her son. She didn't mind Junior coming to the gym, it was keeping him off the streets. Just so long as he didn't fight. So Junior would go with the lads George was taking to fight in various tournaments and he was happy doing that. He would sit and watch the fights and tell Gainford afterwards, 'I could have beaten some of those kids in there tonight, no trouble.' And big George knew he was right.

One night in Kingston, New York, Junior's dream came true. The Amateur Athletic Union (AAU) organiser asked Gainford

---

6 Gene Schoor *Sugar Ray Robinson* 1951

if he had a flyweight in his pocket as he was short of a bout. Gainford said he didn't have a flyweight on the team, but then Junior 'reminded' him. 'Put me in,' he pleaded. The trainer thought for a moment, then called the guy back, telling him he had a flyweight ready to fight. Junior didn't have an AAU card but Gainford quickly rifled through a handful of cards he always carried with him and held one out, 'This is Ray Robinson, here.' he said. 'This is his card.'

'Minutes later, he found himself in the ring, surrounded by noise and lights and the whispering which suddenly seemed loud and George Gainford standing over him and his Salem-Crescent mates cheering him on. "As scared as I was," he would recall, "I was happy." He swung; some of his punches were wild, but more often than not he connected. Gainford yelled from the corner; his boxing mates yelled; the lights got in his eyes, but he moved about the ring with a quickness that surprised even Gainford. He was antsy between rounds, like someone who had been wound up. In the third round, he let loose with a barrage of jabs that excited the gathered boxing fans. The judge had seen enough; "Robinson" was declared, at the end of the third, a unanimous winner. Gainford was happily surprised, grabbing his fighter, wrapping a towel around his neck, grinning wide.

'It is that first amateur victory that the prizefighter remembers with nostalgic rapture. He had done something solid and enviable with his hands; he was flush with talent and knew it. He did not know exactly how he had done it for his fists had been flying so fast. That was the magic and sweetness of it. It was almost beyond explanation. For years and years afterwards, Robinson would regale writers with the story of this fight in Kingston, as if it were the beginning of his realisation of being on earth.'[7]

That was how Walker Smith Jr became Ray Robinson. He would use the name from that time on. 'I knew the real Ray Robinson,' recalled Ray, 'and in the years that followed he liked

---

7 Wil Haygood *Sweet Thunder:The Life and Times of Sugar Ray Robinson* 2009

to tease me that I'd stolen his name. I couldn't argue with him. The last time I saw him, he was a bartender.' After that, the new Ray Robinson fought all around the bootleg circuit. The bouts were supposed to be amateur. The boxers would get a watch, then the guy would buy it back and give them $10. There were bouts for him in Waterbury, Danbury, New Haven, Hartford, Bridgeport, sometimes he fought three times in a week, and loved it.

'I don't know how many bootleg fights I had,' he said. 'Maybe a couple of hundred. We got maybe $10 if we won, maybe eight if we lost. Ray didn't lose. George Gainford would add, "I made a living with them fights during the Depression."'

'We used to fight out of Norwich, Connecticut,' Willie Pep recalled, 'sometimes at this place called DU-WELL A.C. I always got a kick out of that. I was amateur flyweight champion of Connecticut at the time and we used to fight the Salem-Crescent A.C. from Harlem, New York. Black kids who could really fight. Anyway, I saw this real tall kid come in and when I said to my manager, "Who's that?" he said, "That's the guy you're gonna fight." I said, "Be serious, look at that guy." You see, at that time I was a flyweight. I weighed about 105 pounds, and this guy was about 128, a featherweight. So Buster said, "Don't worry, don't worry. He can't be any good fighting you."

'Well, I fight this guy and he's all over me. He's too good. Too big. He's punching me and punching me and I'm just trying to hang in there. When it ended and the guy won, I heard his name was Ray Roberts. Later on I find out that, too, is a phoney name because he was really Ray Robinson. Since Ray, who fought his amateur career under his real name, Walker Smith, was amateur, he couldn't pick up any money in New York, and he came to Connecticut, where amateurs were allowed to fight for money. This was in 1938.'[8]

Robinson would remember that fight. 'I was with George in Hartford, Connecticut. The promoter there had George bring

8 *Friday's Heroes* Willie Pep with Robert Sacchi 1973

me up to fight this kid who was unbeaten. I got the decision, a close one. It broke his winning streak. But he was some fighter, a little Italian kid. "What's his name again?" I asked somebody after the fight. "Willie Papaleo," he said, "but around here, Willie Pep." In later years, Willie Pep would win the world featherweight championship, and he was the best boxer I ever saw. After that victory, I was getting dressed when a Hartford policeman marched in with one of the local amateur boxing officials.

"Gainford," the cop said, "you and your fighter better come with me. Some of the people around here think your fighter has to be a pro if he beat Willie Pep here. I'm going to have to lock you both up for the night until the people here can check with the AAU in NewYork in the morning." George exploded but it didn't do any good. We went to jail. Next morning, the Hartford promoter checked with Ben Levine, the AAU boxing man in New York, and he vouched for my amateur standing.'[9]

The night of 5 January 1939 was a significant one in the career of Ray Robinson. He was in the little town of Watertown in upstate New York, about 30 miles from the Canadian border, leading the Salem-Crescent team into battle. Ray's opponent was a tough brawler, Dom Perfetti, an Eastern States champion. Scheduled for five rounds, it was all action from the opening bell with Robinson going at top speed, outboxing and outpunching the bantamweight. It was over in the fifth, the champion beaten, and Gainford was in the ring wrapping a towel around his neck. Watching from the press row was Jack Case, sports editor of *The Watertown Times.* As Ray came down from the ring with big George behind him, Case told George, 'That's a sweet fighter you've got there, a real sweet fighter.'

A woman spectator heard Case, and smiled. "Sweet as sugar," she said. Next morning, Ray would read Case's report. 'Sugar Robinson, clever little New York mittman, proved to be everything his nickname implied at the Starbeck Avenue arena Wednesday

---

9 Sugar Ray Robinson with Dave Anderson *Sugar Ray* 1969

night where he boxed his way to a five-round decision over Dom Perfetti, Eastern States champion.'

A boxing legend was born that night. Sugar Ray Robinson. 'It rolled almost liltingly from the lips, as if the three names were a stitched-together appellation of something elegant and athletic,' wrote Wil Haygood in his book. 'He said the name to himself over and over again. He was his own man now. The kid in the mirror, the kid who had tramped along the streets in Black Bottom in Detroit, the kid who had sat staring out over Manhattan's East River wondering about his fate, began to feel as if he had reinvented himself. The name was his now and it made him smile when he heard it uttered. "Walker Smith Jr was a forgotten man," the young fighter would declare.'[10]

10 Wil Haygood *Sweet Thunder: The Life and Times of Sugar Ray Robinson* 2009

2
BEATING A CHAMP

HER NAME was Marjorie Joseph and Junior called her Marjie when he met her at a local dance and they started dating that night in early 1938. He had money in his pocket from the bootleg fights and was able to take her to the movies and to dances. Sometimes he would visit her when she was home for lunch and that became a regular thing for the two lovebirds. And that's how the trouble started. Marjie got pregnant and Junior was in a spin. He had to tell somebody and he told sister Marie, who usually saved him when the other kids chased him all the way home. Marie said he had to tell Mom. He didn't want to but he had to and Leila did what she thought was best. Next day, she marched Junior round to Marjie's home and laid her cards on the table. But when she told Marjie's parents that her son would marry their daughter, Mr Joseph shook his head and asked them to leave.

A few days later, Leila and her errant son were back at the Joseph house and she convinced Marjie's parents that marriage was the best option for the sake of the unborn child. It was agreed the youngsters would marry to give the baby a name, but they wouldn't live together. So the sad little ceremony was performed and the lovers went their separate ways. On 25 September, Marjie gave birth to a boy, who would be called Ronnie, and soon afterwards the marriage of Walker Smith Jr and Marjorie Joseph was annulled.

When Junior started making money in the bootleg fights, five, eight, ten dollars at a time, he asked Marie to hide it for him so that his mother didn't know he was fighting. Marie hid it in a shoe in her wardrobe. When Junior checked it one day, it was less than he thought it should be. Marie had to confess she 'borrowed' some one day to buy an outfit for a party. While they were arguing about it, Mom heard them and demanded to know what was going on. Junior had to tell her he was boxing. Her jaw dropped when she learned that he had close to $900 saved. She was making $20 a week as a seamstress. She agreed he could fight so long as he didn't get cut up. Then she would stop him.

When he begged her to let him quit school, she knew what to do. Leila knew that Dr Vincent Nardiello worked for the New York Commission so she went to see him, asking if he thought Junior could box and keep going to school at the same time. The good doctor weighed his words before saying to Leila, 'I doubt if your son ever will be a good student, but he might be a very good fighter.' So everything was all right. Leila even started making his boxing kit for him, new satin trunks and a blue bathrobe. And when she saw him shadow boxing at home one day, she said to punch at her but not to hit her. He laughed and started to call her Punch. Now they were all happy!

'I was boxing in the 1939 Golden Gloves tournament and George Gainford had warned us that anybody who got into trouble with the police was out of the tournament. No appeal. Out, man. Gone. I wasn't about to risk that. I was a featherweight then and my best buddy, another featherweight named Spider Valentine, was in the tournament too. We each kept winning, and the night of the city finals we were matched in the old Madison Square Garden.'[11]

Daily News sports editor Paul Gallico had a passion for amateur boxing and believed a boxing tournament would be as successful a promotion for the paper as the wildly popular Silver Skates Derby,

---

11 Sugar Ray Robinson with Dave Anderson *Sugar Ray*, 1959

an annual speed skating tournament that had been run by the paper since 1922. Prior to 1926, boxing in New York was limited to local bouts, with gambling, set-ups and fixed matches. Boxing had a bad name, in fact. Chicago had run a Golden Gloves competition organised by Arch Ward of the *Chicago Tribune* in 1922 before it was legislated out of existence in Illinois due to the illegal activities surrounding the game. Boxing was again legal in the state in 1928 and the Golden Gloves tournament was set up as a rival to the New York competition. The inter-city rivalry between New York City and Chicago lasted into the 1960s, drawing crowds of 20,000 wherever the matches took place.

It was at an informal meeting of top editors at the Villa Penza restaurant in New York's Little Italy in late 1926 that Gallico pitched his idea of a boxing tournament to publisher Capt. Joseph M. Patterson. As the paper had the Silver Skates, Gallico suggested, 'We'll call it the Golden Gloves.' 'Okay, Paul,' said Patterson. 'Get it going. But make sure it's good.' It was better than good, it was sensational. Within days, Gallico's desk was buried under more than 1,000 entries, so much so that he had to shorten the entry period. Overwhelmed, Gallico had to enlist sportswriter Al Copeland to help sort the entries and Dr Thomas DeNaouley to set up a medical programme. The first bouts took place at two venues in Brooklyn on 11 March 1927. Within a week, 15 new venues were added. Punches were flying all over the city and the soaring circulation of the *Daily News* made Capt. Patterson a happy man.

The eventual winners of the tournament would receive a pair of Golden Gloves, which were diamond studded and cost $65 – nearly double the $35 value limit set by the Amateur Athletic Union for prizes. Gallico argued for his Golden Gloves and got his way. Finals night was Monday, 28 March at Madison Square Garden and the cops had to shut down traffic on Eighth Avenue. If you didn't have a ticket, you couldn't get near the Garden. A record crowd of 21,594 was crammed inside the huge arena when the first bell rang, with an estimated 8,000 to 10,000 disappointed fans turned away. The Golden Gloves were here to stay.

Robinson's first year in the Gloves tournament, 1938, saw him beaten over three rounds by Pasquale 'Patsy' Pesca in the junior 118lb division at St Nick's Arena on 16 February. A year later, Sugar Ray Robinson was the talk of the city as he racked up knockouts on his way to the final. The papers were calling him 'Death' Ray Robinson. There was a roar from the capacity crowd as Ray entered the ring ahead of his stablemate Louis 'Spider' Valentine. They had trained together, palled around and done roadwork together. Now they were going to fight together and one of them would be the champion in three rounds or less. It looked like being less when Sugar dropped Spider with a left hook in the opening round. Then he did a funny thing. He walked forward and helped Spider get to his feet. 'You can't do that,' yelled the referee as the punches started to fly again. Trainer Harry Wiley was in Robinson's corner and when Ray got back to his stool, Wiley growled, 'The next time he falls, let the referee pick him up.'

Spider didn't fall again and the boys waited anxiously for the decision. It was for Sugar Ray and as he stood there in the centre of the ring a spotlight shone down on him, and a trumpet blared, 'The *New York Daily News* Golden Gloves featherweight champion for 1939, Sugar Ray Robinson!' 'He was so happy, he didn't want to leave the ring, or stop waving at the crowds as they applauded, but Wiley hurried him out of the ring. "You'll be back here soon enough," he said as they headed for the dressing room.'[12]

Harry was right about that. Robinson won the Tournament of Champions, beating Armand Dascenza, and the Intercity title at featherweight, beating Tony Ancona. Still growing, a year later he swept the board at lightweight in the Tournament of Champions, against Jimmy Butler, the Intercity title, beating old foe Tony Ancona, and the *Daily News* title, besting Andy Nonella.

---

12 Sugar Ray Robinson with Dave Anderson *Sugar Ray* 1959

Professional fight managers were circling like sharks, but they weren't just after Robinson.

The Salem-Crescent club had another star hitting the headlines. Heavyweight Buddy Moore was being touted as another Joe Louis after winning the *New York Daily News* open heavyweight championship, the Tournament of Champions and the Intercity match against Chicago. He was a knockout and Gainford already had a manager lined up for him. Curt Horrmann dressed well, drove a 16-cylinder Packard, dined at the Stork Club daily, and as Big George said, 'He can come up with a $100 bill faster than any man alive.'

Horrmann's family owned a brewery on Staten Island, Rubsam and Horrmann, and he was a millionaire looking to sign Buddy Moore to a contract. 'I might just let him,' said Gainford when Robinson asked who the stranger was hanging around the gym. 'He's talking about a lot of money.' Buddy Moore was no Sugar Ray. He turned professional with Horrmann and in a nine-year career lost 11 of 27 fights, seven by KO. Within a year, Horrmann had lost interest and was chasing Sugar Ray Robinson, and Ray wasn't running too fast.

When he made the change, Robinson's amateur career with George Gainford was listed as 85-0 with 69 knockouts, 40 in the first round. He had lost to Billy Graham and Patsy Pesca under his given name, Walker Smith Jr. He was 19 years old when he had his first fight for money on 4 October 1940. Horrmann's money and Sugar Ray's reputation got the new boy a four-round bout at Madison Square Garden on a world championship card, welterweight champion Henry Armstrong defending his title against Fritzie Zivic, a rough, tough guy from Pittsburgh.

Robinson's first opponent was Joe Echevarria, a Puerto Rican-born New Yorker with a 4-17-4 record, and he was no better than many of Ray's amateur victims. A sizzling left hook ended it in the second round. Robinson was happy, but he had noticed there were many empty ringside seats, not like in the amateurs. The people who had bought those seats would be in them for the main event. They would see a vicious 15-round battle as Zivic cut and slashed his way to a unanimous decision over Armstrong. Henry was a mess, with both eyes almost closed, and he was saved by the bell as the final round saw him dumped on his head by a smashing right from Zivic. In a ringside seat, Sugar Ray cried at the defeat of his idol. On the way home, he horrified his mother by saying he wanted to fight Zivic. 'I don't want you to ever fight that man, do you hear me?' she said. Ray heard, but he would get his wish in time.

In the dressing room after Ray had showered and dressed, Horrmann handed him a bundle of dollar bills. Ray counted $150, his entire purse for the fight, and when he protested, the manager said, 'It's your first pro fight, you keep all the money. I'll take care of George.' Pop had another surprise for Ray. He was going to box on the undercard of the Joe Louis-Red Burman fight at Madison Square Garden, and he would be training alongside his Detroit hero at Greenwood Lake in New York. Jack Blackburn, Joe's trainer, took a shine to the kid just starting out and gave him a few tips. The one Ray remembered was, 'Chappie [Blackburn called everyone Chappie and they called him that also] said, "Just keep your hands up and your ass off the floor."' Sugar Ray Robinson could do that better than anybody.

The young fighter had another surprise one night in Detroit. With 11 fights under his belt and eight knockouts, he was in the Motor City to fight Gene Spencer. He got a phone call the night before the fight, a man's voice saying, 'Is that Ray Robinson? It's your pop, Junior.' It was Walker Smith Sr. They hadn't seen each other for eight years and were still talking when George looked at his watch and sent Junior to bed. Next night, at the Olympia Stadium, Ray got rid of his man in four rounds and father and son went out on the town.

'In bars and restaurants and people's homes and on street corners, there was no prouder man than Walker Smith telling everyone he met, "This is *my* son." He had to swallow his pride next morning when he saw Junior off at the railroad station, telling his son, "Things have been a little hard for me, lately. I wonder if ..." "He didn't have to finish the sentence," recalled Ray. "I had a few hundred dollars in my pocket. I pulled them out and stuffed them into his hand. In the years that followed, he always showed up when I fought in Detroit or Cleveland or Chicago. I always gave him some money, whether he asked for it or not."'[13]

Sugar Ray asked Gainford to get him a few more fights in Detroit so that he could see more of his father, but Big George and Curt Horrmann had other plans for their young star. They signed him to meet Sammy Angott, the National Boxing Association lightweight champion, for promoter Herman Taylor at Shibe Park in Philadelphia. To protect his title, Angott insisted they both weigh over the 135-pound limit for the ten-round bout. The morning of the fight, Horrmann phoned room service and ordered half a dozen bananas and two quarts of milk. It was not the lunch Ray fancied but when he weighed in with the champ he hit the scales at 136½ pounds, as did Angott. Angott was born Salvatore Engotti in 1915 in Washington, Pennsylvania and by the time he climbed into the ring with Sugar Ray Robinson on 21 July 1941, he had won 60 of 80 professional fights. He was recognised by the NBA as their lightweight champion by virtue of a 15-round decision over Davey Day in May 1940. He had an unfortunate nickname, 'The Clutch', because of his habit of grabbing his opponent after landing a clean blow. Robinson suffered that for three minutes then chastised Sammy in the second round.

The United Press described the knockdown: 'Sugar's lashing right found its mark, hurling Angott to the canvas. The blow smashed Angott off his feet and he landed on his face, burning his cheek, and not a spectator in the house expected him to rise. Instinct alone raised him to his knees at the count of six and to his feet at nine, and he clung to Robinson with a cloud over his eyes throughout the rest of the round. Sugar Ray took the unanimous decision and said afterwards, "That punch was just too high in the

13 Sugar Ray Robinson with Dave Anderson *Sugar Ray* 1969

second round. If it had just been a little lower, I'd have knocked him out." Angott didn't know whether it was high or low. He didn't even know what hit him.'[14]

Having reeled off 21 unbeaten fights, Robinson collected his purse, $6,000. First thing he did was retire his mother from her job with the Modern Silver Linen Supply Company. Leila never worked again. Ray moved the family into a nice four-room apartment in St Nicholas Avenue, and next day a delivery van brought two bedroom sets, a parlour set and a kitchen set. His mother sat down and wept. She had never had new furniture before.

There was more good news. Ray was to fight his first main event at Madison Square Garden, ten rounds against Maxie Shapiro on 19 September 1941. He had bought a new blue Buick convertible and when his name went up on the Garden marquee, he drove around the city block twice to enjoy that moment. There would be many more. Shapiro was a New York boy but this wasn't his night. Maxie was down twice in the second round and twice in round three before referee Arthur Donovan stopped the fight. It was Maxie's first knockout and promoter Mike Jacobs announced he would match Robinson with the winner of the forthcoming lightweight title bout between champion Lew Jenkins and Sammy Angott.

When two unbeaten fighters clash, something has to give. It was that way in Philadelphia when Robinson met Marty Servo, the Schenectady, New York lightweight with 44 bouts behind him. Sugar Ray was riding a 24-bout win streak and in a bitterly fought ten-round thriller, the Harlem boy had it all to play for coming out for the last two rounds. Ray turned it on in a blazing finish to come out with a unanimous decision over an awkward opponent. They would fight again.

Just a year after making his professional debut in the Garden, Sugar Ray defied his mother by going back there to fight former welterweight champion Fritzie Zivic before a sellout crowd of

---

14 *Dubuque Telegraph Herald* Iowa 22 July 1941

22,000. Next morning, it was all over the New York papers – 'Sensational Negro Scrapper Earns Shot at World Crown: This victory gives slender Robinson a title tilt with champion Red Cochrane in January, but it also avenges Zivic's two triumphs over Henry Armstrong, who was Robinson's idol and friend. Zivic took a terrific battering in the ninth round, and it seemed to the roaring crowd that he could not last the distance, but the game Croatian from Pittsburgh never left his feet. A feature of Robinson's performance tonight was his superb demonstration of left jabbing. His flashing left fist beat Fritzie to the punch in every round and set him up for right bolos or following left hooks.'[15]

The sportswriter W. C. Heinz recalled Robinson telling him once, 'Fritzie Zivic taught me more than anybody I ever fought.' 'What did he teach you?' said Bill. 'He taught me that a man can make you butt open your own eye,' replied Sugar Ray. 'And how does a man do that?' asked Heinz. 'He slipped one of my jabs,' said Ray, 'and reached his right glove around behind my head and pulled my head down on his.' Young Otto, who boxed the best lightweights during the first two decades of this century, refereed that fight. One day in Stillman's, Bill Heinz asked him about it. 'In the sixth round,' he said, 'Robinson said to me, "He's sticking his thumbs in my eyes." I said, "You ain't no cripple." After that, he gave it back to Zivic better than Zivic was givin' it to him. I said to myself then, "This kid is gonna be a great fighter."'[16]

Two months later, Jacobs put them together again in the Garden, which didn't sit well with Philadelphia promoter Herman Taylor, who appealed to the New York Supreme Court. 'Taylor sought to halt the rematch on the grounds that Robinson refused to go through with a fight with Marty Servo, originally scheduled for November. Robinson twice had the fight postponed because of injuries, then ran out on Servo to accept the New York match. Curt Horrmann, Ray's manager, told the court he signed for the New

15 *Nevada State Journal* 1 November 1941

16 W. C. Heinz *Once They Heard the Cheers* 1979

York match prior to the date Taylor contended he gave him an oral agreement to the Servo fight. The court upheld this version. Taylor had charged that he built Robinson up to the headline fighter he is (Ray had fought 11 times in Philadelphia) and now he is taking advantage of him by refusing to go through with a match that he agreed to fight.'[17]

Robinson, going for his 27th straight win and a shot at the welterweight title held by Freddie 'Red' Cochrane, trained at Greenwood Lake for the Zivic fight, slated for 16 January 1942. A crowd of 15,475 paid their way into the Garden to see the return fight, over 12 rounds this time, and they were treated to another intense battle.

At ringside for Associated Press, Sid Feder reported, 'Fritzie Zivic has no complaints today about the speed and "Sunday shots" with which Rapid Ray Robinson whipped him, but Fritzie and a lot of other folks are mighty curious over what made referee Arthur Donovan stop the fight. Referee Donovan stepped in with Zivic on the floor in the tenth round last night in Madison Square Garden and gave Robinson a technical knockout victory. Possibly the most amazed man in the place was Luke Carney, Fritzie's manager, who declared today that Donovan's decision was "too fast". Said Carney, "At least my man was entitled to be counted over."

'Now, there's no denying that Harlem's Skinny Hammer was considerably out in front up to that point, The AP scorecard gave the negro five of the nine completed rounds. What's more, he floored Zivic with a looping overhand right for a nine count in the ninth. But when Ray let go both barrels and dropped the Pittsburgher early in the tenth, Fritzie wasn't hurt. Like the brainy boxer he's always been, the youngest of Smoky Town's five flying Zivics was figuring on taking a count – and a rest. But Donovan stepped in and called it off after 31 seconds of that round even as the flat-nosed flailer was struggling to his feet. It marked the second time in ten years that a knockout was scored against Zivic.

---

17 *The Afro-American* Baltimore 17 January 1942

'"Gee," Zivic told his handlers, "when I was just about slaughtering Henry Armstrong and taking his title away a year ago, Donovan wasn't in such a hurry to call a technical knockout. But don't get me wrong," Fritzie added in praise of his rival at the finish, "he's too fast for most guys and if and when he gets hold of Cochrane, he'll stiffen Red in six heats, no more."'[18]

Robinson never did get hold of Cochrane. Marty Servo, with his only two defeats, both by Sugar Ray, got the title fight with Cochrane in the Garden in February 1946 and knocked Red out in four rounds to become champion. Cochrane got $50,000 for the fight and promptly retired – his last fight of 112. Robinson was still out in the cold.

18 Sid Feder *Warren Times-Mirror* Pennsylvania 17 January 1942

3

MEET JAKE LAMOTTA

THEY NAMED the boy Normando Rubio Correa when he was born at Arecibo, Puerto Rico in May 1916 and 25 years later he was in New York City to fight Sugar Ray Robinson in the main event at Madison Square Garden. They announced him as Norman Rubio, from Albany, New York, winner of 30 of his 39 professional fights, but he wouldn't win this one. Sugar Ray was the hottest young fighter in boxing, undefeated in 118 amateur and professional bouts, and he was looking for a shot at Freddie 'Red' Cochrane's welterweight title.

'Rubio,' reported United Press, 'a game, awkward club fighter, tried desperately to wage a good battle, but he lacked the weapons to cope with 21-year-old Robinson's blinding speed and explosive punches. Rubio's bulling attack took the first and fifth rounds by narrow margins, but never was there any question that the bout would end before the scheduled 12 rounds.

'Robinson, operating with the deadliness of a Joe Louis on dancing feet, staggered his man with two straight rights to the head in the fourth and battered him on the ropes until Rubio wilted to the canvas just as the bell rang. The rugged Spaniard rallied surprisingly in the fifth, but Robinson in the sixth broke out of a clinch in a corner and barraged Rubio until he was groggy at the bell. One minute of the seventh had elapsed when the "Sugar" kid stunned his man with a left hook. Another portside hook smashed Rubio half through the ropes with his shoulders on the ring apron. Rubio was back on his feet at the count of nine, but Robinson's furious attack had him bloodied and helpless at the bell. Referee Arthur Donovan halted the bout with Rubio sitting on his corner stool before the bell could ring for the eighth round.'[19]

In the dressing room after the fight, Robinson's manager Curt Horrmann announced a series of five matches, including bouts at Detroit, Cleveland and Boston, but as he showered, the young fighter was thinking it was time he was handling his own business.

'Robinson was actually loathe to relinquish so much of his potential income to Horrmann and thought Horrmann took too much of his earnings. Robinson also thought Horrmann acquiesced too much when dealing with fight promoters. But Horrman loved all of it. He grinned like the men who owned baseball teams, like racehorse owners, like tycoons even. His daddy had founded a brewery, he had discovered a fighter, a fighter who had already jumped on to the cover of *The Ring* magazine! But then Sugar Ray – blinded by Horrmann's old-money wealth, the kind of deep wealth he wanted, and that he believed promoters were keeping him from attaining – wished to be rid of his manager. The contretemps caught Horrmann by surprise. He tried reasoning, but Robinson was determined. He wanted independence: he believed he and Gainford could handle his career, and Gainford bent to his wishes. He had to pay Horrmann $10,000 to buy back his contract.'[20] Ray borrowed the ten grand from promoter Mike Jacobs against future purses. 'I guess you can just say Mr Horrmann was too busy with his other affairs to give enough attention to my end,' Robinson told reporters. Now it was just Ray and Big George, and Mike had them back in the Garden in May 1942 fighting Marty Servo, Al Weill's entry from Schenectady, New York. In their first fight eight months previously, Servo had suffered his first defeat in 45 bouts when Robinson finished like

---

19 *Uniontown Evening Standard* Pennsylvania 21 March 1942

20 Wil Haygood *Sweet Thunder: The Life and Times of Sugar Ray Robinson* 2009

a train to snatch the ten-round decision, but the 10,000 crowd in Philadelphia's Convention Hall booed loudly. When Jacobs signed them for the Garden, the Philadelphia promoter, Herman Taylor, had Ray suspended in Pennsylvania for running out on a contracted return. Robinson would later say he 'really wanted to keep that agreement but my manager thought otherwise and there was nothing I could do about it'.

The Garden fight was another sizzler and another disputed decision that was greeted with thunderous booing by the 13,678 fans. For the United Press Jack Guenther wrote, 'Robinson entered the ring a 5-1 favourite and climbed out of it 45 minutes later no better than an 8-5 shot. The bout was a thriller in spots. Servo, who appears to be almost as old as a high school basketball player, gave Robinson a full evening in their first meeting and he was busier than a lion tamer at feeding time again in this second go-round. He forced the action, but Robinson landed the harder blows. The pattern was fashioned in the first round. Robinson circled his smaller opponent like a hawk circling a henhouse. Ray has no real love of a brawl and as usual he preferred to stay at long range, where his looping smashes could be shot over with a minimum of danger. Servo, however, was all for in-fighting. And so it went. Servo would force the fight for the first two and a half minutes of the round, Robinson would stage a spectacular flurry in the last 30 seconds and do his damage then. Referee Billy Cavanagh gave the bout to Servo but both judges voted for Robinson.'[21]

Whitney Martin was ringside for the Associated Press and he was watching Servo's manager with interest. 'Al Weill sat hunched on a lower step of the stairs leading to the ring at Madison Square Garden, eyes fixed stonily on the floor and perspiration forming in small puddles on his brow before trickling its roundabout course to drip from his chin. Above him sounded the sandpaper shuffle of shoes on canvas, the grunts and sniffs of men in violent exertion, and the sudden thud of leather against flesh. At each thud Weill

---

21 Jack Guenther *San Mateo Times* 29 May 1942

would wince a little and his round body would twitch involuntarily. Every 15 seconds or so, without moving his head, he would ask apprehensively of a second who was watching the fight: "How's he doing?" His Marty Servo was meeting Ray Robinson for a second time, and suffering far less than his rotund manager.

'Al Weill sat in his office overlooking Broadway. He was explaining, with quick, emphatic gestures, why he had refrained from watching Servo in action against the stout-punching Robinson. Was he afraid to see his boy get licked? "No," Al said seriously. "It's just that I like him so well and didn't want to see him get hurt. I felt the same way about Lou Ambers, like a father feels toward his sons. The boys' welfare comes first with me."'[22]

Two months after his second victory over Servo, Robinson hammered out a second win over the NBA lightweight champion Sammy Angott in the Garden ring, and three weeks later had Cowboy Rubin Shank back on his horse at 2.26 of round two, again in the New York ring. In that fight, just over five minutes in duration, Sugar Ray convinced United Press sportswriter Jack Cuddy to write, 'Accumulating evidence today tells us that the time has arrived to indulge in the ultimate in superlatives and admit that Ray "Sugar" Robinson – a slender young Negro from Harlem – is the greatest all-round fighter we have ever seen. Robinson tackled one of the most dangerous men he ever faced in awkward, bobbing, weaving young Shank. The unorthodox youngster was battering Robinson from rope to rope for the first minute and a half of the second round, proving himself a mighty tough kid – a kid who had licked the former welterweight champions Henry Armstrong and Fritzie Zivic – a lad who never had been knocked out.

'But when Robinson – Harlem's dancing dynamiter – finished with Cowboy Shank, he left his spurs jingle-jangle-jingling in such fashion that referee Billy Cavanagh could have counted to 50 over him instead of stopping the scheduled ten-round fight with Shanks on the floor for the fourth time in that second round,

---

22 Whitney Martin *Hagerstown Morning Herald* Maryland 28 September 1946

belted out quickly by the most explosive puncher the welterweight division has known since the heyday of Jimmy McLarnin almost a decade ago. But the 21-year-old Ray Robinson of today shapes up as a greater fighter than McLarnin ever was because he couples blinding speed afoot with just as much dynamite as McLarnin ever packed. And he's a smart, deadly effective boxer. McLarnin was a good boxer, too. No doubt of that – but he never did have the panther-like footwork of Robinson.'[23]

When Sugar severed his connection with Curt Horrmann, he considered his future in the fight business. 'I wanted a manager who would be tough in negotiations and who would be honest with me,' he told biographer Dave Anderson. 'The more I thought about it, the more I came to the conclusion that only one person in the world was capable of succeeding at that: Sugar Ray Robinson. My decision shocked George. He had assumed he was taking over. "Don't you trust me?" he complained. "George," I replied calmly, "I don't want to *have* to trust you. I want you to stay as my trainer," I told him, "and you can do the negotiating, but I make the final deal."'[24]

Mike Jacobs triggered off one of the ring's fiercest rivalries when he matched Robinson with Jake LaMotta for his ten-round main event at Madison Square Garden on Friday, 2 October 1942. 'Robinson gave plenty thought to the proposition before signing to fight LaMotta,' related the *Baltimore Afro-American*. 'It was not that Ray, a welterweight who boxes at about 144 pounds, was reluctant to oppose a middleweight scaling in the neighbourhood of 158. On the contrary, Robinson was quite willing to meet Georgie Abrams or even champion Tony Zale, if either was available. The factor that made Robinson hesitate about signing for LaMotta was the Bronx middleweight's style. Sugar Ray simply does not relish the idea of meeting opponents who employ the aggressive fistic tactics of LaMotta.'[25]

---

23 Jack Cuddy *Dunkirk Evening Observer* 22 August 1942

24 Sugar Ray Robinson with Dave Anderson *Sugar Ray* 1969

25 *Baltimore Afro-American* 3 October 1942

'Jake LaMotta,' wrote historian Bert Randolph Sugar, 'was a throwback to the old barge fighter, one to whom every fight was a war with no survivors taken; a rough-and-tumble fighter who gave every fan his money's worth. But LaMotta was a curious piece of goods as well. His fists were as delicate as those of a concert pianist, forcing him to eschew the head and direct his attack almost exclusively to the body. And his style was that of a street kid, no subtlety, no finesse, just straightforward, unabashed balls-out mauling.'[26]

'Ray Robinson made his bow against middleweight competition Friday night by taking target practice at Jake LaMotta and galloping off with a one-sided ten-round decision in Madison Square Garden as he ran his winning string to 125 fights in a row. Robinson weighed 145; LaMotta 157¾. Putting on a dazzling show of speed and slugging for the entertainment of a near-capacity crowd, Robinson solved the Bronx belter's peculiar style in one round and from there on he did just about all the punching. The Bronx croucher was a willing and rugged workman, but he was completely outclassed. Except for the first round, in which his style bothered the Harlem hammer, and the seventh, when he connected with several wild hooks, Jake had a rough crossing throughout. The Associated Press scorecard gave the never-defeated Robinson seven rounds, LaMotta two and called one even.'[27]

Frank 'Blinky' Palermo was an organised crime figure who controlled prize-fighters and fixed fights. Palermo was an associate of the Philadelphia crime family and also ran Philadelphia's biggest numbers racket. Blinky's partner was mobster Frankie Carbo, a soldier in New York's Lucchese crime family who had been a gunman with Murder Inc.

Sugar Ray was in Philadelphia to fight Al Nettlow. After the weigh-in, Robinson was standing near Lew Tendler's saloon when

---

26 Bert Randolph Sugar *Boxing's Greatest Fighters* 2006

27 *Winnipeg Free Press* 2 October 1942

Palermo approached him and said gruffly, 'Is it all set?' Ray didn't know what he was talking about. 'Didn't George tell you?' Blinky said. When Ray said no, Palermo said, 'He will,' and walked away. Back at the hotel, the young fighter asked George, 'What's going on with Blinky?'

Big George did his best to explain to his fighter how things were, with Blinky anyway. 'Well, now, Robinson, it wouldn't be good for you to knock out this Nettlow. You're knocking out too many guys. Nobody wants to make a match with you any more. The only way we got Nettlow was to agree that you wouldn't hurt him. We got to live with boxing people, Robinson, and we got to do favours now and then. This is one of those favours.'' But what if I *can* knock him out?' said Ray. 'I agreed you wouldn't,' said George, 'I agreed.' 'That's the whole trouble,' snapped Ray. '*You* got no right to agree to anything.'

That night in the Convention Hall, as Robinson related to his biographer, 'I was content to carry Nettlow for ten rounds. He was a nice little guy, and I didn't have any reason to measure him. For two rounds he was no trouble, but in the third he swatted me with a good right hand and I let go a left hook. It nailed him on the jaw and he went down. Nettlow was moving but not enough to beat the count and when the referee waved his hands, George hopped into the ring with my robe. "You double-crossed me, Robinson," he growled. "You tell Blinky it was an accident." Later that night, Ray told Palermo he hadn't meant to knock Nettlow out, it just happened. Blinky just shrugged his shoulders, said there was nothing more to do, and walked away.'[28]

That was the story Robinson related to Dave Anderson, but it read differently in next morning's papers. The Associated Press reported, 'Ray "Sugar" Robinson, hard-hitting Harlem welterweight, battered Al Nettlow at will tonight to score a three-round technical knockout over the game chief boatswain's mate from the Navy's Jacksonville, Florida base. A crowd of nearly

28 Sugar Ray Robinson with Dave Anderson *Sugar Ray* 1969

10,000 watched in horror as the Negro administered such terrific punishment that Nettlow's manager Al Weill ordered referee Mat Adgie to stop the bout after the third round. "He didn't have a chance," said Weill. It was Robinson's 40th straight victory as a professional and his 29th knockout.

'Robinson rushed Nettlow into a corner at the opening bell and let fly a flurry of savage lefts and rights that floored Nettlow. The Detroiter, game to the core, bounced to his feet before timekeeper Joe Cervino could start to count, but from there on it was only a question of how long Nettlow could last. All through the first round, Robinson kept swinging at the back-pedalling Nettlow. It was the same story in the second round, with Robinson landing left after left as he chased Nettlow around the ring. The crowd started to yell, "Stop it. Stop it." Starting the third, Nettlow landed his first blow, a weak right to the face. Robinson appeared tired, but unexpectedly cut loose in the middle of the round and stunned Nettlow with three consecutive lefts. It was a mystery that Nettlow stood up the rest of the round, but after he got to his stool, Weill beckoned to Adgie and told him to stop it. The fight was scheduled for ten rounds.'[29]

The United Press carried a similar report, 'Ray (Sugar) Robinson, New York welterweight, won his 40th straight professional bout last night by scoring a technical knockout over Sailor Al Nettlow of Detroit in the third round before 7,868 at Convention Hall. Nettlow weathered a hail of punches from Robinson in the first two rounds. But the Detroit fighter's manager, Al Weill, asked that the bout be stopped after the bell sounded, ending the third round. Although he was severely battered by Robinson, Nettlow went down only once, in the first round. He got up, however, before the referee could begin his count.'[30]

So whoever stopped the fight, Sugar Ray or Al Weill, Al Nettlow went back to the Navy and never fought again.

---

29 *Helena Independent* Montana 15 December 1942

30 *Evening Democrat* Madison, Iowa 15 December 1942

'Shortly after the Nettlow accident, I was training in Grupp's one afternoon when the phone rang. It was for me, but I was working on the light bag and George answered it. When he hung up, he was grinning and hopping. That wasn't like George. He usually was much more dignified, much more serious. "Robinson," he yelled. "*The Ring* magazine just voted you the outstanding fighter of 1942." The honour pleased me, but it also annoyed me. I was the year's outstanding boxer, but I wasn't a champion. Not only that, but I wasn't even getting a title shot. It didn't make sense. The next day I went to see Mike Jacobs. "I'm the Fighter of the Year," I snapped at him, "and I deserve a shot at Cochrane's title." Red Cochrane had won the welterweight championship from Fritzie Zivic midway through 1941, but more than a year later he enlisted in the Navy without having defended it.

'"He's not available," Mike said, "and pretty soon, you won't be available either. Any day now you'll be getting your army induction notice." "But how do you know?" I said. "I know," he said. "I *know*." "How much time before I leave?" "Time enough for a couple paydays," Uncle Mike said, wrapping me around his little finger again. "You're not the type to live on a private's $50 a month. I'll get you LaMotta in Detroit." "Good," I said. "We'll draw money."'[31]

31 Sugar Ray Robinson with Dave Anderson *Sugar Ray* 1969

4

SUGAR RAY'S REVENGE

THE DETROIT Olympia stood at the corner of Grand River Avenue, a monument to civic pride that would be affectionately known as 'The Old Red Barn', home to the Detroit Red Wings ice hockey team from 1927 until 1979. There was no single opening day; on 15 October 1927, an eight-day rodeo began, while on 26 October, 15,000 fans crammed into the new stadium to witness the first of many boxing matches. 'Detroit has leaped into big-time fight circles as a result of the first boxing card staged at this city's new sports palace – the Olympia,' the *Detroit Times* reported. 'Fifteen thousand persons last night jammed the big building and saw Tom Heeney, New Zealand heavyweight, defeat Johnny Risko of Cleveland in ten rounds. Just how much money the fight drew is still in doubt. But there isn't any question that it smashed all Detroit records.'

On this February night in 1943, the record would be smashed again as promoter Nick Londes hung the 'standing room only' sign over the Olympia box office as the first sellout crowd in two years – 16,000 persons – shelled out $50,000 to see if Jake LaMotta could avenge his New York defeat by Sugar Ray Robinson.

Londes was the man bringing big-time boxing back to the Motor City. He had stowed away on a ship leaving the Greek seaport of Patrae, aged 12. 'I wanted to come to the United States,' he would tell the United Press in 1954. But that move didn't immediately bring Londes to America. First he joined the British Navy, then he enlisted with the US Shipping Board. Upon his discharge, he chose Chicago as his home and became a real estate salesman, although he could speak little English. 'I made a $200 commission on my first sale,' he said, 'so I opened my own office.' During his free moments, Londes tried his hand at booking concerts, fights and wrestling matches. With the Depression came a decline in the real estate business. He closed his office and ventured to Detroit. Boxing in Detroit grew rapidly with the arrival of Londes as he made the Olympia his headquarters.[32]

'To stage this super-dooper attraction, matchmaker Nick Londes had to lure young Robinson away from promoter Taylor of Philadelphia, who had the young Negro under contract for another bout,' wrote Jack Cuddy for the United Press. 'But Londes knew Robinson wanted to make one last "touch" before going into the army, so he offered the Harlem Negro 30 per cent of the net gate, and Robinson forgot about the Philadelphia contract. Londes also took good care of LaMotta, who was being ogled by promoter Mike Jacobs in New York.'[33]

The fight would be Sugar Ray's third appearance in Detroit; he would see Pop again and all his old friends from the Brewster Centre as he carried his winning streak of 129 fights, amateur and pro, into the Motor City arena. It was also Jake's third fight in Detroit and he would become a favourite with the crowds, having 22 of his 106 career bouts there. In his first fight with Robinson in New York, he complained that he had been forced to scale 157 pounds, leaving him weak at the weight. This time, Big George told the press they were taking Jake at the middleweight limit so that 'when we beat him he won't have any excuses'.

On the day, LaMotta weighed half a pound over the 160-pound limit, with Robinson still under the welterweight class limit at 144½.

---

32 *Pacific Stars and Stripes* 31 March 1954

33 Jack Cuddy *Nevada State Journal* 14 March 1943

The bout was expected to draw a capacity crowd to the Olympia and a gate that would compare not too unfavourably with the $60,000 that was drawn by the bout between Johnny Risko and Tom Heeney when the Olympia opened 26 October 1927. When the doors closed that Friday night in February 1943, a crowd of 18,930 was jammed into the arena, the largest ever to attend a boxing event at the Olympia, beating the attendance at the fight between Mickey Walker and Johnny Risko, which drew 18,916 in November 1930.

The bout, scheduled for ten rounds, was made at the middleweight limit of 160 pounds, but Big George Gainford said that the Robinson camp would have no objection if Jake weighed more than that, adding that LaMotta, 'who puts on weight easily, probably would put on four more pounds before he entered the ring at 10pm.'

Mike Capriano, manager of LaMotta, said, 'Jake hasn't been paying too much attention to his weight, but has been concentrating on getting into condition. I think he is in first-class shape and a little lighter than he has been. That means he should be faster.'[34]

'Before the bout thousands of dollars were wagered in the lobby of Olympia, the closing price establishing Robinson as the favourite at 3¼ to 1. Old-timers who were regular patrons in the flourishing twenties said they never saw the betting of last night equalled in Detroit. Robinson was a 2 to 1 favourite until a few hours before the fight, when a flood of Robinson money sent the price soaring.'[35]

'The fight was the kind of bout it was expected to be. Having a 16-pound pull in the weights, LaMotta decided to make full use of it and charged into Robinson at every opportunity. Ray, on the other hand, tried to box LaMotta, just as Charley Hayes tried to box him in Jake's last bout in Detroit. Robinson had more success than did the blond Ferndale youngster, but he did not

---

34 *Detroit Free Press* 5 February 1943

35 Dale Stafford *Detroit Free Press* 6 February 1943

have quite as much as his well-wishers hoped he would have. The crowd let out a roar of expectancy as the men came out of their corners fighting in the first round and it roared from then until the finish. Robinson tried to box LaMotta, flicking him about the head with his left hand and occasionally trying to stop his rushes with a right uppercut or a straight right that was thrown from West Grand Boulevard. Jake managed to get under most of the jabs and avoided most of the long rights. But he was jarred a couple of times by the right uppercuts.'[36]

'Despite the odds, Sugar Ray did not take Jake lightly. He went to work at the opening bell, stabbing with jolting left jabs, mixing sharp hooks and uppercuts. But LaMotta shook them off and kept whaling away at Sugar Ray's body. The scrapping was hot and heavy through the third, fourth, fifth and sixth rounds, never changing in pattern – Sugar Ray boxing in his classic stand-up style and LaMotta charging in with bull-like rushes, flailing away to the head and body with both hands. So intent were the fighters that several times they did not hear the bell, continuing to punch away until they were separated by referee Sam Hennessey.

'By the sixth round, LaMotta's powerful body attack had slowed Ray down a trifle and Sugar was getting hit with punches he ordinarily would have parried or slipped. In the eighth stanza, Jake blasted Robbie to the ropes with solid lefts and rights. Ray was now fighting desperately, trying to keep LaMotta at long range, but the Bull kept driving in close, landing his sledgehammer blows on the target. A right to the body, followed by a pile-driving left hook to the jaw, slammed Ray through the ropes and out on to the apron of the ring. Although he was hurt, Robbie kept his senses. Just as he was getting to his feet at the count of ten, the bell saved him from further punishment. The men slugged it out through the ninth and tenth rounds with no further knockdowns. The huge crowd was on its feet during the entire ten rounds.'[37]

---

36 Charles P. Ward *Detroit Free Press* 6 February 1943

37 Gene Schoor *Sugar Ray Robinson* 1951

'Although the bout was a real battle from start to finish there was no doubt as to the winner, for referee Sam Hennessey and judges Joe Lenahan and Michael H. Butler gave the decision to LaMotta unanimously. Butler gave the third, fourth and ninth rounds to Robinson and the sixth, eighth and tenth rounds to LaMotta. He called all the rest even and gave the decision to LaMotta by a score of 57 points to 49. Lenahan gave the first, second, sixth, eighth, ninth and tenth rounds to LaMotta and the third, fourth and fifth to Robinson. He called LaMotta the winner, 55 points to 45. Referee Hennessey gave the first, third, fourth and sixth rounds to Robinson, and the second, seventh, eighth, ninth and tenth rounds to LaMotta. He called the fifth round even and gave the bout to LaMotta 52 points to 47.'[38]

The gross receipts were announced as $47,280 and the net receipts $39,399. Both Robinson and LaMotta expressed the desire to meet again and, of course, promoter Nick Londes was willing to put on the rubber match. Any fears of Londes that the bout might go to New York were dissipated by Nat Rogers, matchmaker for Mike Jacobs. 'I haven't got a spot for the fight,' Rogers said. 'Robinson is fighting California Jackie Wilson in Madison Square Garden 19 February and after that he isn't available.'

The defeat of Sugar Ray shattered his sensational winning streak at 129 fights, including 40 in the pro ring. 'SUGAR ROBINSON'S LOSS BLAMED ON LAMOTTA'S EDGE IN WEIGHT' headed Jack Cuddy's column for United Press next day. 'Never in the history of boxing was the importance of weight stressed as it was last night at Detroit. Before a record local indoor crowd of 18,930 fans, middleweight Jake LaMotta, 3 to 1 underdog, gave welterweight Ray Robinson the first defeat of his career as an amateur or professional, largely because LaMotta was permitted to come into the ring outweighing the unbeaten New York Negro by 15¾ pounds. It must be mentioned that recently in New York the same middleweight who licked Robinson at

---

38 Charles P. Ward *Detroit Free Press* 6 February 1943

Detroit last night scored a similar upset victory over welterweight contender Sgt Jackie Wilson of Mitchell Field, New York after Wilson permitted LaMotta to come into the ring enjoying a weight advantage of 16 pounds.

'We recall Wilson and LaMotta for a good reason. Wilson tangles with Robinson at Madison Square Garden on 19 February. And promoter Mike Jacobs has his usual luck because the defeat of Robinson – who would have gone in a top-heavy favourite against Wilson – now makes this bout such an attractive affair that the two grand Negro welters may attract a crowd approaching 21,000 at the Garden. Thus, weight becomes ultra-important when a fighter of one division is matched with a scrapper of a lower class. New Yorker LaMotta, for example, is a mediocre middleweight. We're confident that Tony Zale, the middleweight champion who now is in the Navy, would belt his brains out. But the LaMotta who went in against welterweight Robinson last night and welterweight Wilson recently enjoyed such poundage advantages that his opponents were forced to pack a pull of at least 15 pounds – pull in the weights throughout the bouts ... When a welter fights a middleweight, the welter expends almost twice the energy of the middleweight before the final bell, if the difference is 15 pounds, the limit permitted by the New York Commission. LaMotta exceeded this difference in his Detroit bout with Robinson and his New York bout with Wilson.'[39]

'I have no alibi, but I'd like to fight him again,' Robinson told the reporters who jammed his dressing room after the fight. 'And I'd like the bout to be right here in Detroit, too.'

LaMotta said it was just another fight and he was ready for another Robinson engagement – 'tomorrow if they want it.' 'No, I wasn't in trouble. After our first fight in New York, I had a feeling that Robinson couldn't take it in the stomach. And after the second round tonight, I was sure of it.'[40]

39 Jack Cuddy *Amarilllo Sunday News-Globe* Texas 7 February 1943

40 Dale Stafford *Detroit Free Press* 6 February 1943

A couple of weeks before joining Uncle Sam's Army, Sugar Ray figured this was as good a time as any to give a sergeant a good belting. So, still working for his Uncle Mike Jacobs, he hammered Sgt Jackie Wilson all over the Garden ring in New York to cop a majority decision after ten rounds.

'California Jackie Wilson didn't make any mistake in showing up at Madison Square Garden last night,' reported Associated Press, 'although it's a matter for argument as to whether the $10,000 or so he got for turning up was worth the thumping he absorbed from Ray Robinson. But he made several other mistakes in the course of the evening's beak-busting, and the chief one of these cost him the fight. This slight error was in trying to trade long-range artillery with the Harlem Sugar man at odd moments during the ten rounds. Sugar may be rationed, but the Sugar man's Sunday shots definitely aren't, a fact he proved in the fourth round when he floored Sergeant Jackie for a nine count. The way he walked out against Wilson from the word go last night, tossing his blockbusters and pulling the trigger on his big guns, he resembled his hero, Joe Louis, the night Joe all but took Max Schmeling apart in a couple of minutes.'[41]

One week after the Wilson fight, Sugar Ray was back in Detroit to fight LaMotta again in their rubber match at the Olympia. With three ten-round fights in three weeks, two of them with teak-tough Jake LaMotta, who almost knocked him out in their last bout, it was a gruelling programme Ray had set himself but he wanted desperately to avenge the LaMotta defeat and a crowd of 15,149 crowded into the arena that Friday night to see if he could do it. Once again, the Bronx Bull was a solid middleweight going against a natural welterweight, 160¾ to 145 for Robinson, but this was a fitter, stronger Robinson, hell-bent on revenge. From Detroit for Associated Press, Watson Spoelstra reported, 'Lanky Ray (Sugar) Robinson, probably the best fighter never to have won a championship, is ready to step into a real fight Tuesday as

---

41 *LaCrosse Tribune and Leader-Press* 20 February 1943

Pvt. Walker Smith of the US Army after wiping his slate clean with a decisive victory over tough Jacob LaMotta. The verdict received the unanimous support of referee Sam Hennessey and the two judges, and it amply avenged Sugar Ray's only setback in a 132-fight career at LaMotta's hands three weeks ago. Hennessey gave Robinson five rounds, LaMotta three – including the seventh when he had the Sugar boy on the deck for an eight count – with two even. Neither judge gave LaMotta more than two rounds. In his dressing room, Robinson just bubbled all over with elation. Many customers had roundly booed the verdict, probably because LaMotta had gathered a huge personal following here, but Robinson didn't seem to mind.'[42]

'I lost the third Robinson fight,' recalled LaMotta. 'That's not right. I didn't lose it, he got the decision. You can ask anyone who was there, or if it means that much to you, you can read the newspaper stories. I know the date of this fight, it was the last week of February in 1943 and Robinson was going into the army the next day. I'm not knocking him on it. I would have done the same thing in his shoes, but he got every newspaper inch there was about the story of this brave boy off to fight for his country.

'He didn't fight up to his best in the ring that night, but he got a decision by one miserable vote after I decked him once. That's when I began to think about Robinson as a nemesis. Well, no, not really, but if you score the only knockdown in a really tough ten-rounder and the judges give the decision to the guy you knocked down, you got to figure that things aren't really going your way. At the time, I figured what the hell, I flattened this guy once before and I'll get him again when he comes out. I didn't figure he was going to use his army career as one long training camp.'[43]

---

42 Watson Spoelstra *Sheboygan Press* Wisconsin 27 February 1943

43 Jake LaMotta *Raging Bull* 1970

5

IN AND OUT OF THE ARMY

'"PRIVATE SMITH," I remember a corporal saying that day, and I ignored him until he pointed to me and yelled, "You!" Suddenly I was Walker Smith again. *Private* Walker Smith. I had changed names again. I had changed uniforms, too. Instead of white trunks, I was wearing olive drab, all over. I was in an olive drab world. The morning I was inducted at the Whitehall Street centre near the lower tip of Manhattan Island, our group boarded an olive drab bus. The bus took us through the Holland Tunnel to New Jersey and down US 1 to Fort Dix. There, a sergeant marched us into an olive drab building, where we were issued our olive drab uniforms. Then he marched us to our olive drab barracks.'[44]

'Now it was up at the first blast of Reveille and out at Fatigue Call. It was "Column right – haarch!" bellowed by a leather-lunged drill sergeant. It was hot, sweaty hours on the bayonet course and days on the rifle range. It was march and sweat, and grumble and sweat, and dig and sweat. It was the army. To millions of draftees, this schedule was hell. But to Sugar Ray, there was little difference between this training and the regular routine he had been going through to get ready for his bouts. Ray was in fine shape – his reflexes razor sharp, his muscles like springs of steel, his eyes keen. He always kept himself in top condition. The basic training was

44 Sugar Ray Robinson with Dave Anderson *Sugar Ray* 1969

no chore for him – not after weeks of arduous preparation for the LaMotta fights.'[45]

Basic training finished, Robinson was assigned to an Army Air Corp base at Mitchell Field in Hempstead, Long Island. One duty he enjoyed was coaching the boxing team, between spells of guard duty and other army chores. Being Sugar Ray Robinson helped ease his time in uniform. Officers went out of their way to talk to him, to shake his hand, and even get an autograph. He usually managed to get a few days' leave now and then, and even managed to find time to get himself married. He had been seeing Edna Mae, a showgirl, in Harlem and in May 1943 she was dancing in a Chicago club. Ray fiddled a weekend pass, took a train to Chicago, where he and his girl were married 29 May 1943, at the home of a friend of hers, Ann Helm.

Back at the Mitchell Field base in Long Island, Robinson was able to get in a couple of fights, helped by Mike Jacobs. In Boston, he knocked out Freddie Cabral in one round and took a ten-round decision over Ralph Zannelli. But Ray wasn't happy when Jacobs suggested a match with Henry Armstrong, who had been his boyhood idol. In 1938, Hammerin' Hank was the idol of all the kids training with young Ray Robinson at the Salem-Crescent gym in Harlem as he did what no other fighter had done in holding three world championships at the same time. He knocked out featherweight champion Petey Sarron, whipped Barney Ross over 15 brutal rounds to become welterweight champ and beat lightweight boss Lou Ambers. Three titles in ten months.

Now, in 1943, Armstrong was pushing 34, the titles were gone and he was broke. Mike Jacobs, with an eye on a box office winner, convinced Robinson he would be doing his idol a big favour in boxing him over ten rounds in the Garden. On 27 August, a crowd of 15,371 paid $60,789 to see if Henry could get the glory years back.

---

45 Gene Schoor *Sugar Ray Robinson* 1951

This is what Whitney Martin wrote for Associated Press: 'Most of the fight fans present had the idea that Ray Robinson was spilling a little of the milk of human kindness in his bout with Henry Armstrong at Madison Square Garden last Friday night. That is, that out of sympathy and respect, he refrained from knocking out the worn and weary warrior. If such was the case it was history making ditto marks, with Armstrong drawing the interest on a little investment in chivalry on his own part. It wasn't too many years before that Armstrong, then at his peak, had met a fading Barney Ross. Those who saw that battle, memorable because of the refusal of Ross to quit when hopelessly beaten, carried away the vivid impression that Armstrong eased up in the late rounds out of tribute to his gallant opponent, who was determined to go out as a champion should go out – doing his best and asking no quarter. Those who saw that battle also probably never imagined that some day, a few years away, this same Armstrong would be in a position similar to that of Ross, saved from a knockout by the compassion of a younger and stronger rival.'[46]

With the Armstrong fight behind him, Sugar Ray had finished working for Uncle Mike Jacobs and started working for Uncle Sam. The military authorities had come up with the idea of having the world heavyweight champion, Sergeant Joe Louis, organise a boxing troupe that would tour camps and bases across America, entertaining the army and air force personnel with exhibitions of training and boxing. It was a brilliant morale booster for the soldiers and airmen, thousands of whom were preparing for duty in the European Theatre of Operations.

Following orders from the War Department, which were backed by President Roosevelt's administration, 'good soldier' Louis gathered his troops. Long-time sparring partner George Nicholson was joined by California Jackie Wilson, who like Robinson was a top welterweight contender. What had been announced as a 100-day tour started at Fort Devens in Massachusetts, where 'upwards

---

46 Whitney Martin *Lethbridge Herald* Alberta 31 August 1943

of 7,000 soldiers whooped and hollered at the sight of the group. In the ring set up outdoors at the rural military camp, GIs piled on jeeps, tall pine trees rising in the distance, Joe and George went at it for a few rounds, then Sugar Ray and California Jackie took a turn. The GIs on the ground, as if inside a fevered arena, howled and whistled as the fighters landed punches. The group got a lot of questions about their weight, their past opponents. Joe and Sugar Ray signed autographs at the Fort Devens army hospital. Many of the patients were arrivals from battles in North Africa. The fighters scrawled their names on the plaster arm and leg casts of soldiers.'[47]

The show was a tremendous success and the nationwide tour kicked off. 'Coming to a camp near you, the Joe Louis Troupe.' Camp Grant, Illinois ... Fort Meade, Maryland ... Lincoln Air Base, Nebraska ... Camp McCoy, Wisconsin. By the time the boys were ordered to Fort Hamilton, Brooklyn, where preparations were being made for the overseas tour, it was reckoned that they had entertained a million servicemen at 110 camps in America from August 1943 to January 1944.

'At one of the camps, the world heavyweight champion was asked, "Do you have any plans for the future?" "Nope," said Joe, "all depends on the war." When the group landed in London in April, the war was still going on, and they were short one man. Ray Robinson. "Sugar began complaining of headaches a few months ago," explained Captain Fred Maly, special service officer from San Antonio, Texas, who is in charge of the party, "so we left him at a hospital in New York."'[48]

'On Friday, 5 April, 1944, a lithe, muscular black man lay in a too-small, railed bed at the one-thousand-bed Halloran General Hospital on Staten Island. "That's Sugar Ray Robinson," a nurse whispered. He had been there a week, and still a few staffers hadn't gotten the word about the star in their midst. Not that

47 Wil Haygood *Sweet Thunder: The Life and Times of Sugar Ray Robinson*

48 *Stars and Stripes* Belfast 12 April 1944

there was much to look at even for those who did know. When awake, he was groggy, and he spent most of his time on his left side holding on to his bed for dear life, seemingly consumed by dizziness and nausea.

'According to the chart at the foot of the bed, the patient, an army sergeant named W. Smith, had fallen down a flight of stairs at Fort Hamilton. Robinson did not even recognise his wife and manager when they came to visit … "You've had an attack of blunt trauma amnesia," was the first explanation he received from the parade of white-uniformed doctors and nurses who came and went from his room. They probed, poked, and prodded him; they shoved thermometers in his mouth and shined tiny flashlights in his eyes. They listened to his heart. They measured his blood pressure and took blood and urine samples.

'"So what do we do now?" Ray asked after receiving his diagnosis. "We wait, Sugar," the doctor said with confidence. "There's no medicine for this one, but it should blow over pretty quickly." The funny thing about amnesia, Ray learned, was that you can understand you have it without knowing much about anything else. When Robinson recovered, he remembered the accident and the names and faces of his friends and family. He was then promptly arrested by the military police. He was in such hot water because he had not been on the ship that was supposed to carry him and the Louis troupe from Pier 90 to Europe.'[49]

For 38 years, Dan Parker was a highly revered and respected columnist for the *New York Daily Mirror* and Damon Runyon called him 'the most constantly brilliant of all sportswriters'. Mr Parker wasn't exactly flavour of the month with Sugar Ray Robinson when he wrote in his column 7 April 1944, 'Robinson is in a bit of a pickle. Leaving the ship which was to carry him overseas with a group of other boxers to entertain the fighting men on foreign fronts, Ray was picked up by the military police after the ship had sailed and now awaits court-martial.'

---

49 Kenneth Shropshire *Being Sugar Ray* 2007

In his autobiography with Dave Anderson, Robinson stated, 'There is nothing in my army record that mentions me leaving the ship. As far as I know, I was never even on the ship. I was never court-martialled.' When Ray was at Halloran, Lieutenant V. H. Gill stated that in his opinion, 'I had seemed upset that I wouldn't be able to accompany Joe Louis on the trip to Europe. I do not believe,' added Lieutenant Gill, 'that this patient is a malingerer.'[50]

In a further column dated 27 April, Dan Parker wrote, 'It seems to me that the army authorities who have been uncommunicative about the Robinson case should issue a statement which clarifies his status. If Robinson went AWOL from the boat, the army should say so. If he didn't, he should be cleared of the stigma attached to his name since stories about the incident began to circulate.'

'Meeting behind closed doors, army officials decided to thank Sugar Ray Robinson for his military service. He would be granted an honourable discharge. On 3 June 1944, Sugar Ray Robinson left the army. Louis and the others were in war-scarred Europe, rallying the troops for the last big push.'[51]

In his 'Sports Patrol' column, veteran sportswriter Oscar Fraley wrote, 'Joe Cummiskey, able sports editor of PM [a New York City daily] reasoned that Robinson couldn't have been the fighter he was in the ring without possessing a number of qualities that go together to make up a man. As a result of his reasoning, Cummiskey refused to believe the stories he has heard and read about Robinson until he did a little checking up on his own hook.

'The stories, or rumours as they turned out to be, had Robinson jumping ship when he was supposed to accompany Joe Louis to England; had him AWOL; had him slugging a superior officer; had him beating up MPs, and any number of other equally false accusations. The facts as discovered by Cummiskey when he interviewed Robinson, the fighter's friends and army public

50 Sugar Ray Robinson with Dave Anderson *Sugar Ray* 1969

51 Wil Haygood *Sweet Thunder: The Life and Times of Sugar Ray Robinson* 2009

relations officers presented an entirely different story. Robinson is in a government hospital under medical observation, never has been and so, of course, was never AWOL. Neither had he been beat up, nor had he beaten anyone. The rumours started flying when Ray entered the hospital after his boxing troupe was known to have left the country. It so happened that, during the final physical check-ups, Robinson was found unfit for overseas service and as a result was disqualified from making the trip. He was under orders to say nothing about being unable to go with the others because such a statement could reveal the departure time of Joe Louis and the other soldiers until they were safely at their destinations.

'At any rate, Sugar Ray proved himself as good a soldier as he was a boxer by keeping his mouth shut while his name was being slandered across the country by those who are always anxious to make up for their own deficiencies by finding fault with champions.'[52]

The name of Sugar Ray Robinson was no sooner back in the 'Fights Last Night' column than it was back in the news pages across the country. 'ARMY CHANGES MIND ABOUT ROBINSON'S SECTION EIGHT – Sugar Called Up Again. Army Looking at Robinson.

According to an INS report from New York dated 28 February 1945, 'Ray (Sugar) Robinson, New York Negro welterweight, today was at Fort Jay, Governor's Island, for observation and possible re-induction into the army. Robinson was discharged a few months ago because of "ineptness" under Section 8 of army regulations, reportedly, but has returned to the pugilistic limelight as one of the outstanding fighters of these times and may be headed back for another hitch in uniform. According to reports, he will remain at Fort Jay several days and doctors there will report back to the local induction centre, recommending that he be redrafted or deferred. In the latter instance, his case will be subject to review by the War

52 Oscar Fraley *Montana Standard* Butte 18 April 1944

Department in Washington in keeping with regulations governing the rejection of athletes.'[53]

Ten days later, it was reported that Robinson was rejected by the Army at Fort Jay, where he had been undergoing tests since a reinduction physical examination at Grand Central Palace. However, a new mandate from Washington required that any athlete rejected for military service must get his final disposition from the War Department.

W. C. (Bill) Heinz was asked to do an article for the *Saturday Evening Post* in 1950, which they were going to entitle 'Why Don't They Like Sugar Ray Robinson?' '"This is a tough assignment for me," I said to him. "How's that?" he said. "I have to ask you the tough questions," I said. "That's all right," he said. "Go ahead." I really believed it. I believed it for about five minutes. "All right," I said. "Let's get the army thing out of the way first."

'It wasn't any good. We went around and around, as in a ring, and when Robinson couldn't counter my leads or even slip them, he professed only astonishment that I should hold such documented assertions to be facts. There was something to be celebrated in his army record. He had been a member of Casual Detachment Z, known as the Joe Louis Troupe. Joe and he and four other fighters spent seven months touring camps in this country and putting on boxing exhibitions. In Florida, Robinson refused to box unless black troops were allowed to attend, and he, an enlisted man, faced down a general.

'It was a matter of army record and common knowledge, however, that when the troupe sailed for Europe, from Pier 90, New York, on 31 March 1944, Robinson was not aboard. It was also in the record that he had previously declared his intention not to go, and that the Articles of War as they applied to the punishment for desertion had been explained to him. "But why would a man say such a thing?" he said when I had read to him from the affidavit.

---

53 *Lowell Sun* Mass. 28 February 1945

'"He not only said it," I said, "but he swore to it."'[54]

It was the summer of 1944 and Sugar Ray Robinson was back home in Harlem. In his book *Pound for Pound,* Herb Boyd would write, 'Out of uniform and back in civilian life, Sugar had to redeem his standing both as a citizen and as a top contender for the welterweight title. He was being branded a deserter and less than patriotic in some newspaper columns because of his failure to stay with his unit when it was shipped abroad. It would take years before the jeers on this matter subsided, though he had been honourably discharged. The path was equally difficult in his pursuit of a title shot. Each time he requested a title fight, he was told that he could make more money without the crown because he'd get more fights. But Sugar insisted that it was no longer about the money so much as it was about fame, glory and international acclaim. He wanted to be known, like Louis, all over the world.[55]

Robinson was now generally recognised as the uncrowned welterweight champion. The guy holding the title officially was Freddie 'Red' Cochrane, out of Elizabeth, New Jersey. As a kid, he lived a few houses from where Mickey Walker lived, a kid with bright red hair, blue eyes and a stubby nose. Walker was the welterweight champion at the time and Red would recall scrambling for pennies and nickels tossed by Mickey when he came home from a fight. With other neighbourhood kids, he would sit on Mickey's porch waiting for him to get up in the morning

In July 1941, Cochrane pulled off a stunning upset when he took a 15-round decision over favourite Fritzie Zivic to become welterweight champion of the world, emulating his boyhood idol. But before he could defend his title, Japan bombed Pearl Harbour and America was at war. The first boxing champion to don a uniform was Frederick James Cochrane, who enlisted in the Navy, but he was exempt from combat because he was born with one arm shorter than the other. That hadn't stopped him

---

54 W. C. Heinz *Saturday Evening Post* 9 December 1950

55 Herb Boyd with Ray Robinson II *Pound for Pound* 2005

reaching out to grab Zivic's title, and it didn't stop him serving Uncle Sam either.

Fast forward to January 1945 and manager Willie Gilzenberg announced that Cochrane had been honourably discharged. That was good news for Sugar Ray Robinson and it was also good news for Miss Jeanette Peterson, who charged the boxer was the father of her daughter born 21 May 1943. Red was held in $500 bail immediately after his release from service. He would appear voluntarily on a warrant issued while he was out of the country.

Robinson finally got some good news when United Press announced from Chicago that Cochrane had agreed to defend his title against Sugar Ray some time in June. Promoter Jack 'Doc' Kearns said he was able to stage this long-awaited match by offering a $100,000 guarantee and that he would hold it in one of the Chicago baseball parks or at Soldier Field. This did not sit right with Sugar Ray, however, glad as he was to be getting a crack at the title. 'When I fight for the title,' he told reporters, 'it won't be in Chicago, it will be right here in New York.' Back to the drawing board.

Kearns was out of the picture and into the frame stepped the portly figure of Al Weill. Al and his fighter Marty Servo, twice a loser to Robinson, cooked up a deal whereby they would take 60 per cent of the $72,000 net gate at the Garden and pay champion Cochrane a flat $50,000. It cost Marty roughly $7,000 to buy his title shot but it was worth it.

'Servo went out after Cochrane as if he owned him,' wrote Sid Feder. 'He staggered Freddie the Red in the first round, plastered him liberally in the second, had a baudy red stream running from Cochrane's nose in the third and then hit the jackpot in the fourth with a left hook followed by assorted mayhem. Red slumped to the floor and was counted out. Cochrane had kept the world welterweight title on the shelf for four years and 187 days – and lost it in exactly 11 minutes and 54 seconds.'[56]

---

56 Sid Feder *Hattiesburg American* Mississippi 2 February 1946

'The New York Commission,' wrote Jack Cuddy for United Press, 'had permitted Servo to bypass Ray (Sugar) Robinson as the challenger against Cochrane because Servo had a better service record than Robinson. However, Servo was forced to sign for a title defence against Robinson on 24 May in case he took the title from Cochrane. Marty suffered nose injuries on 29 March when he was knocked out in the second round of a non-title bout by middleweight Rocky Graziano. He notified the New York Commission that these injuries would prevent a defence against Robinson on 24 May because an operation was necessary.

'The commission, in irritation, set 6 September as a deadline by which Servo would have to defend against Robinson or have the title vacated. Servo notified the commission on 3 September that he could not defend, and the title was vacated. In addition, Marty and his handlers were suspended indefinitely in New York State.'[57]

Robinson had already started training at Greenwood Lake for the Servo fight when he was visited in his dressing room by two white strangers. One of them 'moved in closer to me. "Robinson," he said, "you can make an easy $25,000 cash if you don't fight Servo." "Don't fight Servo?" I replied. "Man, all I want to do in the world is fight Servo." "Now take it easy," he said. "All you have to do is say you can't make the weight." "Get away from me," I snapped. Soon after that, the fight was off anyway.'[58]

Ray would still later be suspended for 30 days and fined $500 by the New York Commission for not telling them of the bribe offer. Commissioner Eagan would organise elimination series with stipulation that Sugar Ray be one of the title contenders. The other one to be eventually agreed on was Tommy Bell of Youngstown, Ohio, a guy Ray had already beaten over ten rounds.

With the title fight looming at last, Ray figured a warm-up bout was in order. He chose Artie Levine, a 21-year-old middleweight from Brooklyn with 50 fights on his dance card.

---

57 Jack Cuddy *Dunkirk Evening Observer* New York 25 September 1946

58 Sugar Ray Robinson with Dave Anderson *Sugar Ray* 1969

Halfway through the ten-rounder in Cleveland, Sugar wished he had picked a different partner.

'For eight tumultuous seconds last night, it seemed that young Artie Levine was about to achieve the biggest upset in post-war boxing,' reported United Press. 'It seemed to the frenzied 12,102 fans in the Cleveland Arena that the fair-skinned middleweight was about to tag the great Ray (Sugar) Robinson with a knockout. But at the end of those eight seconds – at the count of eight in the fourth round – Robinson rose from the canvas. He weathered an immediate hurricane of blows. He came on, through one of the most thrill-packed battles ever staged in this lakeside city, to knock out Levine at 2.41 of the tenth and final round. Going out for that tenth round, Levine had ignored the advice of his handlers to box cautiously. He replied, "Nuts. I'll knock him out now. He's getting tired." Robinson staggered him with a left hook to the head, and then drove him to the ropes. Robinson barraged him there and finally smashed him on the chin with a straight right. Levine grasped desperately at the ropes and he held himself in a half-sitting position as referee Jackie Davis counted him out.'[59]

Big George Gainford started breathing again. 'That warm-up was too warm, Robinson. You got a big fight coming up. Time to get ready.'

Back in New York City, there was good news. The fight for the world championship would be in Madison Square Garden on 20 December 1946. The dream was coming true for a little black kid called Walker Smith Jr from Detroit, five days before Christmas.

59 *Ames Daily Tribune* Iowa 7 November 1946

6

SUGAR RAY IS THE CHAMPION – OFFICIAL

GEORGE GAINFORD was a worried man. He was at the training camp at Greenwood Lake, New York preparing Sugar Ray Robinson for the biggest fight of his life, for the vacant world welterweight championship against Tommy Bell in Madison Square Garden. Big George was worried because Ray wasn't focused on the job. There was something on his mind and it wasn't Tommy Bell. What it was was the site of his new café, which would be called 'Sugar Ray's' on Seventh Avenue between 123rd and 124th Streets. Workmen were toiling night and day to have the place ready for the night of 20 December – Ray's victory party.

'I almost blew the Bell fight over it,' he recalled in his autobiography. 'Every time the workmen needed me, I drove down from Greenwood Lake to make the decision myself. Whenever I did, George started to scream that I wasn't training properly. I knew I wasn't. Nevertheless, I wasn't about to let anybody make a decision on Sugar Ray's except Sugar Ray.'[60]

Somebody else hoping to make a decision on Sugar Ray and his plans for a victory party was Tommy Bell. From Youngstown, Ohio, he had won 39 of his 52 fights with 26 knockouts. At Ehsan's training camp at Summit, New Jersey, where he had boxed a total

60 Sugar Ray Robinson with Dave Anderson *Sugar Ray* 1969

of 85 rounds, Bell talked to columnist Red Smith of the *New York Herald Tribune*. 'What did you think of Robinson after your other night with him?' he was asked. Robinson knocked him down in the last round of a close bout. 'Well, I just wish I'd been in better shape.' 'Tell 'em what you told me,' Solly King said, 'about his punch.' King managed Bell with Ernie Braca. 'Well,' Bell said, 'he was knocking out everybody, see? I figure if he hits me I'm gone, so I was extra careful. Then, in the tenth, he catches me coming out of my corner and hits me a right and a left hook to the chin. I didn't go down and I couldn't believe it. But then he moved back and I tried to move away and my legs kind of wouldn't work and I fell on my head. But I got up and it was a hell of a round after that.'[61]

On Wednesday, examining physicians from the New York State Athletic Commission pronounced Robinson and Bell fit for the Friday night fight at the Garden. Sugar Ray had declared an end to sparring on Tuesday, a day early, after working one round each with Jackie Cooper, Jimmy Taylor and Clarence Wilkinson. He weighed 149 pounds and expected to dry out the two pounds necessary to make the 147-pound limit at noon on Friday. Bell worked one round against Johnny Eagle and two against Art Robinson and hit 147 pounds when winding up camp at Ehsan's. Robinson was being quoted at 1 to 4 to take the title.

The day of the fight, veteran sports scribe Oscar Fraley wrote, 'There wasn't anything "going" at Madison Square Garden as Sugar Ray Robinson met Tommy Bell for the welterweight championship. On the heels of the football gambling scandal, the palace of punch failed even to come up with its usual low-talking groups which gather before the main event and discuss the odds. You couldn't wager a dime in the joint, according to one veteran who usually knows where you can get a price.'[62]

It was a lousy night that Friday as rain and snow hit Manhattan, but there was still a good crowd numbering 15,670, who paid

---

61 Red Smith *New York Herald Tribune* 19 December 1946

62 Oscar Fraley *Salt Lake Tribune* 21 December 1946

$82,948 into the box office. Writing of Rocky Graziano, Ted Carroll observed, 'No one has ever seen him wear a hat. The night Tommy Bell boxed Ray Robinson for the welterweight title, a blizzard hit New York. Forced to park his car some distance away from the Garden, Rocky strode into the lobby with a head full of snow that made him look like an ice cream cone.'[63]

With former champions Jack Dempsey and Gene Tunney and current king of them all, Joe Louis, at ringside, the judges were announced as Arthur Schwartz and Jack O'Sullivan, with referee Eddie Joseph in charge of the action.

The first round followed the expected script, with Bell forcing the action and Robinson countering with the cleaner, more effective punches from his upright stance, gloves up high, as Tommy shuffled forward with menacing hooks and right hands.

'For a while there in the early going,' wrote Sid Feder from ringside, 'it looked as though what was regarded as a sure-pop win for Robinson, as soon as he showed up, was going to turn out to be the largest rabbit pulled out of the little hat since Max Schmeling made the eyebrows pop clear off all over the place by knocking out Joe Louis. Tommy, who lost a close decision to Robinson nearly two years ago, came on in the last moments of the first round, and pulled the trigger on his big one in the second. After a short, slugging session near the ropes, he suddenly came winging in with a long, larruping left hook and there was the uncrowned champion flat on the floor.

'Ray shook his head, pulled himself together, and was up at seven and flailing away before the round ended. In the third, Ray opened a body attack, but was nailed a couple more of those four-star hooks which did him absolutely no good. In the fourth, Bell found the range again, took two lefts to the face to work his way into firing range, then cut loose with the left once more. Tommy ripped in after him, but on the way in Bell slipped to his knees on the ring floor. By the time he righted himself, the lean man from

63 Ted Carroll *The Ring* October 1947

Harlem had shaken the cobwebs off and was ready to go again. That was Bell's high spot of the fight. If he hadn't slipped right then, there's no telling what further damage he might have done to a Robinson who was definitely staggered and shaky on his pins and no end astonished at the way things were turning out.'[64]

'Uncrowned king of the welterweights,' wrote veteran scribe Oscar Fraley from his ringside perch. 'That's what they have been calling the slim Harlem dynamiter who has lost only one fight in his career. But for five rounds in the glaring circle of light at Madison Square Garden last night, Sugar Ray was no better than the crown prince. The crowd was cheering violently, hungry sounds which roared through the rafters as Bell chased Robinson about the ring. This Robinson was a man with glowing bruises on his face and confusion in his eyes, and the frenzied fans were rooting for the underdog.

'But then came the sixth round and retribution for the man who had dared humiliate the mighty Sugar Ray. Robinson banged him with everything in the book and claret flowed freely from Bell's nose. By the tenth, it had blossomed like a ripe tomato. And in the 11th, his face was a gory mass through which Bell peered as Robinson sent him crashing to the canvas for an eight count. He was on queer street then and through the 12th. Bell was a tottering target which absorbed all the battering from those flailing fists of the uncrowned king about to be crowned. He shook them off and clutched and staggered and fell back and then still had the courage to come back swinging. He was there on sheer guts. And he had enough of them to surge back and win the 13th round with a surprise attack. But nobody in the house felt he could win and it was no surprise when Robinson whaled him at will again through the 14th and 15th.'[65]

At the final bell, the decision and the title were for Sugar Ray Robinson. Judge Artie Schwartz had it ten rounds to five for Ray,

---

64 Sid Feder *Troy Record* New York 21 December 1946

65 Oscar Fraley *Ogden Standard Examiner* 21 December 1946

judge Jack O'Sullivan saw Robinson a winner eight rounds to six, while referee Eddie Joseph cast a 10-5 verdict for Sugar Ray. In registering his 74th victory in 76 professional bouts, Robinson weighed 146½ pounds, Bell 146.

'Bell, who never had been knocked out in his career, menaced Robinson until the seventh round. And going into the seventh session, the United Press scorecard had Tommy ahead, three rounds to two, with one even. Bell had taken the second, third and fifth and he had fought on even terms in the sixth. Robinson took the first and fourth. However, after the deciding seventh session, Bell took only the 13th. Bell was bleeding freely from his nose and lower lip during most of the milling, and Robinson suffered slight gashes on both brows.'[66]

The uncrowned champion for five years was finally crowned. 'The only trouble was,' Ray said in his autobiography, 'my throne room wasn't ready. I had purchased the building a few months before. It had to be renovated. The target date was the night of the Bell fight. I wanted to open my café with a celebration. "No way we can have it ready until Christmas Eve," the foreman told me. About two hours after I won the title, I drove up outside my café. Inside the workmen were installing the lights behind the bar and when I walked in with Edna Mae, they cheered and called me "champ". "Hey, champ," one of them said, "the sign's hooked up. Turn on the sign. It lights up like Coney Island." I turned the switch and went outside. Above me, in red neon, "Sugar Ray's" lit up the avenue. Man, my own café, with my name on it. Everything was starting to come together the way I'd dreamed when I was a kid. Winning a title. Owning a business.

'Rushing inside, I got out a couple of bottles and put them on one of the new wooden tables. No tablecloth. No glasses, but there were some paper cups around. I found a Coke somewhere, and one of the workmen poured drinks for Edna Mae and the other men. "To Sugar Ray's," one of them said, lifting his cup. "To Sugar

---

66 Jack Cuddy *Salt Lake Tribune* 21 December 1946

Ray's," I said, raising my bottle of Coke. It was one of the nicest celebrations I've ever had.'[67]

There was no celebration for his opponent. 'Tommy Bell, who was defeated by Sugar Ray Robinson in a welterweight title bout at Madison Square Garden last night, left today for Reading, Pennsylvania after receiving word that one of his brothers was in a hospital after an automobile wreck. The brother, Shed Bell, apparently was driving into New York from his Youngstown home for the fight. The wire to Bell read: "Auto wrecked. In hospital. Please come as soon as possible." Bell left immediately after settling the financial accounts for the fight, for which he was paid about $13,000.'[68]

An Associated Press item datelined Reading, Pa. 23 December 1946, read, 'Major Hall, 20, a navy veteran and former trainer for welterweight boxer Tommy Bell, died Saturday night of a fractured skull sustained in an auto accident while en route to New York to see Bell's losing fight against Sugar Ray Robinson. Two of Tommy's brothers, Shed and Isaac Bell, also were injured in the accident but were discharged from the Reading hospital. The three are from Youngstown, Ohio.'[69]

Tommy Bell would carry on fighting for another five years, winning 14 of his 33 fights with one draw. He was knocked out seven times in his 18 losing bouts. He did it the hard way, meeting such tough middleweights as Jake LaMotta, Steve Belloise, Anton Raadick and top welters like Kid Gavilan, Jackie Wilson and Frankie Fernandez. But he never got another crack at Robinson.

'Now that I had the title,' Ray said, 'I had to defend it. George Gainford had always told me that a fighter had to keep busy, had to stay sharp. I had three easy non-title fights and I was about to go against another middleweight, Georgie Abrams, when a welterweight title bout was arranged. The challenger was Jimmy Doyle, a nice little guy out of Los Angeles. The date was 30 May

67 Sugar Ray Robinson with Dave Anderson *Sugar Ray* 1969

68 *Zanesville Signal* Ohio 22 December 1946

69 *The Evening Sun* Hanover Pa. 23 December 1946

in Cleveland, but Abrams messed up the schedule. He messed me up, too. I got the decision without too much trouble, but Abrams cut me over both eyes. The Doyle fight was only two weeks away. George called the Cleveland promoter, Larry Atkins, and told him that it would have to be postponed. The next day, Atkins announced a new date, 10 June. I got on the phone. "That's still not enough time," I told Atkins. "You've got to make it the end of the month."

'Atkins agreed, but when Tony Palazolo, a one-legged guy who was Doyle's manager, heard about it, he started hollering that I was trying to duck the fight. Anyway, Atkins made 24 June the new date. That satisfied me and it quieted Palazolo. About 14 months earlier, Doyle had been through a bad experience. He had been knocked out by Artie Levine, the Brooklyn middleweight, and had to go to the hospital with a concussion, but he soon recovered.'[70]

Ray's argument with Tony Palazolo over the date of the fight never happened. The veteran fight manager and promoter from San Francisco died on Saturday, 23 March 1946 after undergoing an abdominal operation in Polyclinic Hospital in New York. The 57-year-old manager, who had developed Jimmy Doyle, was upset that week because he wanted to leave his hospital bed and fly to Cleveland, where Doyle had suffered a brain injury after being knocked out by Artie Levine in the ninth round after taking three counts. Had he lived, peg-leg Tony would not have allowed his boy to be in the same town as Sugar Ray Robinson, let alone share a boxing ring with the welterweight champion, already being hailed as one of the best fighters in the world.

The 22-year-old Doyle, real name Delaney, did recover from the Levine fight, but he was out of the ring for nine months before coming back to win five bouts prior to fighting Robinson. 'Edward Delaney said of his brother that he was a changed man after the Levine fight. He said that before that knockout, Jimmy was active, a great dancer and was always sparring around the house. After

70 *Sugar Ray with Dave Anderson* 1969

the bout, Jimmy sat for hours reading books, was always quiet and insisted he would never return to the prize ring.'[71]

Considered a great prospect when he left Los Angeles after being trained by two former heavyweight greats, Jim Jeffries and Jack Johnson, Jimmy Doyle had won 42 times in 51 bouts, losing six with three draws. That night in the Cleveland Arena, Doyle fought a good fight against the champion. The sixth was his best round. The eighth was his last.

'When I got to Cleveland,' Robinson recalled in his autobiography, 'I stayed at the house of a buddy of mine, Roger Price. And it was there, the night before the fight, that I had a dream, a premonition. In the dream, Jimmy Doyle was in the ring with me. I hit him a few good punches and he was on his back, his blank eyes staring up at me, and I was staring down at him, not knowing what to do, and the referee was moving in to count to ten and Doyle still wasn't moving a muscle and in the crowd I could hear people yelling, "He's dead, he's dead," and I didn't know what to do. Then I woke up.

'In the morning, I told George Gainford about the dream. But George didn't want to hear about it. "Forget it, Robinson," he said. "That's a dream, that's all." At the weigh-in, I quietly told Larry Atkins, the promoter, about it. "I don't want to fight Doyle," I told Atkins. "I don't want anything to happen." "Don't be ridiculous," he said. "Dreams don't come true. If they did, I'd be a millionaire." As much as I didn't want to go through with the fight, I decided to do it after being persuaded by a priest whose name I've forgotten and who was summoned by the commission.'[72]

'Jarred by a stiff left hook in the opening round, Doyle had the worst of matters for two further sessions, in which he was freely punished about the body and head. He started forcing the action in the fourth, only to be met by some heavy counter-punching from the champion. Jimmy was twice staggered in the fifth, but

71 *The Laredo Times* Texas 27 June 1947

72 Sugar Ray Robinson with Dave Anderson *Sugar Ray* 1969

was strong and full of fight. He came back fiercely in the next, opening a nasty cut over Robinson's right eye, and for the first time he appeared to have a chance. Jimmy seemed to have destroyed some of Ray's timing and sapped his strength. The champion was very lethargic in the seventh and Doyle took the round.

'Then, late in the eighth, Robinson produced new vigour. Two quick rights to the body made Doyle quake and Ray pressed his advantage as the Los Angeles boy attempted to fight back. They were in mid-ring when Jimmy launched a right. It brought him close in, and Ray promptly countered with a left hook to the chin, short and shocking. Doyle toppled backwards and went down heavily, his head striking the floor with a thud. He lay unmoved while the count proceeded, but at nine the bell clanged to end the round, and he was removed to his corner. Every effort was made to bring him round, but he was still unconscious when the gong sounded to start the ninth. It was then apparent that his condition was serious and he was immediately removed to the dressing room on a stretcher and afterwards taken to hospital.'[73]

The loser was carried on a stretcher to an ambulance, which sped him to St Vincent Charity Hospital. Seventeen hours later he was dead. Coroner Samuel J. Gerber reported, 'Doyle died from a cerebral hemorrhage. There was general hemorrhage in the brain, considerable in the back of the brain. There was concussion also. The evidence of the old brain injuries are there.'[74]

Sugar Ray's dream had become a nightmare. Coroner Gerber said Robinson would be arraigned immediately on a technical manslaughter charge and police homicide members ordered the champion not to leave town. Simultaneously, Mayor Thomas A. Burke demanded a full report of the fight from Andrew Putka, chairman of the Cleveland Boxing Commission.

The Associated Press reported from Cleveland 25 June: 'Whether Jimmy Doyle died from a punch or from striking the

---

73 *Boxing News* London 27 June 1947

74 *Vincennes Sun Commercial* Indiana 25 June 1947

ring floor was disputed by medical authorities tonight as a coroner's probe into the fatal welterweight championship fight deepened. Dr A.F. Hagerdorn, physician for the Cleveland Boxing Commission, said the brain injuries that caused the Los Angeles boxer's death yesterday resulted from his head hitting the floor when he suffered an eighth-round technical knockout by champion Ray (Sugar) Robinson. "If I give you a push and you fall and hit your head awfully hard on the floor, what kills you?" he said in explaining. Coroner Samuel R. Gerber said that although the ring floor might have added to the damage, the left hook to the jaw caused the injury.'[75]

Veteran scribe Oscar Fraley wrote from New York, 'The clay that was Jimmy Doyle became additional evidence today against the greed and corruption of boxing. The guy from Los Angeles had been in the death house of the ring for 15 months, ever since the night he suffered a critical concussion against the feathery taps of Artie Levine. So they threw him in against Ray (Sugar) Robinson, one of the hardest hitters in the history of the game. And the execution came off as might have been expected.'[76]

With all due respect to columnist Fraley, the 'feathery taps' of Artie Levine gave him a 53 per cent knockout average, with 38 knockouts in 53 winning fights. Levine did have ten pounds on welterweight Doyle and he almost knocked out Sugar Ray Robinson a few weeks before Robinson beat Tommy Bell for the world title. But I agree with Mr Fraley when he wrote, 'Taking away a fighter's licence in the case of cerebral injuries would have saved the life of Jimmy Doyle.'

'At the inquest, Sugar was asked if he had intended to get his opponent "in trouble". Sugar replied dejectedly, "It's my business to get him in trouble." Later, Sugar was more contrite and compassionate. He wrote a note to Doyle's mother in Los Angeles. "I wanted to do something more for her." Out of the proceeds from

75 *Titusville Herald* Pennsylvania 27 June 1947

76 Oscar Fraley *Winnipeg Free Press* Manitoba 27 June 1947

a fight against Flashy Sebastian at the Garden several weeks later – nearly $25,000 – he sent her half. There was another benefit for Doyle, and Sugar donated $6,500 more, from which a trust fund was established to give Doyle's mother $50 a month.'[77]

A United Press bulletin from Cleveland dated 27 June announced, 'No blame was attached today to welterweight champion Ray (Sugar) Robinson in a report by coroner Samuel Gerber on circumstances which led to the death of challenger Jimmy Doyle from a blow suffered in a title fight here Tuesday night.'[78]

'By the time Sugar Ray Robinson left Cleveland, his poise had begun to return. Edna Mae had wrapped her lovely arms around him. George Gainford was calling him champ, champ, champ. "I don't know how it will affect Ray's fighting in the future," Gainford said before departing Cleveland. "He's just like anyone else and is bound to have some reaction. How it will manifest itself, time will tell."'[79]

---

77 Herb Boyd with Ray Robinson II *Pound for Pound* 2005

78 *The Laredo Times* Texas 27 June 1947

79 Wil Haygood *Sweet Thunder: The Life and Times of Sugar Ray Robinson* 2009

7

KID GAVILAN AND STEVE BELLOISE

A COUPLE of months after the Doyle tragedy, Big George had Robinson back in harness in Akron, Ohio, where Sugar was boxing the first of a series of benefits for Jimmy's family. In a steady drizzle, the welterweight champion jabbed Sammy Secreet dizzy before a sizzling right cross had Sailor Sammy all at sea. By the time he was rescued, it was all over at 1.50 of round one. Middleweight champion Rocky Graziano boxed an exhibition bout with Cliff Kierkle of Paterson, New Jersey and promoter Bob Heath announced that about $700 of the $9,542 gate would go to the Doyle family.

A week later, 29 August, Sugar Ray was back in familiar surroundings at Madison Square Garden, where some 17,000 witnessed one of the quickest main-event knockouts in the history of the famous New York arena. Robinson belted out Flashy Sebastian of the Philippines at 1.02 of the first round. 'This kayo did not equal the record of 59 seconds established for a Garden main event on 23 May 1946 when Gus Lesnevich, light-heavy king, stopped Melio Bettina, but it earned second ranking.

'Brown-skinned Robinson stunned the squat, broad-shouldered Filipino with a left hook to the chin. Then Sugar Ray battered him into the ropes with a hooking barrage to body and head. As Sebastian came off the ropes, Robinson exploded a left hook under his chin that lifted his feet from the floor and dropped him on his back on the canvas in a neutral corner. Referee Ruby Goldstein counted him out. The scheduled ten-rounder was finished so quickly that most of the legionnaires and notables had scarcely settled in their chairs after singing *The Star Spangled Banner.*'[80]

Many years later, writer W. C. Heinz was talking to Robinson. 'In that Sebastian fight,' I said, 'you came out of your corner for the first round and he threw a wide hook, and you brought your right glove up and blocked it. He backed off, and came in again and did the same thing. This time you threw the right hand inside the hook and followed it with a hook of your own, and he went back on his head. Then he tried to get up and he fell forward on his face, and the photographers at ringside were hollering, "Get, this! Get this! This guy may die, too." "I know," he said. "I said, 'O, Lord, don't let it happen again.'"'[81]

A few months later, 19 December 1947, Sugar Ray was in Detroit defending his title against Chuck Taylor of Coalport, Pennsylvania and again his challenger ended up in hospital. This time, Dr H. A. Lichtwardt, at Woman's Hospital, was happy to report, 'The young challenger suffered no serious injury and no surgery will be needed. However, Taylor must stay in hospital for several days for rest and observation of the kidney injury which he said occurred in the second round.'[82]

Robinson had to take off seven pounds in five days to come in just under the division limit of 147 pounds. He admittedly tired during the fight, but his punching power seemed as potent as ever when he finally found an opening. Midway in the sixth round, Robinson sent a left hook to Taylor's body and then fired a right cross that sent the challenger down for nine. It was only moments before Robinson repeated the performance and sent Taylor down again. As referee Johnny Weber tolled off the count, Jack Laken, Taylor's manager, threw in the towel. Throwing in the towel is

80 *Associated Press Oakland Tribune* California 30 August 1947

81 W. C. Heinz *Once They Heard the Cheers* 1979,

82 *New Castle News* Pa. 20 December 1947

not recognised in Michigan rings, so Weber continued the count until Taylor regained his feet at nine, and then waved Robinson away at 2.07 of the sixth round.

Sugar Ray Robinson, welterweight champion of the world, was fast becoming a middleweight. In June 1948, Associated Press reported from Chicago, 'Ray Sugar Robinson's 15-round decision over young Bernie Docusen to retain his crown is the story of a steak. The machine-like Harlem slugger starved himself for two days to make the 147-pound weight limit. Then, after tipping the scales at 146½ at yesterday's weigh-in, he drank a quart of beef broth and gnawed through a two-pound broiled steak. This was his first solid food in 48 hours of forced dehydration to shed four or five pounds. That hunk of beef did it. During most of last night's title defence in Comiskey Park against the 21-year-old New Orleans challenger, six years his junior, Robinson was a blur of power and precision. He had to be to beat the "Dook", a dead-pan, polished little Filipino who made the champion go the route. The decision was unanimous.'[83]

Standing in for the ailing Mike Jacobs, relative Sol Strauss had booked the Yankee Stadium in the hope that some 25,000 fans would chip in a gate of $100,000 to see champions Ike Williams and Sugar Ray Robinson in action. Lightweight champ Williams was defending his title against California Mexican Jesse Flores while Robinson was going against the flashy Cuban Kid Gavilan.

Jack Cuddy, United Press, wrote from New York, 'Champions Ike Williams and Ray (Sugar) Robinson had new title defence opportunities today as a result of victories achieved during the 20th Century Club's financial fiasco at Yankee Stadium. Brown-skinned Williams kept his lightweight crown last night by knocking out Jesse Flores at 2.04 of the tenth round before a sprinkling 15,413 chilled fans in the Yankees' huge ball park. It was the smallest crowd that ever witnessed a title fight at the stadium.

'Meanwhile, welterweight champion Robinson discovered a formidable challenger during his ten-round non-title exploration

83 *San Antonio Light* 29 June 1948

in the nearly-empty stadium. Kid Gavilan, the "Cuban Clipper," gave Robinson a hell-for-leather fight before slender Ray wound up with the unanimous but unpopular decision. Gavilan's American manager, little Angel Lopez, declared, "If Robinson doesn't sign to defend against Gavilan [again], I'll keep Robinson's forfeit of $5,000 that he lost yesterday when he weighed 150½ pounds. Sugar Ray had posted $5,000 with the 20th Century Club, under a private agreement with the Gavilan camp that he would weigh not more than 150 for the Cuban, who scaled 140¼.

'Although Robinson was a 5-1 favourite over Gavilan, the Cuban Negro carried the fight to Harlem Ray in every round. Only Robinson's greater experience and fast footwork enabled him to wind up with the decision. Gavilan's flashing left hooks to body and head and his "Bolo" right uppercut nearly brought the second defeat in the champ's long career. And at no time was the bobbing and weaving Gavilan in danger of suffering the first knockout of his own career.'[84]

In the May 1949 issue of *The Ring* magazine, Al Buck recalled two fights Robinson had in February, 'sucker fights' Al called them. 'Ray Robinson didn't have a care in the world when he drifted into Buffalo. He was going to honour an old contract by fighting Henry Brimm. He had outpointed him in ten rounds the year previously. Just a soft fight – a sucker fight. What Robinson didn't know was that Brimm had been left for dead on the Normandy sands on D-Day. Although reported killed in action, he had survived. He was a man who knew he could come back.

'After the fury of the ten-round battle was over, the official decision was a draw. The welterweight champion didn't alibi, but instead remarked with charming frankness, "Brimm is a really good fighter." Henry Brimm was the second "sucker" opponent Robinson took on in a month's period, the first being veteran Gene Buffalo. Ray boxed Gene at Wilkes-Barre, Pennsylvania and when they met on the scales, Buffalo weighed 148 pounds. When they

84 Jack Cuddy *Altoona Mirror* Pa. 24 September 1948

were in the ring, Robinson heard the announcer say that Buffalo scaled 145¾ pounds. That meant the welterweight championship was at stake.

'"What's going on here?" Ray asked. He was told that Buffalo had weighed in with his shoes and tights on, contrary to the rules of the Pennsylvania Commission. "What am I going to do?" the startled champion inquired of George Gainford, his manager. "If you don't want to lose the title, you'd better knock him out," Big George answered. Robinson made it short and sweet, settling the issue in the first round.'[85]

Like most married couples, Sugar Ray and Edna Mae had their problems. The champion was handsome, charming, a ladies' man. His café on Seventh Avenue in Harlem was a babe magnet and he was never without feminine company. There was this time he had separated from Edna Mae and was living with his mother. 'One night in my café,' he recalled, 'I was strolling around, greeting the customers, when I noticed this long pair of legs. The rest of her was all there, too. I guess I was staring. "Hi," she said to me, "I'm Dolores." By the time I got her home that night, I had her phone number. We soon got to be a twosome.'[86]

Parked in a lovers' lane one night, overlooking the Harlem River, Ray's twosome became a threesome. Edna Mae, knowing where to find Ray, stepped from a taxi and asked him to come home. Both ladies were in tears and the champ was in a dilemma. He was due in camp to train for the championship return with Kid Gavilan, set for Philadelphia 11 July 1949. Sugar did what he had to do. He went to training camp at Pompton Lakes, New Jersey, where his pal Joe Louis trained for many of his fights, and got himself into top condition. Ray remembered his first fight with the Cuban, a tough ten rounds, and this time it would be for 15 rounds. The Kid had something he called the 'bolo' punch, a long, looping right he developed swinging the heavy seven-pound

85 Al Buck *The Ring* May 1950

86 Sugar Ray Robinson with Dave Anderson *Sugar Ray* 1969

bolo knife to cut the cane back home. The Kid also had a concrete chin, as Johnny Williams found out. Williams, from Montgomery, Alabama, fought Gavilan in his first two fights in New York. The Kid won both decisions and Johnny told reporters, 'I belted him right on the chin, but he came right back and floored me. I told Gavilan I broke seven jaws with that punch. Anybody who stands up like you did is going to be a champion.'[87]

Kid Gavilan did become a welterweight champion but he had to wait until Robinson gave up the title to fight at middleweight. That night in Philadelphia's sprawling Municipal Stadium, the Cuban found the sugar back home easier to cut down than the Sugar in the ring with him. He tried but Robinson staged a magnificent fight to come out with the unanimous decision. 'Some 28,000 fans paid more than $175,000 to watch the spidery champion's rapier-like left chop the Cuban to ribbons as it flicked into his swollen, blood-smeared features with the speed of a striking rattler. Occasionally, Gavilan managed to shake the Harlem slugger with whistling right-hand smashes. He rocked the champion twice and in the 14th Sugar Ray was on the ropes and in bad shape at the bell.'[88]

'In the 14th, though Ray won the session,' recorded Nat Fleischer in the September 1949 issue of *The Ring* magazine, 'he gave Gavilan an opportunity to gain the cheers of his followers when he remained against the ropes for almost a minute and permitted the Kid to let go a volley which ringsiders noticed did little damage, but which those in the grandstand seats figured to be most effective. Ray weaved his head, his guard down, and let most of the volley strike the air or his shoulders.

'But after that volley was over, the champ took command again. He opened up in the 15th with everything he had and for a time it appeared that the Cuban might be dropped, so effective was the defending title-holder's attack. He staggered the Kid with a left

---

87 Hugh Fullerton Jnr. *Lowell Sun* Mass. 12 July 1949

88 Tom R. Brislin *Lowell Sun* Mass. 12 July 1949

hook to the jaw and followed with a beautiful uppercut that almost took the Cuban off his feet. Ringsiders could hear the groans of the Cuban reporters as the blow landed. Then came a straight left that crashed flush on Gavilan's jaw and again the Cuban was shaken by the punch. That round was Ray's best, a finish which was quite unexpected because of the difficulty that the champ had in making weight. He tipped the beam at exactly 147, the top limit of the division, as against 144½ for his opponent.'

'What they didn't know was that Sugar had received an injection of glucose from Dr Vincent Nardiello, the one-time New York state boxing commission's doctor. This provided him with extra pep after the struggle to make the weight, though the glucose was known to dehydrate and reduce salt content. When the sweat dropped into your mouth, as Soldier Jones had taught him, and tasted stale and not salty, it meant your sugar content had also dropped.'[89]

Robinson still had enough sugar left to thwart the sugar cane cutter from Cuba.

Referee Charley Daggert called it nine rounds to six for Robinson, as did Harry Lasky, one of the judges. The other judge, Frank Knaresborough, saw Robinson a winner 12 rounds to three, as did James P. Dawson for the *New York Times,* who wrote, 'Gavilan just is not in the same class with the Harlem Negro, though the Cuban has more endurance, determination and fearlessness than any other in Robinson's limited field of challengers. What Gavilan lacks is the boxing skill and paralysing punching power of the champion. Robinson admitted after the battle he was taking no chances, though he might have in the eighth round when he staggered Gavilan. Robinson's play was to win and that he did without exposing himself to any more danger than a slight cut over the right eye sustained in the fourth round.

'Following the battle, a contradiction developed in the champion's quarters. Manager George Gainford said from the ring

89 Herb Boyd with Ray Robinson II *Pound for Pound* 2005

that Robinson would be ready again to defend his welterweight title 24 August. Robinson, however, indicated he might surrender the welterweight crown and seek the middleweight title, now held by rugged Jake LaMotta. "I was in the best shape of my career for this fight," said Robinson. "I never tired and he never hurt me." Gavilan, crestfallen, nevertheless had little complaint to offer. "I didn't see too many rounds for Robinson," he said in his broken English. "The judge who gave him 12 rounds, he crazy. He hit me hard several times, but I was surprised at the decision and would like to make one more fight with heem.'"[90]

The fight was better than the organisation, which was a mess, a new outfit doing outdoor boxing for the first time. The ringside press had to fight for their seats and the car parking was a free-for-all. Matchmaker Johnny Attell had taken a stand against television. When local fans discovered there was no TV, they rushed the stadium's two box offices. One of them was tipped over, and inside the stadium the ushers couldn't handle the crowd. The aisles were clogged and people were coming down out of the stands to the ringside. The show was a financial success with a gross gate of $175,754, but Attell said he could have taken another $50,000 had he been prepared for such a crowd. Ray was happy with his biggest purse to date, $51,740. His previous biggest purse was $25,000 and it was the first time he'd cut into a gate of $100,000 or more.

'Although he didn't get beyond the first year in high school,' wrote W. C. Heinz in an article for the *Saturday Evening Post,* 'Robinson has a quick mind and strong business instinct. When, in April of 1949, he signed with the Tournament of Champions, a pro-tem promotional organisation then challenging the Jacobs dynasty, to fight middleweight Steve Belloise for a guarantee of $25,000, he immediately obtained $5,000 for training expenses. It could not have cost him half of that to train, he was merely protecting himself in the event the promotion fell through. The Jacobs organisation, then representing the Garden, and the

90 James P. Dawson *New York Times* 12 July 1949

Tournament of Champions were competing for the match. Jacobs and his lawyer, Sol Strauss, called Robinson to their office. "He agreed," a Garden spokesman says, "to fight Belloise for $20,000. Then he borrowed $1,000. Strauss wanted him to sign the contract right away, but Robinson said he'd come in the next day and sign. Strauss objected, but Mike said, "Forget it. You don't think a guy who just borrowed a thousand will go back on his word, do you?" Then Robinson left, walked one block and signed with the Tournament of Champions for a $25,000 guarantee. We couldn't believe it.'[91]

On a chilly November night in 1940, Bronx middleweight Steve Belloise was fighting the main event at Madison Square Garden against Ken Overlin, recognised by the New York Commission as world champion. Belloise was pitting his 31-2-1 pro record against the veteran Overlin, who brought a 115-18-6 record to the ring. In what the *New York Times* called a 'furiously contested' bout, Belloise decked the champ in round six and was looking for the title after 15 rounds. When the referee scored a draw, with both judges going for the New York titleholder, the crowd erupted. Six weeks later, they were at it again in another blistering 15 rounds and this time referee Arthur Donovan saw Steve a 9-4-2 winner. But once again, both judges voted Overlin the winner and still champion.

That night in the Garden, after a sensational amateur career, Harlem lightweight Sugar Ray Robinson was boxing a four-round prelim bout against Oliver White. In round two, the fans saw a boxing rarity, a double knockdown. Both lads got up and Robinson ended it in the next round, his sixth pro bout. Now, in August 1949, world welterweight champion Sugar Ray Robinson was going into the Yankee Stadium ring for his 100th pro bout against Steve Belloise, the Bronx veteran of 103 pro fights, still looking for a title shot. The winner of this one was promised a shot at world champ Jake LaMotta after the Bronx Bull's return with

91 W. C. Heinz *Saturday Evening Post* 9 December 1950

former champion Marcel Cerdan. Helping boost the fight, Cerdan watched both fighters at their training camps and forecast victory for Steve, telling reporters, 'Belloise hits too hard for Robinson; besides he'll have an advantage of about eight pounds.'

On the big night, Ray weighed 153½ to 158 for Belloise, and was 28 years old against Steve's 30. Robinson came into the ring with a brilliant 96-1-2 record, including 63 knockouts. He had already beaten LaMotta (his only conqueror) four times and was looking forward to what would be their final bout. On this night, Steve Belloise was standing across the ring at Yankee Stadium and a crowd of 28,812 eager fans who had paid a gross gate of $121,131.45 were impatient for the first bell.

'They've been saying for some time now,' wrote Joe Williams from ringside, 'that pound for pound Sugar Ray Robinson, the Harlem Hotshot, is the best fighter in the fight game. Well, last night he came into the ring with several more pounds than he customarily carries and he was simply superb. He had old-timers like James (Bow Tie) Bronson drooling. "He's the best to come along since Joe Gans' time," said Mr Bronson, who goes that far back and then some. When you compare a fighter with Joe Gans, another Negro, you are putting him right up there with the Olympians. There may have been some who were as good but none was ever better.

'The crowd that gathered under the lights in Yankee Stadium last night saw Robinson at what is very likely his absolute peak. There isn't anything he can't do and do superlatively well. He is what you'd call a finished fighter in the truest sense. His footwork is excellent and he has ring cunning. Belloise went as far as he could on what he had, which wasn't much. He fought with resolution and gallantry up to the very end and when he landed squarely, he hurt and shook the Negro. And once – in the fourth – he made Robinson quit and back away.

'It is not too far from the facts to say that Robinson knocked him out three times, first in the third when the bell saved him, again in the sixth when the bell once more saved him and, finally, in the seventh when, helpless and insensible on the floor, the bell bonged at the count of five, but this time it meant more than a reprieve. It meant finish.'[92]

Veteran scribe Oscar Fraley, for United Press, wrote, 'The lithe welterweight champion, whose added poundage boosted him to the fore as a middleweight challenger, has knocked over a lot of guys – some good, some bad, and a lot of them excellent – in his nine-year career as a canvas decorator. But he didn't expect to do it in the cool darkness at Yankee Stadium last night. Yet he did, with the balding Steve Belloise's battered head lolling on his shoulders as he wandered through a punch-inspired darkness at the end of the seventh round. They carried Belloise to his corner at the bell – sound asleep. Dough-faced Eddie Walker, his manager, called off the fight before the bell could sound for the eighth, simply because there wasn't time to shake Steve awake.

'And in the dressing room a few minutes later, Robinson no longer was his usual cocky self, even in victory. He was an amazed young man, awed by his own power. "I was as surprised as he was when he went down," Robinson said. "I didn't expect to knock him out. I'd have been satisfied with a decision." Belloise knew finally, and irrevocably, what Sugar Ray's hammering fists have been etching into the records for nine years.'[93]

Editor Nat Fleischer wrote in *The Ring* magazine, 'In disposing so thoroughly, so artistically, so sensationally, of the dangerous Steve Belloise in their Yankee Stadium meeting, Robinson turned in one of the finest all-around performances of his career. It was Robinson's 100th professional bout, and the Harlem Hotshot couldn't have celebrated the momentous event in more auspicious fashion. Ray Robinson, no matter what he does from now until the time that he last steps out of a ring, has proven his right to a place among the all-time greats of the prize ring.'[94]

---

92 Joe Williams *El Paso Herald Post* 25 August 1949

93 Oscar Fraley *Abilene Reporter News* TX 25 August 1949

94 Nat Fleischer *The Ring* November 1949

8

THE FLAMINGO PINK CADILLAC

SYDENHAM HOSPITAL began as a private hospital in a Harlem brownstone house in 1892, serving mostly African-American patients. In 1924, the hospital moved to a new 200-bed facility at the intersection of Lenox Avenue and West 125th Street, and in one of those 200 beds on 14 November 1949, Sugar Ray's wife Edna Mae gave birth to a son. He weighed seven pounds four ounces and would be named Ray Jr. Ray Sr had weighed 150 pounds for his fight with Vern Lester the night before, in faraway New Orleans. He had offered to cancel the fight but Edna Mae assured him she would be all right.

Al Silvani was one of the top trainers around New York. 'In 1949, Silvani was watching Robinson work out in a Harlem gym when Robinson asked him to work with a veteran middleweight named Vern Lester. "Lester," Silvani recalls, "was a pretty good middleweight at one time. He had a bad eye. He couldn't see. But he needed money, so Robinson accepted a fight in New Orleans to fight Vern Lester. To get him a payday, you know. He [Robinson] said, 'Al, would you work with him and come down?' So all well and good, you know, the guy is gonna make a payday. He's gonna carry him and all that. And I think it was about the fourth or fifth round. All at once, he catches Robinson on the ropes. And he starts to throw punches at him and all that. And the bell rings and he's still throwing punches. I'll never forget it. I had to take him to the corner. I said, 'What the hell are you doing?' He said, 'I think I got him.' So I said, 'Jesus Christ, the bell rings and you're still fighting.' When the bell for the next round rang, Silvani says, with an appreciative laugh, "Ray comes out of the corner and put his hands up like, 'Forget about it.' Ray hit him with a shot and knocked him dead. Boom! I'll never forget it. He puts his hands up and boom." And that was the end of the fight.'[95]

'The knockout,' records Boxrec, 'was the second of the fight. Referee Battling Ferdie was kayoed when he tried to separate Lester from Robinson after the bell ending the third round. Lester nailed the referee with a left hook and Ferdie was floored for 30 seconds. Robinson, who displayed masterful boxing before 4,000 fans, appeared to be annoyed at Lester for fighting after the bell ended three of the four rounds. At the start of the fifth, Robinson leaped from his corner, smashed a vicious left hook and then connected with a right cross, and Lester was counted out by Ferdie. The end came at 12 seconds.'

'Among the few fighters Robinson has felt strongly [about],' wrote Bill Heinz, 'was George (Sugar) Costner, a welterweight whom he knocked out in two minutes and 55 seconds of the first round in Chicago on 14 February 1945, and who ruffled Robinson's pride before their second fight in March 1950 in Philadelphia. "With that Costner, he was doing a lot of big talking," Robinson says. "He was going around telling everybody he could lick me and that he was the real welterweight champion. When I met him in Philly before the fight, I said to him, 'Listen, boy, you've been doing a lot of big talking. You know you're going to get a chance to back that up.' He said, 'No hard feelings, are there, Ray? I was just boosting the gate.' I said, 'That may be all right, but when I boost the gate I do it by praising my opponent.' He knocked out Costner this time in two minutes and 49 seconds of the first round.'[96]

---

95 Ronald K. Fried *Corner Men* 1991

96 W. C. Heinz *Saturday Evening Post* 9 December 1950

'On 27 October 1949, an Air France Lockheed Constellation left Paris' Orly Airport for New York City. Scheduled for a fuel stop in the Azores, an island group in the mid-Atlantic, captain Jean de la Neue lost radio contact and veered sharply off course. Seconds later, he crashed into the 3,600ft Mount Redondo. All 48 people on board were killed. The most famous of them was former world middleweight champion Marcel Cerdan, who was headed for a return bout with Jake LaMotta. Four months before, LaMotta had dethroned Cerdan by tenth-round TKO. The news of Cerdan's death darkened the entire boxing community. No other fighter had been so full of life.

'Middleweight champion Jake LaMotta's first title defence was supposed to be a rematch with the fighter he had dethroned, France's Marcel Cerdan. After Cerdan's shocking death, promoters scrambled for a replacement. Fittingly, they chose another Frenchman, Robert Villemain. At Madison Square Garden on 2 December 1949, LaMotta's title was not at stake. Having defeated Villemain in March, the "Raging Bull" climbed through the ropes a 3-1 favourite.

'In setting the line, however, the oddsmakers forgot to consider emotion. Villemain was similar in style to LaMotta and on this night he fought with far more energy. He crowded the champion, worked to the head and body, and after ten rounds the judges rewarded the Frenchman with scores of 7-3 twice and 5-3-2. "I did it for my country," he said, "and for Cerdan."'[97]

During his 15-year professional career, Cerdan won 110 of 114 bouts. But win, lose or draw, he always won more friends. He was confident of beating LaMotta in December, so confident that he recently exclaimed, 'This is the fight of my life. I win or die.'

From New York, veteran sportswriter Bill Corum said, 'Marcel Cerdan was so alive that it is impossible to think of him as dead. It seemed to me that he was a bit of France. A personification in his

97 *The Ring Chronicle of Boxing* 1993

small way of the gaiety and, at the same time, haunting sadness that has made Paris the city that men do not forget.'[98]

Mike Jacobs had kept Robinson away from the welterweight title for years before he tangled with Tommy Bell. Now that the backroom boys had finally got to Jake LaMotta, they weren't falling over backwards to give Sugar Ray a chance to do to the Bronx Bull what he had done in four of their five fights – beat him – and become middleweight champion. With Jake sitting in his throne room and not even answering the door, the Pennsylvania Commission stripped the champ of the title and declared that Sugar Ray Robinson would box for their version of the middleweight championship against the gallant Frenchman Robert Villemain, who had beaten LaMotta in a non-title bout in the Garden six months after Jake had beaten Cerdan.

From Philadelphia, Oscar Fraley wrote, 'Black hair hanging lankly over battered brows, Robert Villemain, the Parisian Bulldog, sat stolidly as a storm of voluble French broke around his broad shoulders. Villemain just had lost a 15-round decision to Ray (Sugar) Robinson, and with it Pennsylvania's recognition as middleweight champion of the world. All the way he had come boring in, but Robinson, the dancing dynamiter from Harlem, pot-shotted him handily and then pinned Villemain to the ropes. Now Villemain's camp was protesting explosively that the referee had hampered their squat, square-cut slugger. Villemain said nothing for a few seconds. Then he shook that hair back from his forehead, opened his brown eyes wide and declared, "He is the only man I have met who struck like that. He is a real champion." And over in his dressing room on the other side of sprawling Municipal Stadium, Robinson felt exactly the same way. Sugar Ray's night was well sweetened by the victory but he was looking ahead to bigger things – a shot at the other 47/48ths of the middleweight crown. Jake LaMotta holds the title in the rest of the land, and

98 Bill Corum *Troy Times Record* New York 29 October 1949

the world. "It's great to win this," Robinson smiled, "but now I want LaMotta."'[99]

Ray would get LaMotta, but he had to wait almost two years for the chance. Two years and 11 fights. The first one would be his last as champion of the welterweights. Jim Becker wrote for Associated Press, 'Sugar Ray Robinson, the welterweight champion who frequently has showed up missing on fight nights when a hefty purse was involved, is odds on to keep a date in the ring on 9 August – and he'll only get a dollar for his efforts. Ray will defend his 147-pound crown against blond Charley Fusari of Irvington, New Jersey. The 15-round bout will be held in Jersey City. Robinson is delivering his purse, minus the buck, to the Damon Runyon Cancer Fund. Fusari will be paid for what is going to happen to him. Fusari is a competent workman, probably the second best welterweight around. He is weak on ring generalship but he boxes well and hits hard. But you could search this town until fight night without finding anyone who really thinks he can whip Robinson.

'Vic Marsillo, Charley's manager, naturally thinks his boy has a chance, but he isn't claiming victory. "I took this match," he explains, "because my kid is ready and Robinson can't make 147 pounds and be strong. We might as well shoot for the big purse."'[100]

As related by Teddy Brenner in his excellent book *Only the Ring Was Square*: 'The trouble was that Robinson could no longer make the welterweight limit of 147 pounds. That's where Abe Greene came in. Instead of insisting that Robinson weigh in at the same time as Fusari, who was a natural 147-pounder, he allowed Robinson to step on the scales in another room at another time on the day of the fight. No boxing writers were present. All they were told was that Robinson had weighed exactly 147 pounds. They took Abe Greene's word for it. So on the night of the fight, Robinson came out moving and Fusari, intent on winning the title, went

---

99 Oscar Fraley *Daily Review* Hayward, California 6 June 1950

100 Jim Becker *Bakersfield Californian* 2 August 1950

after him with his best punches. Nobody was a better defensive fighter than Robinson. He could avoid punches by moving inside or out, or side to side, and he put on a hell of a show against Fusari, taking him along for the distance and getting the decision.

'The next day, a boxing writer had it in his paper that Sugar Ray Robinson was the best carrier since Mother Dionne. What was funny about the whole thing was that at the end of the sixth round, Fusari came back to his corner and said to Vic Marsillo, his manager, "I think I got this sucker figured out now. I'm going to open up in the next round and knock him out." Marsillo said, "Forget it. You're doing just fine. Just go out and box. We'll get the decision." He was worried that if Robinson was pressed, he would let fly with his sharp punches and flatten Fusari.'[101]

Robinson would recall in his autobiography, 'Years later, when Teddy Brenner took over as the matchmaker at Madison Square Garden, he once asked me what had been my toughest fight. "The one with Fusari," I said. "Fusari!" he howled. "You've got to be kidding. Fusari never touched you. That had to be the easiest fight you ever had. How can you say it was your toughest fight?" "Because," I said, "I had to fight 15 rounds for me and I had to fight 15 rounds for him."'[102]

In donating his purse to the Damon Runyon Cancer Fund, Sugar Ray was also thinking of his old team-mate of the Salem-Crescent days in Harlem, Louis Valentine, who had died of cancer. Ray grew more preoccupied with cancer and its causes and would support various fund-raising campaigns throughout his life. His eldest sister, Marie, wife of Clyde Brewer, one of his trainers, died of cancer aged 41.

Two weeks after the Fusari bout, Robinson was in Scranton, Pennsylvania to defend the state's version of the middleweight title. He wasted no time on Jose Basora, the Puerto Rican who had taken him to a draw over ten rounds five years previously.

101 Teddy Brenner *Only the Ring Was Square* 1981

102 Sugar Ray Robinson with Dave Anderson *Sugar Ray* 1969

Jose hadn't improved any and he was on his way to the showers inside 55 seconds of round one. Carl Bobo Olson, the balding Hawaiian, was imported by matchmaker Johnny Attell on the strength of an impressive record of 41 wins, 22 by knockout, in 44 professional starts. With an aggressive, awkwardly clever style, vaguely reminiscent of Robert Villemain's, Olson moved forward continuously, his head bobbing and weaving behind a tight defence of arms and gloves. At the close of the 11th frame, the best that could have been credited to Bobo were an edge in the sixth and an even split in the fourth, though he also was credited with the 11th when it was taken away from Robinson for an inadvertent low punch.

The end was spectacular. The 12th round had gone about a minute when Robinson rapped the oncoming Olson with a routine right, then whipped across a terrific left hook to the chin. For a second or two, it seemed to have no effect on Bobo, but then suddenly he began to sag. As he did, Robinson stepped in with an explosive right to the body. Olson doubled up and tumbled to the canvas, face first. He rolled over to his right, then back to his left, and he was still rolling when referee Charley Daggert completed the toll of the doleful decimal. Time of the round was 1.19. They would meet again.

On a trip to Miami, Ray palled up with the renowned columnist of the *New York Daily Mirror*, Walter Winchell, who had got him involved with the Damon Runyon Cancer Fund with the Fusari fight. The columnist enjoyed being seen around town with the world champ and they took in all the shows. They also went to the Hialeah race track, where the fighter became fascinated by the flamingos in the infield. So much so that he figured flamingo pink would look just dandy on his new car. Since 1941, he had bought a dark-blue Buick convertible every year. In 1950, he had ordered a white Cadillac Eldorado. Meeting Willie Pep's manager, Lou Viscusi, one night, he begged Lou to give him his flamingo tie. Lou corrected him, saying it was not flamingo but fuchsia. Back home, Ray took the tie and his white Cadillac to his dealer, showed him the tie and said he wanted his car painted the same colour. The guy thought he was crazy but took him to a garage, where he asked the foreman if they could mix up a batch of paint the same colour as the tie. Five minutes later, the guy came back carrying a paint can that he sprayed on an old fender hanging on the wall. Ray was delighted, that was the colour, even if it put another $300 on the new car.

'When my car arrived,' he said, 'it was not only exclusive, it was a symbol. When people think they recognise a celebrity, they hesitate a moment. But when they saw me in that car, they didn't have to hesitate. They knew. There was only one like it – Sugar Ray's pink Cadillac. Most people called it pink, but to me it was always more than pink, it was flamingo pink. At first, the car was an even bigger attraction than I was. Its paint job made it the most famous car in the world. "Mister Robinson," a man from *Life* magazine, said to me on the phone one day, "we'd like to come up to your café tomorrow and shoot some pictures of your car." "In colour?" I asked. "Of course," he said. "In black and white, it would be a waste of space."'[103]

Madison Square Garden publicist John Condon recalled, 'Ray would leave that Cadillac convertible anywhere, even in the middle of Times Square, for hours on end, and no one would touch it. Sometimes he would park it right in front of the old Garden and come upstairs to negotiate a deal. When he would go down, three or four hours later, he would find the police guarding the car for him. Nobody would ever think of giving Sugar Ray Robinson a ticket.'

Ray's café was booming and he had opened Sugar Ray's Quality Cleaning, Edna Mae's Lingerie Shop and George Gainford's Golden Glover Barber Shop. Next to the café was his office with 'Ray Robinson Enterprises' on the plate glass window. As he said, he was making money, and he was spending it. Edna Mae had a closet full of furs, $30,000 worth. Ray had his own closet – 25

103 Sugar Ray Robinson with Dave Anderson *Sugar Ray* 1969

suits, a dozen sports jackets, a couple dozen pairs of slacks, a couple dozen pairs of shoes, three tuxedos, drawers full of sports shirts and sweaters. His friendship with Joe Louis got him into golf and, of course, he had to wear the full outfit; plus fours; the old-fashioned knickers that Gene Sarazen always wore with the long socks. Ray sponsored several golf tournaments along with Louis.

Robinson was getting a lot of pressure from Lew Burston, who imported fighters from Europe, to cross the Atlantic, have some fights, have a good time and make a bit of money. When Ray said that he didn't know any of the European promoters, Burston said, 'They know you, and they'll take good care of you. Charlie Michaelis in Paris, Jack Solomons in London. But let me give you some advice. Don't take it easy on an opponent, like you did with Fusari. Knock him out as quickly as you can, in one round if possible. Let the European boxing fans see you at your best. There are enough decent fighters to give you all the action you want and you'll be well paid for belting them out. With your style and your punch, you'll be a hero there to the people and the sportswriters. Mark my words, you'll be a hero.'

'Despite my record,' Ray thought to himself, 'one defeat in 117 fights, I had never really been a hero.' His mind was made up; he told Burston to contact the promoters.

'Ray was working out in Harry Wiley's gym when the phone rang. Big George took the call, then walked over to Ray, saying, "It's for you, Robinson." "Well, who is it?" said the fighter, annoyed at his workout being interrupted, 'Can't you take it?'

'A big smile spreading over his face, Gainford replied, "She just said, Paris calling."'[104]

---

104 Sugar Ray Robinson with Dave Anderson *Sugar Ray* 1969

9

LE SUCRE MARVILLEAUX

TRAVELLING WITH a large number of friends and associates was not uncommon for Sugar Ray. He seemed to relish having a crowd around him at all times, and this time was no different from the others. The date on the calendar hanging on the wall of the departure lounge inside the French Line pier on the Hudson River was 11 November 1950. Flash bulbs were popping as news photographers crowded around Vincent Impellitteri, Mayor of New York City, who was there to wish his friend Sugar Ray Robinson *bon voyage* on his trip to Europe. With Ray was his beautiful wife Edna Mae, sister Evelyn, manager George Gainford, trainer Harry Wiley, Honey Brewer, June Clark and Pee Wee Beale, barber-valet Roger Simon and 53 pieces of luggage, each one marked with red string. 'Easier to spot when we disembark,' said June Clark, who had been with Ray quite a few years.

Paris promoter Charlie Michaelis had arranged a series of fights for Robinson and sent four round-trip tickets on the liner *Liberte*. They would need more than four tickets and it would cost Sugar Ray around $50,000 to take his party with him. When he heard the dock workers talking of 'the boxer Ray Robinson and his entourage,' he smiled. He liked the sound of that and he would use the word to describe his travelling party from that time on.

The *Liberte* made a stop at Plymouth as they reached England and some 40-odd newsmen and photographers swarmed up the gangplank to greet the world champ. It was the same when they docked at Le Havre and a hundred or more kept Ray engaged for five hours before he was able to disembark with his entourage.

Veteran Los Angeles sportswriter Jim Murray wrote, 'He put the word entourage on the sports page. I remember how he took more people to Europe than General Pershing. Not since the Nazi occupation had Paris had more hotel suites and floors taken over by foreigners. Ray set a record of luggage held by the late Marie Antoinette. Ray's entourage included "secretaries" who couldn't type, "valets" who were lucky they could dress themselves and "barbers" who had to be paged at the race track when Ray wanted a haircut. He had a bigger budget than some countries. He didn't visit France, he invaded it.'[105]

'French reporters were goggle-eyed when Sugar Ray Robinson ambled into Paris' Claridge Hotel on the Champs-Elysees last November. Following the coffee-coloured champ, like royalty's retinue, was his entourage. Behind the procession, a corps of panting bellboys wrestled with 32 trunks and 15 suitcases, containing (among other items) three radios sets, 140 jazz records, six punching bags, ten pairs of boxing gloves and Sugar's travelling wardrobe of 12 suits, five overcoats and 100 neckties. Explained manager Gainford, "We just couldn't leave anybody, so we all came." It was, the French agreed, quite an entrance.

'Hitting the Paris hotspots on his first night ashore, Robinson rounded out his retinue to an even ten by hiring 4ft 4in Jimmy Karoubi as "bodyguard" and interpreter. He also managed to find time to hammer out some expert drumming with jazzman Sidney Bechet, then joined trumpeter Roy Eldridge for a fast jam session. Appearances with Maurice Chevalier (a duet) and on the French radio (discussing jazz), plus a series of five-course luncheons, rounded out Sugar Ray's rich, full life in Paris.' [106]

Charlie Parrish covered European boxing for *The Ring* magazine, and in the January 1951 issue he reported, 'Seldom

105 Jim Murray *Pacific Stars and Stripes* 1 April 1974

106 *Time* magazine 1 January 1951

has a fighter captured the imagination of the continental sports enthusiasts to such an extent as Ray Robinson. The amiable Sugar has hardly been allowed one moment's privacy since his arrival in France recently, and his every remark, opinion and activity has been carefully reported to the general public. He has been photographed at the golf links, in the street, at night clubs, and even in consultation with mannequins regarding the purchase of clothes for his attractive wife, but very seldom has he been pictured with the gloves on. Main reason for this is the fact that Robinson sparred only three rounds for his bout with Jean Stock, whereas the French slugger participated in no less than 100 rounds.'

Monsieur Stock should have saved his energy. A blazing combination sent him home inside two rounds before a record crowd at the Paris Palais des Sports. Several British sportswriters were ringside and were suitably impressed.

For the London *Daily Express,* Peter Wilson wrote, 'Sugar Ray Robinson proved to me that he is the greatest fighter, pound for pound, in the world. Why they call him Sugar Ray, I don't know. It should be Death Ray.' George Whiting of the London *Evening Standard* reported, 'I do not usually scream superlatives, but should like to emphasise that Robinson showed more class in five minutes against Stock than any other fighter in the last 20 years.' Norman Hurst in the *Daily Graphic* observed, 'Robinson proved without doubt, in spite of the short time he was in the ring, that he is head and shoulders above any boxer in the world at or near his weight.'

'The fans went wild. They carried Sugar triumphantly around the arena, hugging and kissing him while frantic gendarmes tried to restore some kind of order. Sugar Ray had never had such an ovation, and he, in turn, fell in love with the French. Here, in a foreign country, Sugar Ray found that people appreciated him solely because he was a great fighter. His colour and creed were of no consequence.'[107] A couple of weeks later, Robinson knocked out

---

107 Gene Schoor *Sugar Ray Robinson* 1951

Holland's Luc van Dam in four rounds in Brussels. A week later, he was in Geneva to fight Jean Walzack of France, who had stuck with him for ten rounds in St Louis some ten months earlier. And he did it again as a 10,000 crowd watched Sugar trying to get rid of the French tough guy.

Then he was back at a jam-packed Palais des Sports in Paris for previous victim Robert Villemain. They had boxed 15 rounds in Philadelphia for what the commission called the Pennsylvania world middleweight title and Sugar had been decked in the ninth before getting up to win the decision, and the title. This time, as the 15,000 crowd groaned, it was Villemain on the deck in round nine. He got up but Sugar took him to the ropes and dropped him again as the referee stopped it. The night before sailing home, Robinson was in Frankfurt to knock out German middleweight Hans Stretz after 40 seconds of round five. Four knockouts in five fights and the Harlem Hepcat was ready for his nemesis, world champion Jake LaMotta. They were matched for 14 February 1951 in Chicago, with Jake's title on the line.

'I had pocketed nearly $50,000, and I needed every penny,' recalled Ray. 'My entourage had run up a big bill at the Claridge and Edna Mae had been shopping. Her tab at Schiaparelli's and Jacque Fath's was very big. The day we boarded the *Liberte* in Le Havre for our return voyage, Charlie Michaelis saw us off. "And when you take the title from LaMotta," he said, "return to see Paris in the spring." "We'll be back," June Clark assured him. "I'm keeping the red strings on all the bags."'[108]

'They spread the welcome mat for Ray Sugar Robinson the other eve. He and the missus arrived back in town full of French and gaiety – with two poodles and a watch for Mayor Impellitteri of New York. Still in his charitable mood, Ray flew right out for Washington to referee a benefit bout for the family of the late Sonny Boy West. A lightweight from Baltimore, West had died after being knocked out by Percy Bassett in New York.

---

108 Sugar Ray Robinson with Dave Anderson *Sugar Ray* 1969

'Interviewed by the press upon his return from Europe, Ray blamed the Communists for spreading stories about racial discrimination in the United States. "Those people," he snapped, "are capitalising on statements made by Paul Robeson. Mr Robeson speaks for himself and not for the American Negro. He certainly doesn't speak for my race. If the things the Communists say are true, I wouldn't be in the position I'm in today. American provides opportunity for everyone regardless of race, creed or colour."'[109]

Robinson brought back one souvenir from his European trip that tickled him. It was a clipping from the Paris Communist newspaper in which he was called 'a capitalist'. 'That's good,' was Ray's comment.

Before heading off to training camp, there was a pleasant evening spent at the Waldorf Astoria Hotel in Manhattan, where Ray was presented with the Edward J. Neil Memorial Plaque, named after the former Associated Press boxing writer who was killed in 1937 while serving as a war correspondent in Spain. The plaque was awarded to the boxer who had done the most for the sport that year. Joe Louis, an old friend of Robinson's, presented the plaque as some 300 guests looked on.

It was time for work, but instead of going to his normal training camp at Greenwood Lake, New York, Ray and his handlers headed for Pompton Lakes, New Jersey. 'When Joe Louis was the heavyweight champion,' wrote Dave Anderson in his *New York Times* column, 'he put this leafy little town on the map. "Nobody trained like Joe Louis," recalled Lou Duva, the 77-year-old Hall of Fame trainer in 1999. "On the weekends, there'd be as many as 5,000 people around the outdoor ring under the trees next to the big house when he and his sparring partners lived. He always wore white knit trunks with a white tank top, black boxing shoes and white socks. He was all business."'[110]

Sugar Ray Robinson was all business as he trained for his fight with world middleweight champion Jake LaMotta, but there was

109 *Lowell Sun* Mass. 3 January 1951
110 Dave Anderson *New York Times* 30 May 1999

one guy with whom he wasn't prepared to do business – Frankie Carbo, the underworld boss of boxing. The sportswriters couldn't find Robinson at Greenwood Lake, but Frankie Carbo found him at Pompton Lakes and called the house, asking Ray to meet him. 'I strolled down to the gate near the road,' recalled Ray in his autobiography. 'Moments later, a big black Buick sedan slowed to a stop. Into the chill of the winter evening stepped Frankie Carbo, his $100 black shoes gleaming, a knife pleat in his black pants, the collar of his black cashmere overcoat up near the gray hair, and his black eyes shining from under his gray fedora. "Ray," he said, "I represent the Bull." "Yeah," I said, realising that he was referring to LaMotta. "I got a deal for us." "What kind of a deal?" "I want you and the Bull to have three title fights. You'll win the first. He wins the second. The third is on the level." "You mean I take a dive in the second?" "Either that or you don't put out," he said. "Just so the Bull wins. He'll let you have the first one. In the third, you're both on your own, on the up-and-up. The best man wins that one." "You got the wrong guy," I said. "Three fights is a lot of money," he said. "You give the Bull a message," I snapped. "You tell the Bull to keep his hands up and his ass off the floor. You tell him to be sure to do that when the bell rings." Without waiting for an answer, I spun and headed back to the house.'[111]

With Carbo showing his hand, Ray knew that he couldn't trust the decision to the judges if his fight with LaMotta went the 15-round distance. He would have to knock the Bull out or force a stoppage by the referee, something that had never happened to Jake LaMotta. It was his proud boast that he had never been off his feet, never knocked down, and never knocked out in any of his 95 professional fights. But as somebody once said, there is a first time for everything. Sugar Ray liked the sound of that.

Ray did no sparring at Pompton Lakes the first week of training before moving on to his favourite camp at Greenwood Lake in New York State. He would work there until leaving for Chicago a few days

111 Sugar Ray Robinson with Dave Anderson *Sugar Ray* 1969

before the fight. They say that watching Sugar Ray train was as good as watching him fight, sometimes better. Veteran fight manager/ promoter Lou Duva remembered seeing him work out, recalling, 'You'd watch him jump rope, and it was like watching Fred Astaire dance.''Sugar Ray Robinson in Best of Condition,' a headline in the *Bluefield Daily Telegraph* trumpeted on 6 February. 'Sugar Ray Robinson, who fights Jake LaMotta for the latter's middleweight title on 14 February at Chicago, decided he was in such "very excellent" condition after doing a spot of roadwork today that he took the rest of the day off. LaMotta, also confident he is approaching his peak, contented himself with three rounds of boxing with Jimmy Lee in an uptown gym. Both men plan to take light workouts tomorrow and to leave for Chicago Wednesday by train.'[112]

Jake had already beaten Robinson to the punch in starting to train. On 4 January, Jack Cuddy, United Press sportswriter, found the middleweight boss at his hometown gym, reporting, 'LaMotta has been sparring for eight days at Bobby Gleason's gymnasium in the Bronx. Before he began to spar, the "Bronx Bull" did four weeks of strenuous hiking, roadwork and calisthenics to toughen him up. Mike Wittenberg, manager of the gym, said today, "I've never seen LaMotta so eager for a fight or so serious about his training. He's already in good shape. Look for an upset at Chicago."'[113]

Writing for Associated Press from New York, Jack Hand reported, 'Down to 160 pounds "believe or not," Jake LaMotta snorted Tuesday at 3-1 odds favouring Sugar Ray Robinson for their 14 February middleweight title bout at Chicago. Nobody knows how much LaMotta weighs. Nobody outside his cosy family circle in the Bronx. All you have is Jake's word "on or about" tossed over his shoulder with an impish "believe it or not." He is more positive about his chances of whipping Robinson, the welter king, in this sixth renewal of a series. "I figured I beat him three times," he said after boxing four rounds at Bobby Gleason's gym. "I give

112 *Bluefield Daily Telegraph,* West Virginia 6 February 1951

113 Jack Cuddy *Syracuse Herald Journal* 4 January 1951

him the two New York fights, he won them. This time there will be no question about it. I'm going to try to make it decisive."'[114]

'For a guy who has beaten Jake LaMotta four out of five times,' wrote Charles Chamberlain from Chicago, 'Sugar Ray Robinson is being surprisingly demur about his sixth chance at the Bronx Bull. "So I'm a 4-1 or 3-1 favourite?" asks Robinson. "I've never heard of a welterweight challenging for the middleweight title as such a favourite. My only hope is that at the end of 15 rounds, my arm will be raised as the winner. Listen, I know about this LaMotta pretty well. He beat me once – the only guy ever to lick me – and I took him four times on decisions. I've been accused recently of coasting in several of my fights and I've been asked if I think I'll get a chance to coast against LaMotta. That's the biggest laugh I've had in a long time." Robinson has scored 78 knockouts in winning 120 bouts. Now he is talking about a decision. This can be construed as about the best tribute ever paid to LaMotta's ruggedness.'[115]

Well, it looked as though Jake LaMotta was beginning to worry a little about his renowned ruggedness. The two fighters were ordered before the Illinois State Boxing Commission for a special meeting to determine the details for the Fight of the Year. 'Joe Triner, commissioner, said he will probably grant LaMotta's wish for a 10am weigh-in the day of the fight. However, Robinson's manager, George Gainford, said in New York that he will ask for a noon weigh-in. 'LaMotta will have a two-hour advantage with a 10am weigh-in. If he can't make the weight, why should he be privileged with extra time to take it off? Just because he's a champion, is no reason for special favours. I have a champion, too, you know."'[116]

It was possible for Sugar to win the crown from LaMotta *before* he entered the ring in Chicago on the night of 14 February. LaMotta had to make the 160-pound limit by noon the day of the fight. If he did make it, he would forfeit the crown, although

---

114 Jack Hand *Butte Montana Standard* 31 January 1951

115 Charles Chamberlain *Winchester Evening Star* 10 February 1951

116 *Daily Herald Suburban Chicago* Arlington Heights, Illinois 2 February 1951

the bout would go on. In that case Robinson would be the new middleweight champion, win or lose.

'The Bronx Bull now says his only worry is "conserving my strength." As early as last Saturday, five days before he tangles with the welterweight champion in Chicago Stadium, thick-shouldered Jake hit upon how to stockpile his energy. He would simply rest. He called off his Saturday sparring session and went on a shopping tour for loud neckties in the Loop. Yesterday, he also cancelled a scheduled workout exercising only his vocal chords at a press conference. It will be just light drills today and not even that tomorrow. Old-time ringbirds say that a five-day vacation before a title fight is unprecedented. "I don't care what they say," bellowed Jake. "The lower in weight I get, the more strength I lose. Ain't that right, doc?"

'Dr Philip Brunori, LaMotta's one-man entourage, is no man to mince words. "Right!" he snapped."[117]

When he arrived in Chicago, Robinson got in some rounds at Issy Kline's Midwest gym, stepping three fast rounds with Terry Moore, a squatty Baltimore welterweight who matched LaMotta in build and fighting style. Joe Louis was among several hundred fans who jammed the gym for a look at Sugar. LaMotta went two rounds with Ronnie Hoop at his CYO training site and concentrated on his specialty of body hammering.

The fight had brightened the horizon for Chicago fight fans, with the International Boxing Club predicting a crowd of 12,000 and a gross gate of $150,000. At the end of the day, the gross gate would be announced as $186,866 paid by a crowd of 14,802. The Bronx Bull had talked himself into 45 per cent of the net gate, with Robinson happy to take 15 per cent. The accountant reckoned on cheques for Jake of $62,522 plus $1,500 from television, while Sugar Ray would take $20,840 plus $1,500 TV money. An estimated 60 million fans would see or hear the fight via radio or television, starting time 10pm Eastern Standard Time. Everybody wins.

117 Charles Chamberlain *Winchester Evening Star* 12 February 1951

10

TAMING THE RAGING BULL

'I'M WILLING to lose an eye for this fight. I can get along on one eye.' That chilling statement came from world middleweight champion Jake LaMotta on the eve of his title fight with Sugar Ray Robinson in Chicago on the 22nd anniversary of the infamous St Valentine's Day Massacre of 1929, but this one didn't figure to be so one-sided.

'Sugar had used all sorts of tactics and strategies to keep his opponents off balance. Sometimes he psyched them out – as he may have with LaMotta at a luncheon a few days before their fight. Sitting near the Bull, Sugar asked the waiter if he could have a large glass of beef blood. Both the waiter and LaMotta were puzzled by the request. Sugar stressed his order, clarifying that he did not want gravy, but actual beef blood, extracted "before the meat is cooked," he said. The waiter obeyed and returned with a glass full of blood. Sugar downed it in one long gulp. Wiping his mouth, he explained to a bug-eyed LaMotta that he had been drinking it for years on the advice of Chappie Blackburn, Louis's trainer. LaMotta told Sugar that he was out of his mind.

'Sugar would have likewise questioned LaMotta's sanity when he drank two or three shots of brandy before their fight. LaMotta said he did this to give him a sense of false courage to hide his real fear. He knew he wasn't in good enough shape to fight Sugar. One fighter was half drunk on brandy and the other was juiced up on beef blood. If the bettors had known, there would be no guessing where their money would have gone.'[118]

As they waited for the bell, the odds were favouring Robinson at 1-3. He had made the weight comfortably, coming in at 155½ pounds, with Jake just hitting the class limit of 160. Now all Ray had to do was win the fight.

'The familiar voice of Ted Husing, even and sonorous, would be announcing for Pabst Blue Ribbon. "This broadcast tonight is making history," he proclaimed. "Never before has any event been heard and seen by so many people. Not only here in America but right around the globe. It is being short-waved to Australia and New Zealand, 10,000 miles away." The Voice of America would pipe the fight to military camps in Korea; Pan Am flights would begin carrying it at the sound of the bell on their aircraft flying around the world. Press representatives were in attendance from Canada and France. Italian dignitaries were in the audience, representatives of LaMotta's native land. "The bout the world's been waiting for," Husing said.'[119]

This was Robinson's sixth fight against LaMotta and, at 29, he was determined it would be the last. Jake, 28, had handed Sugar his only defeat in 123 professional bouts and this was the one that mattered. This was for the middleweight championship of the world, and Ray was determined not to leave the decision in the hands of the officials appointed by the Illinois State Athletic Commission – judges Frank McAdams, Ed Klein and Referee Frank Sikora.

'At the opening bell, Jake LaMotta moved out as if he didn't care what happened to him. He carried the fight to Robbie, apparently hoping to weaken him with an early body attack. Robbie came back strong in the second with vicious hooks and right crosses to the champ's jaw. The pace speeded up in the third. Robinson set up LaMotta with three successive left jabs and then

118 Herb Boyd with Ray Robinson II *Pound for Pound* 2005

119 Wil Haygood *Sweet Thunder: The Life and Times of Sugar Ray Robinson* 2009

staggered him with his best punch, a hard right to the jaw. In the fourth, Robinson kept LaMotta at long range with lefts, but was driven into the ropes by a furious LaMotta rally at the bell. By the end of this round, Ray seemed to be tiring. And in the fifth, obviously sensing this, LaMotta charged out of his corner, cutting loose with everything he had. He scored with blasting left hooks to the body and then shook Ray with a smashing right to the mouth that brought blood. It was the Bull's best round.'[120]'

Unlike anyone before or since, Robinson's jab as he backpedalled was just as hurtful as when he was on the front foot. From the very first minute, he danced clockwise around LaMotta and with almost every bounce he seemed to sting his opponent's face with that rapier punch. Round after round, LaMotta ate it up, but against a *bona fide* ring genius he had little choice but to keep marching forward and keep swinging. "God gifted me with a big, hard head," LaMotta often said. He'd need it that night of lovers in the Windy City.

'Robinson was three inches taller and had a reach five inches longer, but occasionally he would allow the Bull into range just to counter him with stunning, short, ambidextrous blows. At other times he would suddenly plant his feet, let his toes grip the canvas floor and then dig into LaMotta's ribs with ferocious hooks. Then he'd circle again, stretching the distance, and adding yet more miles on LaMotta's ring shoes, while he doubled or trebled his jab. As always, whatever Robinson did, it was carried out with a seamless grace.'[121]

'Robinson appeared to be taking command in the early stages of the fourth round. But the Bronx Bull rallied in the closing minute, and sent Sugar back to his corner bleeding from the nose. It was that kind of a battle: guile versus guts, head versus heart, combinations versus courage. LaMotta repeatedly charged back from cover, throwing caution to the wind – and punches to

120 Gene Schoor *Sugar Ray Robinson* 1951

121 Paul Gibson *The Guardian USA* 8 February 2016

the head. His own lips already cut, he snarled out at Robinson, who still tried to keep LaMotta at a distance, backpedalling and counterpunching. Before the fifth ended, Robinson was also bleeding from the mouth.'[122]

'In the fifth Jake resorted to a jab – of all things – and surprised Robinson as much as the crowd,' reported Jack Hand for Associated Press. 'Although a left hook seemed to stray low, Jake was not warned. He opened strong in the sixth, driving Robinson around the ring with his hooking, swarming attack. When Robinson was able to manoeuvre at long range, he was superb. But he couldn't always escape LaMotta's persistent attack in the seventh and eighth. Sugar Ray cut loose in the ninth, the turning point of the contest. In the tenth, he bashed Jake's right eye in a furious counter attack after Jake's opening hook. Jake shot his last dynamite in a dying swan gesture to start the 11th. Robinson covered in a corner and rode out the storm. Then he pulled the switch. Shaking Jake with a series of head punches, he made LaMotta back away and look for the ropes. At the bell, Jake was reeling, trying to find a friendly rope to grab. Again in the 12th, Ray teed off with hardly a return. Glassy-eyed Jake, his left eye cut now, bled freely from several slices on his face. Once again he was staggering and groping toward the ropes at the bell.'[123]

'LaMotta, the only man ever to defeat Robinson,' wrote Chicago newsman Charles Dunkley, 'never fought more determinedly. For eight rounds, he actually forced the battle. He bothered the confident Robinson with resounding body blows and jolting lefts to the head and often forced him into retreat. The jolting LaMotta had the spirit, but not the stamina for the 15-round route. The tide turned in Robinson's favour in the ninth round when Jake began losing his aggressiveness and ability to escape Robinson's shattering punches. He turned into little less than a target. In the ninth, Robinson jabbed LaMotta and followed with punishing

---

122 Bert R. Sugar *The Great Fights* 1981

123 Jack Hand *Titusville Herald* PA. 15 February 1951

body blows. Jake stood up under this barrage and merely went through the motions of evasion.

'LaMotta rallied briefly in the 11th when he pinned Robinson in a corner and lashed out with both hands, but Ray stepped into the clear and exploded with sharp jabs.

'Jake was virtually helpless all through the 12th. The contest, now one- sided, continued into the 13th and the crowd was cheering wildly that LaMotta was still on his feet. The impression prevailed that Jake was exhausted from the rigours of making the 160-pound limit and from the furious pace he set early in the fight.'[124]

'Sugar Ray came from behind Wednesday night to give LaMotta a merciless and bloody battering before stopping him on a technical knockout at 2.04 of the 13th round,' wrote Jack Cuddy. 'He became the first welterweight champion in pugilistic history to win the middleweight diadem when referee Frank Sikora mercifully intervened to prevent helpless LaMotta from suffering any more punishment. Mickey Walker had tried to take Harry Greb's middleweight title in 1925 but lost the decision. Likewise, Henry Armstrong failed to wrest the middleweight laurels from Ceferino Garcia in 1940.

'Squat, bull-shouldered LaMotta of New York forced the fighting until the ninth round and at times chased the slender New York Negro about the ring in a manner reminiscent of Joe Louis' pursuit of Billy Conn in their second fight. In the early rounds, LaMotta not only outslugged Robinson, but he actually outboxed him. He was particularly impressive in out-jabbing Sugar Ray. At the close of the eighth round, the United Press had LaMotta leading six rounds to two. However, as LaMotta tired and Robinson concentrated on an upsweeping attack of uppercuts, bolos and hooks against his bobbing opponent, Jake began to wither under the rising fire.

'Because of Robinson's wide margin of victory in every round after the eighth, he was well ahead on points on the score sheets of

124 Charles Dunkley *Charleston Daily Mail* W. Virginia 15 February 1951

the three ring officials when the 13th round opened. Referee Sikora favoured Sugar Ray 63 to 57. Judge Frank McAdam favoured him 65 to 55 and Judge Ed Klein favoured him 70 to 50. LaMotta was so badly battered in the closing rounds that his handlers kept him practically incommunicado in his dressing room for nearly two hours after he had left the ring. He was so near collapse that Dr J.M. Houston of the Illinois Commission gave him oxygen.'[125]

This is how Red Smith described that last, unlucky for Jake, 13th round. 'In the third minute of the 13th round, Ray Robinson hit Jake LaMotta for what was it? – the thousandth time? The five thousandth? Jake was hung on the ropes like a picture on the wall, like an old wrinkled suit in the attic closet. Now he came off the hook, sagged forward, bent double at the waist. He embraced Robinson about the drawers and the referee, Frank Sikora, pushed in between them and motioned to Robinson to desist. The greatest fist fighter in the world was middleweight champion of the world, and one of the toughest had suffered the first believable knockout of his life. Jake LaMotta was slugged, tortured, flayed, bloodied and bludgeoned tonight by a better fighter. He was stripped of his title and nearly detached from his intellect as well. Yet when it was over, he was on his feet and had not left his feet. After 96 professional fights, the lovable character from the Bronx still can say he has never been knocked down.'[126]

'A dash of colour, aside from the reddish-purple welts puffing out of his face, was added to Jake LaMotta's dressing room at Chicago Stadium last night by the presence of Vicki. Vicki is the Bronx Bull's wife. In a vividly blue dress that clung to her like wet silk, and with her Niagara of blonde hair falling below her shoulders, Vicki indeed made a spectacular sight, if not a paradoxical one, in what usually is a man-only place. It was a good thing she was there. The Bull was in no condition to talk. Vicki could. At first, Vicki could hardly look at Jake as he lay

125 Jack Cuddy *Dubuque Telegraph-Herald* Iowa 15 February 1951

126 Red Smith *New York Herald Tribune* 15 February 1951

there exhausted on the training table wrapped in his leopard-spotted dressing gown and his face a mess from Robinson's trip-hammer punches.

'"Doc, tell me fast, how about Jake? Will he be okay?" she asked with desperation in her husky voice. Chairman Joe Triner of the Illinois Athletic Commission and physician J. M. Houston assured her everything was under control. Relieved, Vicki had a few things to say. "Jake had a terrible time trying to make the 160-pound limit," she confided. He laid off too long from his last fight. He'll never try to make 160 again." Vicki couldn't bear to look at the 11th and 12th rounds, "I just put my head down and covered my face with my hands," she said. "I'm glad they stopped it."

'After the oxygen had been depleted and the doctor was fingering Jake's pulse, Vicki quietly perched herself beside her hammered hubby and tried to do more than the oxygen. She stroked his ballooned forehead and eyebrows, she whisked a manicured finger along his vivid cheeks, she took a towel and rubbed his nose. To him, all this must have been old stuff, but brother! There never was a dressing room scene like this.' [127]

Robinson could do his own talking in his dressing room, as he told Jack Hand of Associated Press, '"I kept swinging and Jake kept standing – I didn't think I could knock him out," mumbled a jubilant, but utterly exhausted new middleweight champion, Sugar Ray Robinson, after his brutal battle with Jake LaMotta tonight. "Naw, Jake didn't hurt me in the 11th round when he had me cornered. I came out strong, didn't I? But, believe me, he clouted me a couple of good ones early in the fight. I figure we were even going into the sixth round. I just couldn't level away with him with my right hand. Then, gradually, I began to nail him. But the more I kept punching, the more determined he seemed to stay on his feet." Sugar Ray said it was not his toughest fight. That came, he said, from Fritzie Zivic."[128]

127 Charles Chamberlain *Racine Journal Times* 15 February 1951
128 Jack Hand *Titusville Herald* PA. 14 February 1951

In his 1970 autobiography, Jake would write, 'To this day I don't know whether it was Robinson or weight that actually licked me. I had to get down to 160, and when I started training I weighed 187. I was even above the weight limit for a light-heavy, and I was going to fight middleweight. I swear to God, never had I gone through the hell I did then. For the last two weeks of training, I was eating almost nothing. Five days before the fight, I went to Chicago so I could do some training in public and help build up the gate. Almost as soon as I got there, I collapsed. They put me to bed and put out the story that I was in such perfect shape that to do any more training would only dull the edge. The night before the fight, I weighed 164½ – almost five pounds over the limit. My handlers decided I had to go to the steam baths. When it was time to go to the weigh-in, our scales showed me at 160, and I went over pretty worried. I took off my socks and my boxing trunks and I hit 160 on the nose. I could hear my cornermen let out their breaths.

'The fight was held on 14 February which, besides being St Valentine's Day proper, is also the anniversary of the St Valentine's Day massacre of 1929. Well, Robinson didn't have a submachine gun and there was only one victim, but it was still a massacre.'[129]

Sugar Ray Robinson had never been flavour of the month with the *New York Daily Mirror*'s acerbic columnist Dan Parker, so his eyes might have popped when he read Parker's column after the LaMotta fight. Parker described Robinson as 'the greatest combination of brains, brawn, and boxing skill the modern prize ring has seen.'[130]

---

129 Jake LaMotta *Raging Bull* 1970

130 Dan Parker *New York Daily Mirror* 15 February 1951

11

PARIS IN HIS LEGS

AS HIS right gloved fist was raised in victory over Jake LaMotta, Robinson automatically relinquished his welterweight crown. He was forced to surrender it under a ruling of the National Boxing Association and also by decision of Eddie Eagan, chairman of the New York State Athletic Commission. Although Robinson and his manager, George Gainford, said that they considered Sugar Ray a double champ, a tournament probably would be held to fill the 147-pound vacancy. In any case, grander plans were afoot. Even before Ray had stripped the middleweight title from LaMotta, Ray's manager was telling the press he was going to try to arrange for a boxing grand slam – a light-heavyweight championship fight against Joey Maxim and a heavyweight title bout with Ezzard Charles.

'The husky fight manager estimated that 29-year-old Robinson still had "two or three more good years of boxing left before retiring." Gainford figured that was time enough for Robinson to become ruler of the light-heavyweight and heavyweight divisions.'[131] There was talk of a 15-round bout between Ray and light-heavyweight contender Harry 'Kid' Matthews to take place in Detroit, with Matthews's manager Jack Hurley announcing, 'The match is practically all set except for the weight. Gainford

131 *Austin American* Texas 3 February 1951

wants Matthews to make 170. I told him, not an ounce under 175.' This one didn't make it to the ring.

Another fight that didn't happen was the return bout between Sugar Ray and LaMotta. Many insiders who saw their last fight rightly figured that the Bull had had more than enough of the Harlem Hepcat, and it was no surprise when Jake announced on 27 April that he had released middleweight champion Ray (Sugar) Robinson from his contract for a return title bout and henceforth would campaign exclusively as a light-heavyweight.

LaMotta also said he would be happy to fight Robinson again in an over-the-weight match at 165 pounds. He also issued a challenge to Bob Murphy of San Diego, Bob Satterfield of Chicago, or any top-ranking light-heavyweight to fight him for the right to meet Joey Maxim of Cleveland for the 175-pound championship. Unfortunately, Jake's dream of another world title was just that – a dream. Three months after the Robinson fight, LaMotta was savagely beaten in seven rounds by Murphy, the slugging ex-sailor, and it was Murphy who got the Maxim fight. But he was out of luck there as Pal Joey boxed his ears off for a 15-round decision.

LaMotta would beat Murphy in a rematch, but in his next bout it finally happened. Jake LaMotta was slammed to the canvas for the first time in 103 professional fights by Danny Nardico, an 11-3 underdog in their fight at Miami. LaMotta climbed to his feet but was unable to take Nardico's furious attack. At the end of the seventh round, a doctor examined Jake and his seconds yelled to referee Billy Regan, 'That's all.' Three fights later, LaMotta quit the ring and opened a bar in Miami.

Two months after his brilliant execution of Jake LaMotta to win the middleweight title, the name of Sugar Ray Robinson was consigned to the 'fights last night' column in most of the nation's newspapers. '5 May 1951 Ray (Sugar) Robinson wpts 10 Holly Mims, Miami.' One paper that picked up the AP report was the *Winchester Evening Star*, Virginia. 'In his dressing room after the fight, Robinson was apologetic for "my bad showing". The bout had been postponed a month because of Robinson's illness and he said, "I guess that virus had me more than I thought. A couple of times I had him lined up but I couldn't get him."'

Five days later, Ray was in Oklahoma City and Don Ellis wished he hadn't got out of bed that morning. The first round had gone just 96 seconds when Don's handlers were scraping him off the canvas. Sugar Ray was in a hurry. He had to pack for his trip to Europe, gather his entourage and make sure the dockers didn't scratch his flamingo pink Cadillac as they hoisted it on board the French liner *Liberte* on 25 April. Paris promoter Charlie Michaelis had insisted the car came with Sugar. In fact, he was paying the shipping charges.

'Ray Robinson, who has nobody to fight in America, is about to make a conquest of Europe,' wrote Lawton Carver. 'He hasn't anybody to fight there either, but that is beside the point. The world middleweight champion will box a gent named Kid Marcel in a non-title match at Paris on 17 May, and after a period of European luxuriating will move on down to Milan, Italy. Under the promotional auspices of Saverio Turiello, who used to box in America, Robinson will get $10,000, which supposedly is already on deposit in an American bank. When he gets over there, Europe will be looking at the best fighter of these times at any weight. None of the rest even approach him.'[132]

From Paris, United Press reported, 'Middleweight champion Ray Sugar Robinson, who defeated five European boxers in less than a month during his visit last winter, will fight ten bouts during his current tour, French officials announced today. Robinson will open his swing with a non-title bout against Kid Marcel of France in Paris on 18 or 26 May. Other sites listed were Zurich, Liege, Amsterdam, Brussels, Milan, Rome, Cologne and Berlin.'[133]

'Robinson began training at the Ringside Cafe-Restaurant just off the Champs Elysees, with society women representing the

---

132 Lawton Carver *The Lowell Sun* Mass. 26 April 1951

133 *Long Beach Independent* California 4 May 1951

French Anti-Cancer League looking on. Sugar Ray stepped into the full-size ring in one corner of the bar and went through some shadow boxing and two fast rounds. He appeared in good physical condition and showed off some fancy footwork in the first round against French middleweight Germain Caboche, who escaped unscathed. Danny (Bang Bang) Womber, his American Negro sparring partner, wasn't so lucky, however. Robinson clouted "Bang Bang" with a punch that knocked him down. "Bang Bang" in turn knocked down one of the posts and along with the post went the ropes. The session was called off until the damage was repaired.'[134]

It wasn't all about punching people. 'As half a hundred French notables gathered in a gilded salon near the Arch of Triumph applauded, Robinson made a brief speech in French and handed over a cheque for $10,000 for the French cancer fund from the American Damon Runyon Cancer Fund. France's first lady, Mme Vincent Auriol, got four kisses from Negro middleweight champion Sugar Ray Robinson yesterday, all in the interests of cancer research. Robinson is delivering a series of such donations from the Runyon fund in Europe. He also will donate to the French campaign his share of the purse of his fight next Monday night with Kid Marcel. After the president of the French fund, Justin Godart, replied with more French and a lot of praise for Sugar Ray, the fighter told the crowd, "Hey, now I get to kiss missus president!"'[135]

A few nights later, it was down to business. Before a slim crowd of about 6,000 at the Palais des Sports, the kisses for Kid Marcel were reserved for the end of the bout, which came in the fifth round as Robinson opened up with some hefty punches and the Kid's handlers threw in the towel rather than risk their fighter getting hurt. The only risk for Sugar Ray was when the weights were announced as 155¾ pounds for both men, inside the class limit of 160 pounds, meaning that Robinson could have lost his

---

134 *Long Beach Independent* 18 May 1951

135 *Pampa Daily News* Texas 17 May 1951

world title had the Kid been up to the job. London promoter Jack Solomons was a ringside spectator for the fight and afterwards he talked to George Gainford, Sugar Ray's manager, about a title defence in London against Randolph Turpin, the British and Empire champion.

Robinson would recall to his biographer Dave Anderson, '"You handle this guy," I told George. "Don't accept anything less than $100,000 for a fight with Turpin." But when George mentioned my figure of $100,000, Solomons walked out. The next day, Jack Solomons surprised me. He had returned from London to resume negotiations for a title match with Randy Turpin. He and George were in the room adjacent to my suite. "You got me beat," I overheard Solomons tell him. "I'll give you the $100,000 you asked for." "But the date you mentioned before, July 10," said George, "we're going to have trouble making that date because we've got a fight on 1 July in Turin." "It has to be that date," Solomons said.

"Never mind the date," I said, bursting into the room. "I'll fight Turpin and everybody in England for $100,000. I really want it," I said, shaking hands with Solomons. "July 10, perfect," Solomons said. As soon as Solomons departed, George warned me that Turpin would be a tough opponent. "I'll be ready, don't worry," I said.'[136]

Five days later, the Robinson roadshow was in Zurich, where Sugar Ray was to box Jean Wanes of France. Jean proved to be a tough nut, surviving counts in rounds two, five, seven and nine. Five times he got up and was still smiling at the final bell. The fans in Antwerp didn't see a knockout when Sugar Ray faced Dutchman Jan de Bruin, they saw a walkout! Jan left the ring in the eighth round, claiming 'Robinson hadn't put forth his best efforts when he had his opponent cornered in the sixth and seventh rounds'. Robinson, winning the scheduled ten-round bout on a technical knockout, said he let de Bruin off lightly because he

136 Sugar Ray Robinson with Dave Anderson *Sugar Ray* 1969

needed the workout for his championship fight against Randolph Turpin in London on 10 July.

Back on the road, next stop Liege, Belgium. Opponent Jean Walzack of France, 64 bouts and counting. Well, the referee was doing all the counting, six times in rounds four, five and six, before he got fed up and sent the boys off to the showers. Winner, Robinson. A week later, Sugar Ray's caravan collided with German light-heavyweight Gerhard Hecht and all hell broke loose among the 30,000 Berliners who had packed the Waldbuehne to see their local hero face the American world champion. From ringside, Associated Press reported, 'Hecht went down once in the first round writhing in pain and was given a rest. Then, in the second session, Sugar Ray hit him with two lefts and a right. Down went Hecht again, clutching his back. The bout was stopped and Robinson disqualified. The judges ruled Robinson hit Hecht with kidney punches which were strictly illegal in Germany. After a six-hour session, the commission declared the fight a no contest, which meant the bout was held but nobody had been judged the winner. Robinson said, "I am sorry if the Germans think I'd come all this way to win on a foul. However, I'm glad that many Germans at ringside know it was not so. I don't care if I ever fight here again."'[137]

Final stop on the tour saw the world champ in Turin to fight Cyrille Delannoit, the Belgian 'Iron Man'. More than 11,000 fans in the Torino football stadium voiced their admiration of the American fighter as he registered a technical knockout when Delannoit threw up his hands in a gesture of withdrawal at two minutes 57 seconds of the third round. With the cheers of the crowd ringing in his ears, Robinson headed for his hotel to pack for the trip to London. Randolph Turpin was waiting.

London, 4 July, 1951, United Press reported, 'Sugar Ray Robinson, the world middleweight boxing champion, arrived from Paris today for his title fight against Britain's Randolph Turpin on 10 July and went straight to his training quarters in the shadow of

137 *Monroe Evening Times* Wisconsin 25 June 1951

the royal castle at Windsor. About 150 fight fans were gathered around the entrance to Victoria Station to see the Robinson party. One hundred pieces of luggage and his rose-coloured Cadillac came off the boat train. The party went directly to the Star and Garter Hotel. The whole hotel was placed at their disposal by the owner who, with his wife, had moved out of their eight-room apartment to let Robinson and his wife move in.

'Meanwhile, up at Gwrych Castle, North Wales, Turpin was training hard for the biggest fight of his life. He has shown good form against his sparring partners. Robinson was quoted today as a 4-1 favourite, with odds of 6-4 against the champion winning in the first five rounds.'[138]

This was Tuesday night, 10 July 1951, and the huge exhibition hall at Earls Court Arena in London was jammed to the rafters with 18,000 people, who were there to see British middleweight champion Randolph 'Randy' Turpin make his bid for the world middleweight championship against the man they were calling the greatest fighter in the world, pound for pound, the Harlem Hepcat, Sugar Ray Robinson. The 30-year-old New Yorker would bring a fabulous record of one defeat and two draws in a professional career of 132 bouts against the best lightweights, welterweights and middleweights in the business.

It had cost a tidy bit of sugar to entice Robinson to London to defend his title against Turpin and the man paying the sugar was walking around the ringside wearing a big grin and an even bigger cigar. Jack Solomons, fishmonger and boxing promoter, was ready to show off his biggest catch. When orders for fight tickets started pouring in by the sackload to Jack's office in Great Windmill Street, just off Piccadilly Circus, he had to ask the Post Office to stagger deliveries as his staff couldn't keep up with the demand. The fight was completely sold out in two days and now those 18,000 seats were filled with anxious fight fans, it was time to start the show.

138 *Long Beach Independent* California 5 July 1951

As he waited for the opening bell, Randy Turpin had the words of Len Harvey, one of Britain's greatest boxers, running through his mind over and over. 'I see no reason why you cannot beat this Robinson,' he told Turpin at the *Boxing News* annual luncheon a few weeks before the big fight. 'Remember, he's only made the same as you. He's [got] two arms, two legs and a pair of fists. So have you. Just get in there and let him know who's boss and you'll win the world's title.' And that's just what Turpin did.

He left his corner, 'hands held high, then dashed in to send a flurry of punches at the world's champion, who immediately backed away. Ray dug a left to the body but Randy retaliated with a swift right to the ear and one to the body, only to be pulled up by the referee for an alleged kidney punch. Turpin drove his man to the ropes, got in a stiff left to the face and they clinched. Randy missed with a right, sunk in a left to the body and they clinched again. Turpin hooked his left to the body, then got home a left and right to the head and Robinson ran into holds. Turpin was trying to tug away as the bell sounded. Turpin's round.'[139]

Three minutes into this 15-round fight and Sugar Ray already knew he had left his fight on the boulevards of Paris, left it in the continental bistros of Zurich, Antwerp, Liege and Turin, left it on the road through five countries, six fights in 41 days. And now, just nine days later, he was in another country, in another ring, with a heavy-handed 23-year old who wanted his championship. As American sports editor Harry Grayson would write in his column, 'Robinson's trouble at Earls Court was that his handlers forgot to tell young Turpin that no one had a Chinaman's chance with Sugar Ray. The British-born Negro is half deaf, so might not have heard. Had anyone brought up Robinson's reputation?'[140]

'Round two; Robinson missed with a left swing. Turpin stabbed a left to the face. A right from Randy clipped Robinson on the chin. Turpin got in another left to the face and they clinched

139 *Boxing News* 18 July 1951

140 Harry Grayson *Kingston Daily Freeman* New York 16 July 1951

again. Ray got in a belting left to the body and there was another clinch. Once more, Turpin shook the champion to his toes with a straight left and Robinson missed with a counter. Randy hooked to the head, missed a left swing and they clinched again. Turpin chopped away with his right until they were parted. He hooked with the left, but Robinson rode it. Ray was back-pedalling. Turpin's round.'[141]

'In the first six rounds,' wrote Nat Fleischer from ringside, 'Turpin had rolled up a lead of four to one, and one round even. In the sixth, Robinson appeared to be ready to set Turpin up for a knockout. Ray shot a left to the jaw and followed with a hard right. Turpin's knees buckled. However, he recovered quickly and much to Robinson's amazement, Randy began to throw punches. Ray's big chance was gone.'[142]

London sportswriter Peter Wilson wrote, 'I had no hesitation whatsoever in tipping Robinson to retain his title – I thought he wouldn't need more than six rounds in which to do it. After he had lost the first five, he came back in the sixth with one of those viper-tongued left hooks to Turpin's jaw. The following right made Turpin's knees hinge under him as though his joints had turned to jelly, but he still had enough sense to throw leather bombs of punches until another right nearly dimmed the light in his staring brown eyes. Then the bell went and the round was over and we wondered. Had "Death Ray" just been holding his fire, toying with his man as we've seen him in Paris and Antwerp and Turin?

'The seventh brought the answer. Robinson plunged in. Another left hook and a right which follows it like coffee follows a good meal. Turpin surged into his man. The two black heads bobbed together. There was a sickening crack like two billiard balls being driven together by a giant with a mallet. You could hear it for yards outside the ring. When they came out of the clinch, the soft chocolate skin of Robinson's face was obscured by a thick red,

141 *Boxing News* 18 July 1951

142 Nat Fleischer *The Ring* September 1951

sticky trickle. The incomparable Sugar had got a split left eyebrow and the blood was streaming fast.'[143]

'By the eighth, both the crowd and Robinson sensed an upset in the making, and Sugar Ray – usually a cool, imperturbable workman – began to try wildly to get inside Turpin's flailing arms and take charge. He succeeded briefly in the eighth and again in the ninth, but each time Turpin's hammer-like blows prevented any sustained offensive by Sugar Ray.'[144]

'Round nine: Robinson opened out more and attacked, but Turpin drove him back with a good straight left, followed by a second and then a third. The crowd rose to cheer him. Heavy infighting. Robinson blazing to the body. Turpin belted back and they got pulled apart. Turpin scored with a left to the face, but Ray replied with a heavy right counter, then let both hands go in a rapid tattoo. They were both warned for rough work in the clinches.

'Round ten: Again Robinson attacked, sending light lefts to the face. Turpin walked into him and Ray retreated. He came back to chase Randy, who ducked and made him miss. It looked as though Randy was taking a breather. He sent a left to the face but Robinson replied with a low right for which he apologised profusely. Randy grinned and they touched gloves. Robinson scored best, both at long and short range, without landing any damaging blows. It was Robinson's round.'[145]

'When the ninth round started,' recalled Peter Wilson, 'it was the first time that Turpin had ever had to fight for so long. But he looked as though he had only just begun. He was, in fact, the coolest man in the huge packed arena. Turpin had not a bead of sweat on him. He was brown ice in boxing boots. The thunder was in his gloves, but he was boxing quite brilliantly, too. Slipping punches, countering magnificently to the body and still ramming home the point that he was the boss with that thudding left. Only once more was Robinson in the hunt at all. That was in the 11th.

---

143 Peter Wilson *More Ringside Seats* 1959

144 Joe Thomas *Charleston Gazette* W. Virginia 11 July 1951

145 *Boxing News* 18 July 1951

The champion – he was still just that – lured Turpin forward and as he moved in caught him with half-bolo punches to the body. And although the American took this round, it was only the second that he won throughout the whole fight, with perhaps two even.'[146]

'During the interval before the start of the final round,' recalled referee Eugene Henderson, 'I knew that unless Robinson knocked out Turpin or won the last round by a very decisive margin, Turpin must be the winner. Clang! The bell sounded and I moved forward, arm outstretched, so that Turpin and Robinson would just touch gloves in the centre before entering the climax. Three minutes later, both men were still on their feet as the jarring discord of the bell put an end to their titanic struggle. They automatically stopped, slumped into each other's arms little over a yard away from me. I waited, fully expecting them to turn to me for the verdict. But I was taken completely off-balance when these superb boxers, their brown arms draped around each other's shoulders, turned their backs on me and walked into Robinson's corner. Which was which? I could not afford to grab the wrong arm, and quickly noting Turpin's less luxurious haircut, I thumped his shoulder and then followed his arm down to grab the wrist. I yanked it aloft, and the crowd went crazy. The excited roar hit the ring like the blast of a bomb and, reverberating round the hall, came back again and again with deafening intensity.'[147]

'Never before have I witnessed such a demonstration,' Fleischer would write, 'of singing, hand clapping, cheering and foot stamping as accompanied the announcement: "The winner and new world champion, Randolph Turpin." It was an indescribable scene, and well might the British celebrate as they did, for a 6-1 underdog, given little chance even by his own people, came through with flying colours against a man who hitherto had been recognised as the greatest fighter of his time.'[148]

---

146 Peter Wilson *More Ringside Seats* 1959

147 Eugene Henderson *Box On* 1957

148 Nat Fleischer *The Ring* September 1951

As the fight entered the final rounds, almost everyone in the huge arena knew who was winning, except the BBC commentary team of Raymond Glendenning and W. Barrington Dalby, himself a former referee. 'Rarely have I ever sensed such an atmosphere of expectancy, of impending crisis, as I did that evening,' recalled Glendenning later. He knew that Robinson was capable of a decisive attack at any stage but that, during the second half of the fight, Turpin's courage and skill was making an impact. Equally important, Turpin was rousing the home crowd to believe he was winning.

'In his comments after the penultimate round, Dalby suggested that with a good final round Turpin "could just *snatch* it", the implication being that he was not ahead. Describing the closing minute of the fight, Glendenning left the verdict wide open, "Well, whatever happens, the English boy's got a grandstand finish, whether he can overcome the points deficit at the start, I don't know. Which way will this championship go? It all depends on Mr Eugene Henderson. Turpin scores the last punch of the round. And who has won?"

'Turpin did win and there was a storm of protest from those who felt the commentary team had underestimated Turpin's performance and thereby been guilty of bias against the British fighter. Barrington Dalby later said that he had made a slip of the tongue and had meant to say, "Turpin could *clinch* it."'[149]

Robinson took his defeat like a good sportsman, telling Turpin, 'You were real good, just like everybody said you were. I have no alibis. I was beaten by a better man.'

On that July night in 1951, Randolph Turpin was truly king of the castle, the new middleweight champion of the world.

149 Dick Booth *Talking of Sport The Story of Radio Commentary* 2008

12
GETTING THE TITLE BACK – ONE!

SO WHAT happened to the fabulous Sugar Ray Robinson in that London fight with Randy Turpin? I think Ray's wife, the beautiful Edna Mae, had the answer when she told a United Press reporter, 'He should have fought Turpin when he started the tour instead of when he was ending it. After all, Ray is 31.[sic] But he'll be in shape for the return bout and Turpin will learn plenty in that one.'[150]

Syndicated columnist Harry Grayson wrote from New York, 'Lew Burston, just back from Europe, gives you a round-by-round description of the gaudiest and most action-packed tour ever taken by a prizefighter. Burston says, "Sugar Ray Robinson beat himself in London, but that young Turpin may beat him at the Polo Grounds, 12 September. The Leamington Spa lad has the equipment and the confidence that comes with having done it once, and there are seven long years on his side," he wraps it up in a nutshell. "But Robinson's battery simply ran down in Piccadilly."

'Robinson, who in his 30th year, can't do the things he used to do, and so suddenly and disastrously found it out, made seven fights and did 17 exhibitions in six countries in 51 days. That

---

150 *San Mateo Times* California 11 July 1951

schedule alone would beat down the ordinary combatant, but the whoop-de-do and mileage took an even greater toll.

'"Never was another fighter acclaimed like Robinson," testifies Burston. "From the time Robinson sailed aboard the *Liberte,* 29 May, until just six days before the Turpin match, he was wined and dined until the wee hours of the morning. He neither smokes nor drinks but when not in strict training, he's a stayer-upper from a way back who loves company and to have a fuss made over him."

'Robinson was in a strange country four or five times a week, being mobbed by entirely different people, eating unfamiliar food and drinking water to which he was unaccustomed. He doesn't sleep well in a strange bed, and found himself in one practically every night. "Ray Robinson needs a complete rest," said Burston, "and he had better get it, for Randy Turpin isn't going to give him any."'[151]

Leaving London, Ray took a fortnight on the Riviera at Cannes, getting the sun on his eye injury and losing a few bob in the casino, then it was back home, back to New York, and off to Pompton Lakes in New Jersey. He had a fight in a few weeks' time and this one he had to win. His good friend, Dr Vincent Nardiello, had taken a leave from his work with the New York State Athletic Commission to keep an eye on Robinson. The good doctor said that he had no doubt that Sugar Ray had not trained properly for the London fight with Turpin.

Ray's usual camp was Greenwood Lake in New York State. Big George had taken him there to train for his first professional bout with Joe Echevarria in October 1940 in Madison Square Garden. All that was 11 years ago, 11 years and 133 fights against the best in the business at three weights, just two defeats and one draw. Now he was 30 and he was back at the training grind and it was getting tougher. Could he do it? This report came out of Pompton Lakes:

---

151 Harry Grayson *Portsmouth Times* Ohio 27 August 1951

'Ray Robinson was skipping the rope as only Ray Robinson can. This was a professional dancer going through an intricate routine. There isn't another fighter in the world who can duplicate Sugar's manipulations with the magic rope. "See these feet," he said to a reporter after 15 minutes of the most amazing antics ever witnessed. "These feet are what tell me I'm ready. They feel like dancing. They feel like moving. When my feet move eagerly and easily, then I can fight like I should be fighting. In London last July, my feet weren't dancing. They're dancing now, like a pair of colts ready to be let loose. I won't have any alibis for this one. I'm as ready as I'll ever be."'[152]

His sparmates would vouch for that. 'Sugar Ray stepped his workout up to five rounds today,' reported United Press, 'belting three sparring partners around in a fast, hard workout. Robinson boxed the first round with Dave Green of Chicago. Robinson floored him with a left hook to the jaw. Sugar then boxed two rounds with Sid Edwards of New York, one of his new sparring partners. Edwards weighed 163 pounds. He staggered Edwards with a left to the body. Robinson finished up boxing Terry Moore of Baltimore. Robinson concentrated on the body against Moore and sank many a punch into the pit of his stomach and also batted Moore about the ribs. Robinson weighed 163½ after the workout.'[153]

Champion Randy Turpin was training at Grossinger's resort in the Catskills and members of the American fight mob have voiced different views on the man who beat the New Yorker.

Former light-heavyweight champion Gus Lesnevich watched Turpin spar. 'Turpin's in good condition, he's a smart fighter, he slips a punch well and counters well, but he holds his head high and I don't like that,' said Lesnevich. 'I haven't seen Robinson train yet, but I know nobody can afford to hold his head high while boxing Ray.' James Dawson, writing in the *New York Times,* had

152 *Baltimore Afro-American* 8 September 1951

153 *The Independent* Long Beach California 1 September 1951

noted, 'Holding the head high, or sticking it forward in a crouch, as Turpin did today, would be inviting disaster. Dropping the left arm just before crossing a right could be just as dangerous. The left leg stiffness brings up the question of balance. An off-balance fighter in the ring with a sharpshooter like Robinson is courting a very interesting evening, to put it conservatively.'[154]

'The pro-Turpin following is stronger among those who have seen Randy fight in England. It includes trainer-manager Ray Arcel, promoter Johnny Attell and manager Bill Daly. "He's as strong as an ox," said Arcel, who took Tommy Yarosz to London to box Randy last December. The Pittsburgh light-heavyweight was disqualified in the eighth round for holding. "Tommy told me during the fight that he couldn't hold off this guy," said Arcel. "Robinson has got to get him quick because that guy is never going to let up on him."

'Jake LaMotta growled, "Robinson's got pride, lots of pride. He wants that title back in the worst way. He'll win." Rocky Graziano, former middleweight champ, who saw the movies of the first fight, said, "Jeez, Robinson ain't gonna be that bad again. He'll stiffen the Englishman."'[155]

'In an atmosphere reminiscent of the Jack Dempsey and Joe Louis heavyweight eras, Randy Turpin and Ray Robinson weighed in yesterday at noon in the offices of the state athletic commission. A police detail had to break a path through milling crowds on the Centre Street side of the state office building when the fighters arrived. Additional police were stationed on the fifth floor to maintain order. Detectives with shields pinned to lapels, commission deputies and inspectors augmented the uniformed police squads. All elevators were barred to the curious. Nevertheless, Turpin and Robinson were subjected to an ordeal. Operators of movie and still cameras set up an ear-splitting din demanding poses. Flood lights transformed the

154 *European Stars and Stripes* 8 September 1951

155 *Lowell Sun* Mass. 11 September 1951

weighing-in room into an oven. It was exciting, it was noisy and it was confusing.

'Through it all, Turpin seemed to be more composed than Robinson. Weighed first, Robinson tipped the scales at 157½ pounds, three more than for the battle in London. Turpin's weight was 159 pounds, just under the 160-pound limit and three quarters of a pound more than he weighed in London.'[156]

'The winner, Turpin,' Johnny Addie announced at 9.27pm. It was not premature, because this Turpin was Randy's brother, Jackie, victor in a preliminary contest. The verdict was greeted with a loud cheer from the third-base side, where the large British delegation was seated.

When Robinson entered the ring at the Polo Grounds that night, the smart money had made him the favourite at 8½ to 5. With all eyes glued on the ring, a crowd of 61,370 had paid a gross gate of $767,630, a record for a fight below heavyweight. On that July night in London when Ray lost the title to Turpin, he knew the rematch was safely in the contract for a New York date. Hearing that, Ray's sister Evelyn said, 'I don't think I even want to see that fight. Ray will murder him.' Come the big night and Evelyn was ringside with sister Marie, Edna Mae, Ray's wife, and his mother Leila. They weren't rooting for Randy Turpin.

Officials appointed by the New York State Athletic Commission were judges Joe Agnello and Harold Barnes, and referee Ruby Goldstein.

'A whistle blew to clear the ring ten seconds before the bell at the beginning of each round. Robinson, as usual, danced about in his corner, waiting for the start, but Turpin sat calmly awaiting the first signal and then they came up for round one. There was a short preliminary spar, then Turpin shot a left to the face, then two more and they went into a clinch. Here, Robinson tied up his rival's right arm so effectively that Turpin was unable to chop at his head and then the referee parted them. Robinson sent out a

156 *New York Times* 13 September 1951

light left, then let loose both hands rapidly to the body. There was a sluggishness about Turpin as he allowed the American to beat him to the punch with a light left and then slug hard to the body. Robinson kept darting in with rights and lefts to the mid-section and it did not seem that Randy could get his left hand going. Ray would not go back, but after flicking out a left would smash either hand to the body as Turpin came forward. Robinson's round.'[157]

'In the second round, Robinson jabbed his left to Turpin's head and took one in exchange. Robinson moved after the champion and speared him with three left jabs to the head and a right to the body. Sugar Ray got in another right to the head. Turpin sent a lunging left to Robinson's head, Robinson pressed Turpin and the Englishman smacked a right to Robinson's head. Robinson sent a smashing right to Turpin's head and another to his body. Turpin scored with a left and right, but Robinson tore back and dropped Turpin with a right to the jaw. Turpin got up without taking a count. His knees had touched the floor.

'Into round three and Turpin scored with a left hook to the body and a right to the head. Robinson landed a terrific right to Turpin's head and the champion was shaken. Robinson drove a stiff left jab to the head and a vicious right to the body. Turpin hooked a left to the body and then a hard right to the jaw. Turpin led with a right to the body, Robinson walloped Turpin with a terrific right to the body, then another before Randy smashed a long right to the head just before the bell ended what looked like an even round.'[158]

In his syndicated column, veteran sportswriter Grantland Rice wrote, 'Robinson, the nonpareil fighter of his time, was a far different opponent from the sluggish fellow back in July, when the strong and aggressive Turpin shocked the boxing world by beating its star veteran decisively. Wednesday night in the Polo Grounds, we had another Robinson and another Turpin. It was

157 Gilbert Odd *Boxing News* 19 September 1951

158 *Buffalo Evening News* 13 September 1951

Robinson's skill and experience against Turpin's youth, power and stamina.'[159]

'The fourth and fifth rounds were hard fought,' recorded Nat Fleischer, editor of *The Ring* magazine. 'In the former Randy took a powerful, stinging right that caused a slight swelling over the Britisher's left cheek, and in the fifth, a series of right crosses by each landed with effectiveness. Then came Ray's best round. In the sixth, he put on all he had for an excellent show, chasing Randy around the ring with his attack. Turpin often rushed into a clinch when he wasn't backtracking. Occasionally in that round, Randy landed stiff straight lefts to the face, but he was not displaying the excellent punching power he did in their previous battle. Turpin was not a disappointment in ruggedness, in stolid indifference to punishment, and in heart. But for those who had been accustomed to seeing British boxers demonstrate cleverness, science and strict adherence to the rules of ring technique, Turpin was a disappointment. He was the most unorthodox middleweight since the awkward southpaw Al McCoy, who knocked out George Chip in Brooklyn in April 1914. Those who had seen fighters like Jem Driscoll, Owen Moran, even Bombardier Wells, and in more recent years, Tommy Farr, found in Turpin a marked deviation from the British pattern.'[160]

A. J. Liebling, the brilliant essayist for the *New Yorker* magazine, observed, 'Robinson acting like a young, nervous fighter; Turpin, eight years his junior and fighting for the first time in this country, was calm as a Colchester oyster. Turpin wasn't crowding this time; he was taking it easy, as if sure Robinson would slow down. Jimmy Cannon of the *New York Post* wrote afterwards that Turpin "moved with a clumsy spryness and appeared to be serenely anticipating Robinson's collapse." The trouble with this policy was that it gave the much-older Robinson a chance to make his own pace, fighting in spurts and

159 Grantland Rice *Akron Register Tribune* 13 September 1951

160 Nat Fleischer *The Ring* November 1951

then resting. He is still about the fastest thing in the world for 30 seconds or so, as Turpin was to find out.'[161]

Gilbert Odd, editor of the London *Boxing News,* was ringside hoping to send a glowing report back to the office. He was bitterly disappointed, writing, 'From the start of the battle, he [Randy] disappointed the large British contingent among the spectators by adopting tactics that played right into Robinson's hands. He was so cautious that he accomplished little of note in the first four rounds and in so doing allowed the American to dictate the course of battle and assume the offensive. We thought Randy had found out for himself at Earls Court that the certain way to beat Robinson was to show him from the start who was boss. We expected him to walk into Sugar and jab him back on his heels with a stiff left and keep him on the run.

'But he did nothing of the sort and apparently those in his corner were satisfied that he was conducting the right sort of fight. How wrong they were and we are forced to wonder if brother Dick, relegated to the press seats and watched over by a commission inspector, would not have advised differently. [Dick was barred from Randy's corner because of an old New York Athletic Commission ruling that blood relatives cannot serve as official aides.] When, in the eighth and ninth rounds, Randy employed his left and waded roughly into Robinson, his change of tactics paid dividends and for the first time in the fight, we sat up and watched hopefully. Even then, he did not press matters as he should and what successes he achieved were frequently negated when he allowed the American to set up a countering rally.'[162]

'Throughout the eighth and ninth rounds, the visiting British crowd had a right to optimism yet again as Turpin unloaded devilish right and left hooks to Robinson's face. Robinson's strategy had betrayed him; it was evident that by the start of the tenth he was smarting under the terrific blows the Englishman had landed

161 A. J. Liebling *The Sweet Science* 1956

162 Gilbert Odd *Boxing News* 19 September 1951

in two previous rounds. Robinson himself realised he was not really in charge of the fight. Just seconds into the tenth, during a clinch, Robinson suffered a head butt from Turpin. Blood began gushing from above his left eye. Referee Goldstein closed in for a look. Robinson realised that Goldstein might stop the fight at round's end and that a decision would likely be awarded to Turpin. Robinson pushed himself away from the clinch.

'Immediately – in the time it takes for a light bulb to spill light after a switch has been turned on – he slammed Turpin with a shuddering right hook. Turpin went to the canvas. The referee closed in for the nine count. Turpin rose before being called out. With dread swelling in them, the English crowd watched Robinson as he rushed from the ropes. He immediately punched Turpin into the ropes with a shocking fierceness – an uppercut, a right, a left, another left, a right then a follow-up overhand right. Blood was still streaking from Robinson's eyes, but no matter; another left, another right – more than 30 punches in less than 30 seconds – and the Polo Grounds exploded. Turpin wheeled and stumbled to the centre of the ring as referee Goldstein stepped in; Turpin stared across at Robinson as if he couldn't believe what had gone so wrong so quickly, as if he could continue, but Goldstein put his arms around Turpin's shoulders. It was all over. Sugar Ray Robinson had regained the middleweight crown of the world.'[163]

'It came up like a sudden summer storm,' wrote Joe Williams. 'Without warning, the thunder broke in Sugar Ray Robinson's gloves, lightning flashed in swift-stabbing streaks. Leather blows fell in torrents. And Randy Turpin, 23-year-old British defender of the world middleweight championship, could not escape. This was in the tenth round in the Polo Grounds Wednesday night and the record crowd, which included Gen. of the Army, Douglas MacArthur, rooting restrainedly in the press section, was on its feet, caught in the curious primeval hysteria which is always present when the kill is near.

---

163 Wil Haygood *Sweet Thunder: The Life and Times of Sugar Ray Robinson* 2009

'The punch that decided the fight was a bulls-eye right to the point of the jaw. Very likely the hardest blow Robinson ever has landed in the ring. It turned Turpin's head as if on a swivel. His eyes seemed about to pop from his head. He was knocked flat on his back. That he ever regained his feet was a testimonial to his bravery and his splendid condition. But when he got up, he was merely postponing the inevitable.'[164]

Ted Smits, United Press sports editor, posed the question in the *New York Times*, 'Should Referee Ruby Goldstein have stopped Wednesday night's Ray Robinson-Randy Turpin fight with eight seconds to go in the tenth round? "No," says Turpin, the dethroned middleweight champion. "Yes," says Robinson, who regained the title. When in the tenth round Turpin opened the cut over Robinson's left eye, the New York fighter declared, "It was do or die. I was sure that if the fight had lasted another round, Turpin would split my eye so much worse that the fight would have to be stopped."

'It was stopped, but not a round or two later and not to save Robinson. The finish came with Turpin on the receiving end of Robinson's fear-driven fists. "Ruby had to stop it then," Robinson said. "I couldn't hit that man no more." The tough and game British fighter admitted, "I might have stopped the bout myself – if I had been the referee."

'"He was dazed," said Goldstein. "When I stopped the fight, he started to go to Robinson's corner."'[165]

Gilbert Odd wrote of the dramatic finish, 'Referee Goldstein took no chances – in his view Turpin had taken enough, and in our view his action was beyond criticism.'

Lainson Wood of the London *Daily Telegraph* wrote, 'Turpin did not go down but it was clear that he was out to the world, mercifully unconscious of the battering to which his head and body were being subjected. No referee with a spark of humanity could

164 Joe Williams *Buffalo Evening News* 13 September 1951

165 Ted Smits *New York Times* 13 September 1951

have allowed such slaughter to continue. Mr Ruby Goldstein, America's best, stepped in as Turpin fell like an empty sack, restrained Robinson and directed him to his corner.'[166]

Goldstein's action in stopping the fight didn't go down very well with London promoter Jack Solomons. Nat Fleischer was in Turpin's dressing room when Solomons shouted, '"He had no right to stop the fight. They've had a few deaths here in America and everyone is scared. Turpin wasn't even hurt." Perhaps Turpin wasn't hurt. At least he didn't show any signs of injury in the dressing room, but a helpless fighter such as Turpin undoubtedly was should not be submitted to dangerous punishment and Randy most assuredly was taking plenty in the tenth. Jack apparently didn't feel the punches.'[167]

However, boxing writers for all three of London's afternoon papers backed the referee's move in halting the bout when he did, which helped to soothe bitter Britishers who had been giving out the equivalent of an American 'We wuz robbed.'

Randy Turpin wasn't robbed, he wasn't even dead. He would fight again.

'Down at my café, about 30 blocks from the Polo Grounds,' recalled Robinson in his autobiography, 'most of the rounds were on me that night. By the time I got there, there wasn't any place to park for blocks, except for the spot reserved in front for my flamingo Cadillac. That was a Cadillac night on Seventh Avenue. It looked like an assembly line. "If you ain't got a '51 Caddy," somebody said in the café, "you got to double park."

'In my little corner of the world, Cadillacs were double-parked. But not for long.'[168]

166 Lainson Wood *Daily Telegraph and Morning Post* 13 September 1951

167 Nat Fleischer *The Ring* November 1951

168 Sugar Ray Robinson with Dave Anderson *Sugar Ray* 1969

13

A FIGHT TOO FAR

SUGAR RAY'S good friend and idol, heavyweight champ Joe Louis, had put his 'Bum of the Month' club into the boxing lexicon in the 40s. Promoter Mike Jacobs lined them up and Joe knocked them down. December 1940, Al McCoy in Boston; January 1941, Red Burman in New York; February, Gus Dorazio in Philadelphia; March, Abe Simon in Detroit; April, Tony Musto in St Louis; May, Buddy Baer in Washington. Joe's title bouts in six different cities gave him purses running at $22,000 a fight. In June, he fought Billy Conn, who was not a bum, and Louis picked up $152,905. Joe earned that one. Conn ran him ragged for 13 rounds before he got careless and Joe had another knockout.

In 1952, Sugar Ray figured this sounded like a good idea. On 14 March, Russ Newland reported from San Francisco, 'Middleweight champion Sugar Ray Robinson successfully started his series of monthly title fights by decisively defeating Carl (Bobo) Olson of Honolulu last night. The tap dancing master of the 160-pound division had to travel at top speed to score a 15-round unanimous decision over his younger rival. He next defends against Rocky Graziano in Chicago on 16 April and against Paddy Young in New York on 16 May. Robinson, obviously tired after exchanging punches with the rugged 23-year-old Honolulu-born fighter, said he finished in good condition.

'Ray was tired but jovial after defeating Bobo Olson. "Would he like to fight light-heavyweight champion Joey Maxim?" he was asked. "Maybe my manager wants to fight him," Ray grinned. "I'm not interested." Pressed, Sugar Ray said he "might" be talked into a Maxim fight, but "I'm about ready to retire. I'm just plain tired of fighting. I don't even watch fights any more, not since Joe Louis quit." And he joked about getting only $1 for defending his crown against Olson. The rest of his purse went to the Damon Runyon Cancer Fund. "I'll have a hard time explaining that $1 fight to my son (two-year-old Ray II) when he grows up. He'll ask, 'Dad, how come you fought for $1 if you weren't a preliminary boy?'"

'Robinson's fast finish, when he belted Olson with some stiff head punches, appeared to have Bobo slightly wobbly at the final bell. The champ said he considered this fight a needed tune-up. "I hope for the best against Graziano in Chicago," he said.'[169]

Lester Bromberg, boxing writer for the *New York World-Telegram and Sun* since 1937, did not think Rocky, a former champion, a suitable contender for Robinson's middleweight title in April 1952. 'Graziano had been a superb animal, without boxing skill but with an electrical punch in his right hand and a set of reflexes out of a steel trap. Time has robbed him of the reflexes, for a certainty. There is even serious reason to wonder how much hitting power he has left. Rocky no more expects to go 15 rounds than I do. He knows he will either score a staggering upset within a few rounds or get knocked out within approximately the same distance.'[170]

That was Bromberg on the button. 'The third round found Graziano getting a little cocky. When he floored Robinson with a right hand that spilled the champion so quickly it looked like he slipped, Rocky had made a fatal mistake. Robinson quickly uprighted himself and then, squaring off for murderous

169 Russ Newland *Charleston Daily Mail* West Virgina 14 March 1952

170 Lester Bromberg *New York World-Telegram and Sun* New York 12 April 1952

range, pumped the left-right combination that put the lights out for Rocky.'[171]

New York middleweight Paddy Young was training hard. He was slated to fight Sugar Ray Robinson for the middleweight championship in the Garden on 16 May, his big chance. Paddy didn't figure to beat Robinson, but who did? He was a regular at the Garden and had won 43 of his 54 fights, the last one with tough Ernie Durando. But when he read the sports pages, it was bad news. Robinson was skipping the fight for a better deal, a shot at Joey Maxim's light-heavyweight title at Yankee Stadium for 30 per cent of the gate.

Sugar had protested that he didn't want to fight Maxim, but as manager George Gainford was telling it Sugar Ray considered himself capable of whipping much heavier foes and was desirous of joining Bob Fitzsimmons and Henry Armstrong as a triple champion. Fitzsimmons captured the middleweight, heavyweight and light-heavyweight titles but never held them at the same time. Armstrong simultaneously held the featherweight, lightweight and welterweight crowns, a monopoly that prompted boxing commissions to ordain that only one title could be held at a time. Be that as it may, Robinson still considered himself the welterweight champion, although he had been stripped of that title when he took the middleweight crown off Jake LaMotta. Now he was eyeing the light-heavyweight title.

Joey Maxim wasn't a very good fighter but he had a very good manager. Jack (Doc) Kearns had taken a hobo named Jack Dempsey to the heavyweight championship and a million-dollar fortune in the Roaring Twenties. He blew another fortune with middleweight champ Mickey Walker and now he had another champion. His square name was Giuseppe Antonio Berardinelli, but his name on fight posters was Joey Maxim. 'I was trying to ballyhoo him as "the new Dempsey," recalled Doc. 'I took a lot of kidding about it. Everybody knew that Joey wasn't the greatest

171 *Newport Daily News* Rhode Island 17 April 1952

puncher in the world. They found all kinds of faults with him. But there's one important item they all overlooked. He kept winning.'

Maxim beat Gus Lesnevich to claim the American light-heavy title, which gave Doc a chance at world champion Freddie Mills. He packed Maxim off to London, where his non-puncher knocked out Mills in ten rounds to go back to New York as champion of the world. Now Doc could move and one guy he had his eye on was Sugar Ray Robinson. He talked to Robinson in his Harlem tavern but Ray was against the fight. 'I know what you want, Doc, but the answer is no,' he told Kearns.

In his autobiography, told to veteran sportswriter Oscar Fraley, Doc told Robinson, 'This is probably the greatest chance you'll ever have to win the light-heavyweight championship of the world. No matter what happens, you can't get hurt. Maxim doesn't punch that hard. Now, if we have to fight Archie Moore for the title he'll probably beat us. And, while I think you're a helluva fighter, Ray, I don't think you could whip Archie if they let you carry a meat cleaver. But Maxim, now, well that's another story.'[172]

'The more Jim Norris talked to me about the fight,' recalled Ray, 'the more I knew that he'd come up in price. He started out by telling me how it was Maxim's title, how Maxim had to get the most of the money. He should've known better than that. "Jim," I told him, "you know that I'm the man selling the tickets. Maxim never sold a ticket in his life." When the contract was signed, Maxim was getting 30 per cent of everything. And so was the challenger – me.'[173]

Joe Liebling, the guy from the *New Yorker*, met Kearns in Dempsey's Broadway restaurant a few days before the fight. 'Most managers say "we" will lick so-and-so when they mean their man will try to, but Kearns does not allow his fighter even a share of the pronoun. "Up to now, I had to stuff myself up and fight heavyweights," he said. "Me, the only white guy with a title.

172 Jack Kearns with Oscar Fraley *The Million Dollar Gate* 1966

173 Sugar Ray Robinson with Dave Anderson *Sugar Ray* 1969

But now I got somebody I can bull around." By this he meant, I gathered, that, in order to obtain what he considered sufficiently remunerative employment in the past for Maxim, he had had to overfeed the poor fellow and spread the rumour that he had grown into a full-sized heavyweight. Then, after fattening him to 180, he had exposed him to the assault of more genuine giants, who had nearly killed him.

'But now, he implied, Maxim had an opponent he could shove around and control in the clinches. I said I hoped it would be a good fight to watch, and he said, "I got to be good. I can't afford to lay back. I got to keep moving him, moving him."'[174]

'"I didn't want to fight him at first," confessed Ray at his Pompton Lakes training camp. "My mom didn't like the idea. She figures he's 20 pounds heavier and might hurt me. But my manager thinks I can beat him. So do I." "Maxim don't knock you out," chimed in George Gainford. "That's why we take him. We lick Maxim and we go after the big boys. Walcott? You think he can lick my man? If Mickey Walker fights the big boys, so can he."

'Sugar Ray would be satisfied adding just the light-heavyweight title to his collection. "I'm no Mickey Walker," he reflected modestly and prudently.'[175]

'Dusky Robinson, wealthy businessman of Harlem, and swarthy Maxim, owner of two delicatessen stores in Cleveland, spent last night in New York after motoring in from their training camps. The most sparkling facet of this battle of champions was cut by the ancient ring axiom; "A good big man can always beat a good little man." Will that axiom be upheld? Or are the Robinson supporters correct when they tab Sugar Ray "a great little man" and refer to Maxim as a "mediocre big man?"'[176]

The fight was scheduled for Monday, 23 June 1952 but was postponed until Wednesday night because of rain and cold. Both fighters weighed in on Monday. Robinson scaled 160 pounds,

---

174 A. J. Liebling *The Sweet Science* 1956

175 *Daily Capital News* Jefferson City, Missouri 14 June 1952

176 *San Mateo Times* California 23 June 1952

Maxim a quarter of a pound inside the 175-pound light-heavy limit, but they would have to weigh in again on Wednesday, with the general feeling that the postponement would hurt Joey more than Robinson. There was strong support for Robinson after Monday's weigh-in, changing the odds from 6-5 and 'pick 'em' to 13-10 in favour of Sugar Ray in his bid for a third title.

On Tuesday, Maxim ran four miles in the morning and went through a brisk workout at Stillman's Gym on Eighth Avenue in the afternoon, perspiring freely as he went through three rounds of shadow boxing, a session on the light bag and another with the skipping rope. At the Uptown gym in Harlem, a large crowd watched Sugar Ray go through a light drill of shadow boxing, bag punching and rope skipping.

Wednesday's weather went into the record books before the result of the fight did. It became the hottest 25 June in the history of the New York City Weather Bureau. Joe Liebling, riding the subway up to the Yankee Stadium, where the fight was to be held, observed, 'The men slumped in the seats and hanging to the straps weren't talking excitedly or making jokes, as fight fans generally do. They were just gasping gently, like fish that had been caught two hours earlier. Most of those who had been wearing neckties had removed them, but rings of red and green remained around collars and throats to show the colour of the ties that had been there. Shirts stuck to the folds of bellies, and even the floor was wet with sweat.'[177]

Inside the stadium, Peter Wilson of the London *Daily Express*, sweating like the fighters in the pressure cooker the ring had become, wrote, 'When you reach for cigarettes and matches from the pocket of your shirt and the cigarettes are a wet, brown, unsmokeable stickiness and the book matches won't strike because they are sodden, think of that and then imagine what it's like fighting under the additional heat of 35 ring lamps when your ring shoes feel like a deep sea diver's lead-soled boots and your gloves

177 A. J. Liebling *The Sweet Science* 1956

seem tied to the floor and you have read in the evening papers that it's 104 degrees ringside in the shade and 139 degrees out of it.'[178]

Going into the ring, Robinson weighed 157½ to Maxim's 173 pounds, a difference of 15½ pounds. 'Maxim was very strong and a good boxer,' Sugar Ray said in his autobiography, 'but my plan was simple enough. I was much faster, and with my speed I hoped to keep him off balance. My strategy was working. Through five rounds, Maxim was an easy target. The two judges, Artie Aidala and Harold Barnes, gave me all five rounds. The referee, Ruby Goldstein, gave me four with one even.'[179]

'I scored the first seven rounds for Robinson,' wrote Jesse Abramson. 'Round after round, he was the ring master we have known. No one expected he would be so dominant for so long. He was the master of versatility, the virtuoso. He played on Maxim as though he were a violin. He played up and down his body with left leads, he stormed into volleys and barrages and fusillades. He hit and got away clean, or he erupted into two-fisted body attacks in close when he wasn't tying Maxim up in the repeated clinches. Robinson was tactically the master. He did what he wanted with Maxim, and he wasn't going to let Maxim do anything in close where Maxim, the defensive fighter, is at his best. At long range, Maxim didn't hit Robinson a solid blow until the fight was half over. If Maxim intended to wear Robinson out by letting him do all the fighting and moving, it was an infernally clever and diabolical plan. In the inferno of last night, it worked.'[180]

Joey Maxim had the right man in his corner. Jack (Doc) Kearns had devised the plan in the training camp. 'There wasn't much in the way of compliments written about Maxim while he prepared for the bout. Joey looked sluggish and the flashy Robinson apparently was scalpel sharp. But all I was worried about was condition,' said Doc. 'Just keep boxing him and above everything save yourself as much as possible. Don't worry about the lead he might be piling

---

178 Peter Wilson *Daily Express* London 26 June 1952

179 Sugar Ray Robinson with Dave Anderson *Sugar Ray* 1969

180 Jesse Abramson *New York Herald Tribune* 26 June 1952

up. It's gonna be hot enough to fry sausages under those ring lights and this fight can be won in the last round if you save enough to get the job done.'[181]

Referee Goldstein didn't get to see the last round of this fight. The tenth round was Ruby's last. 'My strength was being burned out of me,' he recalled in his autobiography. 'By the eighth round, I was beginning to get groggy and a haze was forming in front of my eyes. Robinson, too, was slowing down and only the stolid Maxim, who had set an early slow pace for himself, was moving steadily along. As early as I could tell – there were times when I wasn't quite sure who was hitting whom, or how effectively – nothing happened in the ninth and tenth rounds and, to be on the safe side, I called both rounds even. It was at the end of the tenth that one of the commission doctors, who must have been watching me closely, realised that I was about to pass out. He told chairman Robert Christenberry that if I were not immediately replaced, the result might be serious, even fatal, to me. I was ordered out of the ring and left it in a daze, and Ray Miller was assigned to take my place. Although I do not remember having done so, I gave my tally card to Miller, who later said that the markings for the eighth, ninth and tenth rounds had become so blurred on the sweat-soaked card that they were illegible.'[182]

When Goldstein was replaced by Ray Miller, it was an unprecedented occurrence in ring history. The only similar occurrence was the collapse of former lightweight champion Benny Leonard while he was refereeing a bout at St Nicholas Arena, New York on 18 April 1947. That bout, an extra fight put on after the night's main event, was cancelled and Leonard died a short time later in a dressing room.

'Robinson gave indications of fading in the 11th,' observed James P. Dawson for the *New York Times*, 'and the change came soon after Robinson had staggered his rival with a mighty right to

---

181 Jack (Doc) Kearns with Oscar Fraley *The Million Dollar Gate* 1966

182 Ruby Goldstein with Frank Graham *Third Man in the Ring* 1959

the jaw, his best punch of the fight. Through the 12th and 13th, Robinson staggered and stumbled all over the ring. But Maxim was unable to take advantage. Robinson missed awkwardly with punches he had previously sent home unerringly. He sagged into clinches and jabbed and swung aimlessly. He almost fell through the ropes early in the 13th, while in retreat. Ray missed a sweeping right for the jaw later in the round and fell flat on his face. But near the end of the round, when he appeared weariest, Ray crashed a terrific right to Maxim's jaw as Joey came in with lefts and rights to the body and head. Robinson clung to the ropes in a neutral corner as the 13th ended. His handlers leaped in to carry the weary fighter to his corner. His seconds made every effort to clear his head during the one-minute rest period. Ice packs were applied to Ray's head and neck. Smelling salts were used. Physical therapy was attempted under the supervision of Dr Alexander I. Schiff, of the state athletic commission. But all in vain. Then, while the stunned crowd stood in amazement, the bell clanged for the start of the 14th. Robinson made no move to get off his corner stool. Referee Ray Miller stepped to Robinson's corner. Maxim leaped across the ring, only to be waved aside. Dr Schiff had informed referee Miller that Robinson could not continue and the battle was over.'[183]

When the first bell rang that night in the concrete cauldron that Yankee Stadium had become, a perspiring crowd of 47,983 had set record receipts for a light-heavyweight championship, $421,615, plus the approximate $100,000 for theatre TV, beating the mark set in July 1926, when Paul Berlenbach and Jack Delaney drew a gate of $461,789 to Ebbets Field in Brooklyn.

They had dragged the referee out in the tenth round and they dragged Sugar Ray Robinson out in the 13th, leaving Joey Maxim the winner and still light-heavyweight champion of the world.

'Joey Maxim pressed an ice bag to his swollen brow in the oven that was his dressing room and mumbled, "Know he was

183 James P. Dawson *New York Times* 26 June 1952

ahead? I'd have to be a real dummy not to know he was way ahead. I didn't know what happened. I thought maybe he was faking when he started reeling around in the 13th. He was the smaller guy and I guess he couldn't take the heat too good. It was the first time I ever fought anybody so little. I just couldn't get at him."'[184] Maxim was 15½ pounds heavier than Robinson but only an inch taller.

'Burly handlers dragged Robinson to the dressing room. Reporters converged upon the door. Finally, Dr Ira McCown of the boxing commission staff came out. "Robinson is suffering from heat prostration," he announced in a loud voice. "Anything else?" asked a reporter. "That's enough," said the doctor. "He is in no condition to talk. He's way out in left field."

'A few moments later, the door opened again. A cordon of police formed an aisle. Out came manager George Gainford and Mrs Robinson. Sugar Ray was supported by them. His feet dragged, his head hung and he shook it convulsively from side to side. He was dragged in this fashion to a waiting automobile and spirited off. Joe Louis walked by. "They shoulda stopped it in the 11th," he said. "Ray had him enough then."'[185]

It wasn't supposed to end like this. It didn't.

'The scenes of that fabulous night had not ended in the ring,' Peter Wilson would write later. 'When Robinson was finally supported to his dressing room through the milling crowd, the final bizarre happenings of that utterly bizarre night took place. First of all, Robinson repeatedly sought assurance from his friend, Vincent Impellitteri, Mayor of New York, that Maxim hadn't knocked him out. Then his personal physician, Dr Vincent Nardiello, persuaded him to get under a shower in order to reduce his temperature. Robinson agreed to do so, but there was still so much perplexity in his mind that he suddenly grabbed the fully clad mayor and pulled him under the shower with him. When the

184 *Chester Times* PA. 26 June 1952

185 Stan Opotowsky *Lebanon Daily News* PA. 26 June 1952

mayor escaped, Robinson's manager, George Gainford, also fully clothed, remained under the shower with Robinson.

'All Robinson kept repeating was: "The heat didn't beat me. God willed it that way. You fellows think I'm crazy, but I'm not crazy. It was God. He wanted me to lose." People were getting seriously concerned about Robinson, and they asked Dr Nardiello to take him to a hospital. In the end, Nardiello, although admittedly he had never seen a fighter act as Sugar did, said, "He can identify everybody around him. But he just hasn't gained full control of his faculties. I'll let him go home. I'll be up to examine him in the morning. Ray doesn't like hospitals, and I didn't want to do anything that might frustrate his brain. He might have passed out then, and that could have been dangerous."

'A final footnote. It was announced later that Maxim had lost nine pounds and Robinson 11 pounds, which meant that it was a heavy middleweight fighting a welterweight for the light-heavyweight title.'[186]

186 Peter Wilson *More Ringside Seats* 1959

14

THOSE DANCING FEET

VINCE NARDIELLO was a tough Italian kid from the Lower East Side of New York. He was handy with his fists and had about 100 fights at stags and smokers at clubs around the city; Sharkey's, Healey's and the New Polo. Calling himself Jimmy Sheppard, he turned pro and with his purse monies paid his way through medical college. From 1931, he was a representative of the New York State Athletic Commission and would become the chief medical officer for the commission, a well-respected member of the boxing community.

When Ray was starting to make a name for himself as an amateur boxer, he wanted to quit school but his mother was against it. In his autobiography, he recalled, 'When I talked to her about dropping out of school, she went downtown to ask advice from a doctor she had taken us to when we lived in Hell's Kitchen. He was Dr Vincent Nardiello, a small Italian man with a pencil moustache. Mom knew he was around boxing. He worked for the New York State Athletic Commission and for Madison Square Garden. He knew all the fighters, and he had even heard about me as an amateur. He even knew my two names.

'That convinced her. And after that, all she thought about was my career as a fighter.'[187]

187 Sugar Ray Robinson with Dave Anderson *Sugar Ray* 1969

Dr Nardiello would become a great friend of Ray Robinson as he climbed the boxing ladder and in time became his personal physician. He was there when they dragged Sugar out of the ring that sweltering night in June 1952, leaving Joey Maxim still holding his light-heavyweight title. 'He's fine, just exhausted,' Dr Nardiello told reporters. 'It was just the heat.'

The good doctor was not too happy when reading a United Press bulletin a few days later. '"He asked me to get a return bout," said George Gainford, Sugar Ray's manager. "They are going to give him an 'Israel salute to Ray Robinson' dinner at the Astor on 10 July. We sail for Paris on the *Liberte* on 11 July. Robinson will fight Albert Yvel at Tel Aviv in a benefit bout on 2 August. He might even make a movie in Paris later."[188]

'Dr Nardiello announced from New York 6 July, "Middleweight champion Sugar Ray Robinson will not go through with his projected European tour and title fight in Israel." Dr Nardiello said he advised Robinson against making the trip because the champion still has not fully recovered from the effects of the heat exhaustion which caused his defeat in the 23 June bout with light-heavyweight champion Joey Maxim.'[189]

'Sugar had a restless night, and Edna Mae's was not much better,' wrote Herb Boyd in his Robinson biography. 'The next morning, she was alarmed to discover that Sugar's body was covered with fever blisters, which were the result of his boiling blood. Despite reports to the contrary in his autobiography, for several days Sugar was ill, unable to go anywhere. Edna Mae insisted, "The fight had been a sobering experience for Sugar," she wrote. "He later announced his retirement and was now ready to listen to some of the wonderful offers that were being waved in front of his face to try a career in showbusiness. I thought with the right teachers Sugar could do anything."

---

188 *Butte Montana Standard* 27 June 1952

189 *Lubbock Morning Avalanche* Texas 7 July 1952

"Sugar was totally dehydrated after the fight," his son recalled. "People don't know how near dying Dad was. He could not retain anything in his stomach for two days, and he was delirious and was not well for six months after the fight."[190]

'I began to think seriously about retiring, because Dr Nardiello had advised me to take a long rest from boxing,' Ray recalled in his autobiography. 'I had developed a friendship with Joe Glaser, the president of the Associated Booking Corporation, one of the biggest agents in showbusiness. He handled Louis Armstrong and later he would handle Barbra Streisand. "If you're ever interested," he had told me several times, "I'll book you as a dancer when you retire." I was interested now.'[191]

A few weeks later, Glaser phoned Ray with good news. He was booked into the French Casino at the Paramount Hotel, opening on 7 November for four weeks at $15,000 a week. He would follow that up with a similar engagement at the Sahara Hotel in Las Vegas. Sugar Ray was knocked out! He didn't have an act yet and he was signed up for $120,000 for two months.

Ray's autobiography continued, "Ray," Glaser said, seriously, "I used to handle Bill Robinson, 'Bojangles,' and I know what Fred Astaire and Gene Kelly have been paid for their nightclub acts. And you're making more per week than any dancer who ever lived."

'When the story broke in the newspapers about my retirement from boxing and my new showbiz career, I got another phone call, from Pee Wee Beale. "At 15 thou [thousand] a week," he said, "there's got to be room somewhere for Pee Wee." I found room. I had kept June Clark around as my secretary, even though she had never taken or typed a letter. The other members of my entourage had scattered.'

Joe Glaser was the son of a Chicago family of Russian-Jewish origin. As a young man on the make, 'Glaser was an influential fight promoter in Chicago. From his two-room office in the Loop,

190 Herb Boyd with Ray Robinson II *Pound for Pound* 2005

191 Sugar Ray Robinson with Dave Anderson *Sugar Ray* 1969

Glaser ran his boxing empire and zealously protected his turf. When a gambler and part-time journalist named Eddie Borden denounced Glaser in print as a front for the Capone organisation, Glaser had the man run out of town and swiftly returned to business as usual. Glaser's power to fix fights earned him a reputation as the sage of boxing, especially among reporters. Vern Whaley, who covered boxing for the *Chicago Evening Post*, recalls that on the day of a big fight, "Glaser would give me the names of the winners in advance, even the round of a knockout."'[192]

With the help of his alleged mob connections, he started managing Louis Armstrong in May 1935. The success of their association caused other jazz musicians to join Glaser and his agency, the Associated Booking Corporation, which was formed in 1940 by Glaser and Armstrong. Although his clients had a high opinion of him, Glaser was a feared person in the business industry. Associated Booking Corporation, or ABC as it is also known, has at various times represented Duke Ellington, Benny Goodman, Lionel Hampton, Woody Herman, Dave Brubeck, Barbra Streisand and B.B. King, among many others.[193]

'Ever since the days when he tap-danced for pennies as a youngster on the streets of Harlem, Sugar Ray Robinson has dreamed of being an entertainer,' wrote columnist Oscar Fraley. 'That's why, with his fortune made and a lucrative nightclub contract in his pocket, they insist today along the concrete strand known as Jacobs Beach that the middleweight champion will never fight again. There are other reasons too. One of the biggest is that Sugar Ray admires himself as a fashion plate, and one not distorted by facial indignities which go with the pecuniary rewards of the ring. Not too long ago, he went under the knife to remove scar tissue from his brows and acquire a nose unmarked by violent contact.

---

192 Laurence Bergreen *Capone* 1994

193 Wikipedia 2018

'Robinson is a dancer of remarkable professional talent who does not have to trade on his name, although it helps, naturally. The one factor which keeps him from making a clean break with the ring at the moment is that Sugar Ray flinches from retiring as a loser. In his last start, Robinson collapsed from heat fatigue at the end of the 13th round against Joey Maxim. It was only his third loss in 137 fights, but it tells the tale of a declining fighter. Yet the more he remembers the unrelenting rigours of the training camp, the more unlikely it is that he will accept a title bout with Kid Gavilan in February.

'Only two items seem fairly certain. One is that action in the middleweight division should pick up because Robinson had the Indian sign on most of the boys. The other is that Sugar Ray is finished.'[194]

The newspaper stories in November 1952 seemed to indicate the end of one career and the beginning of another. 'Sugar Ray Robinson is worrying about his hands,' Jack Gaver wrote for United Press, 'which ordinarily would be quite a worry for a boxer. But this concern over his fighting tools involves his debut as a dancer instead of another defence of his middleweight championship. "Funny thing about the hands," the perspiring fighter said as he took time out from rehearsal on the floor of a nightclub. "In boxing, they have to be up all the time, if you want to stay healthy. In dancing, you need to keep them down and natural. That's been the toughest thing for me to master."

'The lithe champion certainly doesn't seem to be having trouble with his feet. His practice sessions on the stage at the daytime-deserted French Casino, where he will make his debut as a performer Friday night, reveal a tap dancer with a variety of routines that are really professional. "And he's only been taking serious instructions for a little more than two months," interjected Henry Le Tang, dance teacher who has prepared Robinson for his serious effort at a new career. "I've liked dancing all my life," Ray

194 Oscar Fraley *Altoona Mirror* PA. 18 October 1952

said. "Stepping just sort of comes natural to me, but I really didn't know anything about how to do it right until I began to study under Henry. Far as I'm concerned, it's just as tough as training for a fight, maybe tougher."'[195]

'As a rule, Friday night is fight night,' wrote columnist Red Smith, 'but Madison Square Garden had been pre-empted by the horse show. For men of action, consequently, the place to go was the French Casino, where Sugar Ray Robinson, the Harlem Boulevardier and middleweight champion of the world, was to take on Terpsichore at catchweights in a battle to the finish. It was Sugar Ray's theatrical debut as a dancing man. The French Casino, two flights below the Paramount Hotel lobby, was crowded for the dinner show with a glittering assemblage, some in black tie, some wearing dried apricots for ears.

'The eight o'clock show began at 8.45pm with a production number entitled "Champs Elysees in April" – leggy broilers, chorus boys and a ballerina. Then the prize ring made its newest gift to the theatre, amid tremendous applause. He said the toughest 10 moments of his life had begun backstage when a man said, "Champ, you're on in 10 minutes." He remembered a joke all the way through, introduced a juggler and retired. When he re-appeared, Ray was accompanied by a small comic who identified himself as Slaphappy Scotty. He and Scotty did a tap dance to howling applause. Ray dances well. If the pair of them added up to something less than Bojangles, well, Bojangles never knocked out Rocky Graziano. The programme promised that Robinson would do one more scene entitled, "The Champ." Anyway, the decision was already in the bag. Robinson was so far ahead he couldn't lose unless he collapsed from heat exhaustion. At the curb outside, a Cadillac convertible was parked, bearing the licence plate "27 RR." The car is flamingo pink.'[196]

---

195 Jack Gaver *Huntingdon Daily News* PA. 4 November 1952

196 Red Smith *New York Herald Tribune* 20 November 1952

'The girls,' reported the man from Associated Press, 'as befits a show imported from Paris, wore elaborate costumes part of the time and not very much on other occasions. On the gaudy side, they were rivalled by Sugar Ray, who had seven changes of attire that were positively dazzling. First he came out in a dinner jacket in the now-famous Robinson plaid. Next he wore a two-tone brown number. His third change was into a tap-cream outfit. Then he did a dance in conventional formal attire, tails and white tie. Then came a change into a dark brown suit. Next he wore white with a faintest sort of check in it. And finally, for a sentimental flag-waving United Nations finale, he wore just plain blue serge.'[197]

'The critics who were there were mostly boxing writers who had come out of curiosity. They were kind, if cautious, with their remarks. Some of the praise was of the backhanded variety. "The guy is a superb clotheshorse," wrote Lewis Burton in the *New York Journal-American*, "but if you are going in for horses, Native Dancer is a better bet."'[198]

From Las Vegas, columnist Dave Lewis wrote, 'The man whose fists earned him the distinction of being one of the truly great boxers of all time shook his head and said, "I've never been so scared in my life!" It was Sugar Ray Robinson speaking, and he was talking about his opening show a few minutes before in the beautiful Copra Room of the Hotel Sahara here Tuesday night. Robinson obviously was extremely nervous during what show people regard as his first real test as an entertainer. But, like the champion he is, Sugar Ray conducted himself most admirably. And the "first nighter" audience, which included such famous personalities as Del Webb, owner of the New York Yankees, and Jack Benny, received him in a most enthusiastic manner.

'Frankly expecting a rather crude attempt at tap dancing, we were pleasantly surprised and even impressed by the first of his three dance routines. It was a tap number with his partner during

197 *Austin Daily Herald* Minnesota 8 November 1952

198 Wil Haygood *Sweet Thunder: The Life and Times of Sugar Ray Robinson* 2009

which they dance to several different tempos. One professional dancer with whom we talked remarked that Robinson's taps were remarkably clear. This is his fourth engagement and he's getting $12,500 per week for two weeks from the Hotel Sahara. That's the minimum weekly figure for which he has worked so far and which he will receive for his forthcoming 14-week swing through Chicago, Detroit, Milwaukee, Minneapolis, Indianapolis, Montreal, Toronto etc., starting 13 February in the Chicago Theatre. "I was even more panicky tonight until those good people started applauding," he said. "That really made me happy!"'[199]

Ray could use a little happiness about that time. He had just attended the funeral of his good friend and trainer Fred (Pee Wee) Beale, aged 41. A former dancer prior to 1938, when he joined Henry Armstrong's group of trainers, Pee Wee teamed up with Robinson in 1942 after three years in the armed services.

About the middle of December 1952, Sugar Ray had released his 'complete and unequivocal' retirement through Abe Greene, commissioner of the National Boxing Association (NBA). George Barton, veteran NBA president, told Greene that the American title be cleared up at once by a contest between Bobo Olson and Ernie Durando, Paddy Young and Rocky Castellani, the survivor to meet the winner of a Randy Turpin-Charles Humez bout in Europe. Bob Christenberry, New York chairman, also was making plans for a tournament. Within a year, Turpin had beaten Humez over 15 rounds in London to become European champion, and Bobo Olson had thrashed Turpin over 15 rounds in the Garden to win the title Sugar Ray had given up to tread the boards.

'The kid nobody wanted held the middleweight championship of the world today,' wrote Oscar Fraley from New York, 'but as usual in the hectic life of Carl (Bobo) Olson, everything was just a little late. Ten years ago, the balding young man of 25 was a stray on the dead-end streets of Honolulu. His parents had separated and when you are the offspring of a Swedish-American ex-Army

199 Dave Lewis *Long Beach Independent* California 29 January 1953

sergeant and a Hawaiian-Portuguese mother, whether you like it or not, help is scarce and seldom offered.

'So the plotting of his life was left in the hands of the broad-shouldered youngster who looked older than his 15 years. And a scrap on a bus with a sailor, plus the soon-found ability to handle himself in those dead-end scraps, quickly charted the course which Bobo was to follow. "I wish," he said in a flat undertone which was almost lost in the usual clamour of the winner's dressing room, "that this had happened against Ray Robinson. He was the guy I wanted to beat." To Bobo it was, as usual, everything was just a little late!'[200]

So where was Sugar Ray? From New York, Jack Gaver wrote for United Press, 'Tomorrow afternoon he'll demonstrate still another skill – as a dramatic actor on the first broadcast of "Excursion," the new television show for children put together by the Ford Foundation TV-Radio Workshop on the NBC network. Sugar Ray will play the role of Jim in the programme's dramatisation of the Duke and the Dauphin episode from Mark Twain's *The Adventures of Huckleberry Finn*. Eddie Albert will play the Duke, Thomas Mitchell the Dauphin.'[201] A week later, Sugar Ray Robinson and his New York Revue was playing the Casablanca club in Canton, Ohio. A note on the poster stated, 'For This Attraction – Everybody Welcome – Sunday Inter-Racial Night.'

A United Press bulletin from New York stated, 'Interesting competition during the approaching warm season in boxing may be sparked by Sugar Ray Robinson's return to the ring. Just when everyone was convinced that the former welterweight and middleweight champion had hung up his gloves for good, promoter Jim Norris said Tuesday, "I believe Robinson will come back. I have a hunch he will." He emphasised that his hunch was not based on any word from Sugar Ray. "Robinson should have discovered by now that he can't make money as fast in the role of song-and-

---

200 Oscar Fraley *Oshkosh Daily Northwestern* Wisconsin 22 October 1953

201 Jack Gaver *Kingsport Times-News* Tennessee 13 September 1953

dance man as he could with his fists," Norris explained. "Taxes and travelling expenses leave a performer with little profit nowadays," he said. 'Because of the great interest in middleweight competition aroused by Bobo Olson, Randy Turpin and Charles Humez, I believe Sugar Ray will come back this summer and shoot for a big chunk of dough," he declared.'[202]

Maybe the former champ would be safer back in the boxing ring, if you believed the stuff Dorothy Kilgallen was writing in her 'Voice of Broadway' column – 'This never hit the newspapers, but while touring with the Count Basie band, Sugar Ray Robinson had the nose of a .45 poked into his ribs at the close of a one-night gig in the Quincy High School auditorium in Quincy, Illinois. Why the native drew the gun still remains a mystery – he didn't rob Sugar Ray, just warned him to get out of town as soon as possible.'[203]

The Sugarman made it out of town safely. A couple of weeks later, he was strutting his stuff in Toronto and after his one-week stint in the Canadian city was taking his troupe to New York and Philadelphia. Ray had a court appointment in New York to hear the verdict in his suit against the *Amsterdam News* (the oldest black newspaper in America), which had printed a story that the ex-fighter, now a song-and-dance man, had assaulted his wife, Edna Mae, when the two were in Paris three years ago. Robinson was making an exhibition tour of Europe when the paper printed the story on 6 January 1951. Both Robinson and his wife testified during a three-day trial that the newspaper story was not true. The newspaper's defence to the suit was that it had merely reported rumours that had been circulating in Harlem and that it had published a retraction in its next issue when it learned that the Robinsons were returning to the US together. The paper had reported that Robinson was sending her home alone.

A jury of ten men and two women awarded Robinson $25,000 in his suit against the paper. The newspaper moved Tuesday, 23

202 *Logansport Pharos Tribune* Indiana 6 May 1953

203 Dorothy Kilgallen *Dover Daily Reporter* Ohio 16 January 1954

March in Superior Court to set aside the jury verdict. Supreme Court justice James Gibson reduced the award to $15,000 and gave Robinson 20 days to accept. If he did not, the justice said, he would grant the motion to dismiss the libel verdict.

A few weeks later, Ray's name was being bandied about in Washington, where a subcommittee was looking into 'athlete coddling' in the armed services, with one representative asking how did Private Walker Smith, otherwise known as Sugar Ray Robinson, 'jump from private to sergeant before he was found unsuitable'? Another member of the subcommittee stated, 'The honourable discharge given Sugar Ray Robinson after the boxer allegedly went AWOL smells as much now as it did ten years ago!'[204]

From Vancouver, where he was appearing in a nightclub, the former champion stated, 'I was discharged from the army as a sergeant with four medals – among them a good conduct medal. That doesn't seem to be the record of a deserter. I went where they sent me in the army – a fellow with my colour doesn't buck them. Their investigation shows I was cleared of this charge, but the way it works, even though you are cleared, headlines make you guilty.'[205]

Paris seemed like a good idea at this time and that's where Art Buchwald found him, sitting at a café on the Champs Elysees. Buchwald left California in 1949 with a one-way ticket to Paris, where within a year he had gotten himself hired as a columnist by the European edition of the *New York Herald Tribune*. He was a humorist whose columns on political satire and commentary would win him a Pulitzer Prize and a syndicated column in the *Washington Post*. This day in September 1954, the column would be about Sugar Ray Robinson.

'We told him that we were surprised to see that he was still in Europe. "Man," Ray said, "I been here since 23 June. I been to

204 Jack Walsh *St Louis Sporting News* 19 May 1954

205 *Waterloo Courier* Iowa 9 May 1954

the French Riviera, the Italian Riviera and any other Riviera you can think of."

'We said we had heard about it and had even read some of the reviews in the French papers. They weren't too flattering. "Yeah, I know that, but, you see, I can explain that. The critics came the first night, and then they didn't come back after that. The show was all jumbled up the first night, you understand? And the fact that we were not able to understand French made our comedy limited."

'"Were you sore at the press?" "No, I can't say that. I was disappointed. But the one thing you learn in sports is you have to win or you have to lose."

'"What do you think they expected of you?" "Well, I guess they expected me to come out in my boxing shorts and hit the bag a few times and stuff like that. They didn't dig the tap dancing bit. In Europe, they want you to do what you're famous for. Why man, I stopped the show by coming out in my shorts and skipping rope in time to the music. That's the kind of stuff they liked over here."

'"When you take a beating in showbusiness from critics," we asked him, "does it hurt as much as when you take a beating in a fight?" "Man, when you take a beating in a fight you know you're going to be all cut up and hurt bad. In showbusiness, you take a psychological beating. It hurts, but it don't hurt nothing like being beaten in the ring."

'Robinson told the columnist he would love to stay in Europe, but he had signed contracts back home and if he didn't go back he would be sued, which "he had no intention of being"'[206]

---

206 Art Buchwald *Winnipeg Free Press* 11 September 1954

15

THE COMEBACK

IN OCTOBER 1954, Sugar Ray Robinson was back in America and back in boxing according to the headlines in the sports pages.

'SUGAR RAY MAY TRY COMEBACK.'
'SUGAR RAY TALKS OF COMEBACK – IF PURSE OK.' 'BOXING MEN BELIEVE RAY CAN COME BACK.'

'No champion ever has come out of retirement to win back a title,' wrote Oscar Fraley in his Sports Parade column. 'Yet boxing men – trainers, seconds and managers – find Robinson an absorbing topic as they go about their chores in such spots as Stillman's Gym. And the surprising part of it is that practically all of them believe that Sugar Ray can fight his way right back to the top. "The big item is the legs," says Dan Florio, a trainer who worked with such men as Jersey Joe Walcott, Bat Battalino and Paddy De Marco. "Robinson never smoked or drank and he has kept his legs in shape by dancing professionally, which really requires good legs. A couple of tune-ups and he'd be ready for Olson."

'And it was surprising how few of them had kind words for Olson, who wears the crown which Robinson gave up two years ago. "Look at him against Rocky Castellani, who is a stab-and-run guy and if you hit him, he goes. So Rocky goes 15 rounds with Olson. Robinson beat Olson twice – and give him a couple of fights to get really ready and he'll do it all again."'[207]

'I have the urge to fight again,' Robinson told a press conference in his Harlem café on 15 October 1954, 'but I won't make any final decisions until I see how I make out in training. But if I can't regain the condition that I was once so proud of, then I'll give the idea up.'[208]

Sugar Ray looked pretty sharp a few weeks later when he boxed a six-round exhibition with Gene Burton of New York at Hamilton, Ontario. Syracuse promoter Norm Rothschild had motored up to see him and told columnist Jack Slattery, 'The fellow still has his old class and appeared as feather-footed as ever. True, Gene Burton didn't provide much in the way of opposition, but that was to be expected.' The Syracuse contingent visited at length with the former champion and he assured Rothschild that he very much wanted to fight in Syracuse. Robinson, a highly intelligent man, made quite a denouncement of television and claimed that it has ruined the fight game. A squib in Dan Parker's column of Monday would bear out Sugar Ray's contention. 'In 1949, there were 800 boxing clubs in the country. Today, there are only 40.'[209]

'Close friends have been unable thus far to dissuade Sugar Ray Robinson from attempting to make a ring comeback after two years on the tap-dancing circuit,' wrote Gayle Talbot from New York. 'The once-great fighter is in training and declares he is serious about winning back the 160-pound title. The Sugar Boy says he is 32, the book credits him with 34 years and you probably would be safe in splitting the difference.'[210]

'Some ring veterans, like ex-heavyweight champion Jack Dempsey, would not venture out on the limb regarding Robinson's chances,' reported the *Huntingdon Daily News*. 'Surprisingly, Dempsey said, "I never saw him fight, so I can't express an

207 Oscar Fraley *Monessen Daily Independent* PA 22 October 1954
208 *San Antonio Express* Texas 16 October 1954
209 Jack Slattery *Syracuse Herald Journal* 1 December 1954
210 Gayle Talbot *Lima News* Ohio 26 October 1954

opinion." Other boxing men felt that if anyone could come back in the ring, Robinson was the man to do it. Ex-middleweight Steve Belloise, one of the many fighters Sugar Ray beat while compiling 131 victories, two draws and only three defeats in 136 bouts, was among the majority who felt Robinson had a good chance to make a successful comeback. "I think he'll be the middleweight champion of the world again," Belloise said. Former heavyweight contender Tony Galento put the same idea across another way. "I think Robinson'll come back and lick all the bums they got around today," Two-Ton Tony declared.'[211]

The comeback started badly, with boxing people recalling Robinson's past history of cancelled fights. Detroit promoter Nick Londes stated that Robinson and manager George Gainford withdrew from a fight with Joe Rindone on 8 December after asking for more money than was originally agreed. Commissioner Floyd Stevens handed out an indefinite suspension to the former champion and his pilot. Common sense prevailed, however, as the boys made up and on 5 January 1955, Sugar Ray Robinson climbed into the ring at the Detroit Olympia to fight Joe Rindone in his return to the boxing wars.

Joe Rindone was a 28-year old ex-Marine sergeant from Roxbury, Massachusetts with a 36-13-4 pro record. One of those 13 defeats was a sixth-round knockout by Robinson five years previously. The Associated Press had described Rindone as 'a fairly active club performer with a chin that juts from beneath a battered nose as conspicuously as Cape Cod does off the Massachusetts seacoast'. Sugar Ray found the chin easily enough and Joe was on his way home after 55 seconds of round six. He fared no better in the rematch in the Detroit ring as Robinson lowered the boom again in round six, with his handlers claiming he should be ready for a crack at Olson after a half-dozen fights.

Two weeks later, it was announced that Ray would fight Ralph 'Tiger' Jones at the Chicago Stadium. Joe Glaser, who had told

---

211 *Huntingdon Daily News* PA. 16 October 1954

Robinson immediately after the Rindone knockout, 'I'm the boss now, I'm going to guide you to the title,' didn't want Ray to fight Jones, telling Truman Gibson of the International Boxing Club, 'Jones is a little too tough for Robinson at this point.' But Gibson stated that if Ray wanted to fight in Chicago, it would be Jones or nobody. So on 19 January, the televised main event from the Chicago Stadium was Sugar Ray Robinson against Ralph 'Tiger' Jones.

From Yonkers, New York, the 27-year-old Jones had lost his last five bouts and you could have any odds you wanted if you figured he had a chance of beating the former champion. Well, believe it or not, the Tiger believed he could beat Robinson and he did just that, climbing all over the favourite to take a unanimous decision. Sugar Ray didn't look so sweet at the final bell, bleeding from the nose and a cut over his right eye for most of the fight, and afterwards in the dressing room he said, 'I have no alibis – that's one I lost. Let's get another fight.' His manager, Joe Glaser, was bitter over the selection of such a tough fighter as Jones for Robinson's second comeback fight following a 30-month layoff. Both Robinson and Glaser assured sportswriters and sportscasters that Robinson would continue fighting. Robinson's trainer added a jocular note to the post-fight talk when he said, 'The trouble with Sugar Ray was that he got out of the habit of keeping his hands up while he was dancing during the layoff.'[212]

Robinson went back to Greenwood Lake for a two-month training siege and he needed it for his next fight, ten rounds with Johnny Lombardo at the Cincinnati Gardens. The 26-year-old seaman gave Ray a rough passage and he needed a blazing finish to grab a split decision, one judge voting for Lombardo, who was given a standing ovation for his sterling performance against the former double champion. Robinson praised Lombardo as being a tough fighter and said he was stung several times. Robinson also expressed dissatisfaction with his own timing, saying that he 'just wasn't sharp'.

---

212 *Daily Review* Hayward California 20 January 1955

Ray was in better form a couple of weeks later when he faced 25-year-old local boy Ted Olla in Milwaukee. All the fight was in the third round and it was all Robinson. He stepped from his corner and rammed a right to Olla's head, which was the beginning of the end. The blow sent Olla to the ropes and there Robinson poured in lefts and rights to the head. A left floored Olla, who took the mandatory eight before Ray opened up again to bring the referee's intervention at 2.15 of the round. 'I'm not ready for Olson yet,' Robinson said. 'I'm happy at my progress but I'm just beginning to find myself. I'm not at a point yet where I'd want to or could fight Olson. I want two fights a month until September,' he added while happy followers addressed him as 'champ'.

Three weeks later, Joe Falls wrote from Detroit, 'Sugar Ray Robinson looks a little sharper and a little faster in his ring comeback, but his opposition remains of questionable quality. Robinson recovered from a staggering right to the head to win an easy and unanimous decision over slow-moving Garth Panter of Salt Lake City last night. While his famed combinations were still not in evidence, the former champion showed more stamina and more punching power.'[213]

'I had reached the point where the IBC wanted to give me a shot at Bobo Olson's middleweight title,' Sugar Ray said in his autobiography, 'but first I had to earn it with a good win over a contender. We settled on Rocky Castellani, who was ranked as the number one contender. He was a rangy, hard-hitting guy out of Luzerne, Pennsylvania, who had lost a 15-round decision to Olson in a title bout the year before. He wanted another shot at Olson, and he thought he could take me. So we got Olson to agree that the winner would get a title shot. The match was made for 22 July in San Francisco.

'One morning when I was doing roadwork out there along the beach, Olson jogged by, going the other way. "Hi, Carl," I called. He waved and said, "Hiya, Ray," but when he was out of earshot,

---

213 Joe Falls *Camden News* Arkansas 5 May 1955

Gainford laughed. "Why did you call him Carl?" George said. "That's his name," I said. "Carl Olson." "I know," George replied, "but when a man is the champ, you're supposed to call him champ." "He's not the champ. He just happens to have *my* title."'[214]

In the sixth round of the fight at the Cow Palace, Sugar Ray came within one second of seeing his comeback come to a shuddering stop. Rocky smashed Ray with a left hook followed by a right to the head and Robinson made a three-point landing, got to his knees and listened to the count of referee Jack Downey. Looking out at the crowd through a cut right eyelid, Ray heaved himself off the canvas as the referee shouted 'nine' and he was back in the fight. Castellani moved in for the kill but Ray tied him up inside and fought his way back to be given a split decision after a tough ten rounds. The crowd of 8,230 gave the former champ a terrific ovation at the final bell, drowning out the cries of 'robbery!' from Rocky's corner team, with manager Al Naiman shouting that he would protest the decision to the athletic commission. 'One of the greatest fighting machines in ring history is within one victory of claiming the middleweight championship of the world for an unprecedented third time today,' reported John Kane for the *San Mateo Times*. 'Sugar Ray Robinson, still housing enough fistic craft and slugging ability to outpoint the division's number one challenger, is in line for a shot at Bobo Olson's crown following a close split ten-round decision over Rocky Castellani last night at the Cow Palace in North San Mateo county. The 34-year-old stylist may give the current title holder a tough evening if he continues to regain his old touch.'[215]

'I feel that I have regained much of my former fighting qualities,' said Ray when he visited *The Ring* magazine office following his bout with Castellani. Talking to editor Nat Fleischer, he said, 'There wasn't a reporter in California who gave me a chance against Rocky, yet I had confidence, decided I would fight

214 Sugar Ray Robinson with Dave Anderson *Sugar Ray* 1969

215 John Kane *San Mateo Times* California 23 July 1955

in close to wear him down, and I succeeded. I didn't go into that ring to tap dance my way to victory. Those days are over and no one realises that better than I. The spring I once possessed is gone, otherwise I think I have everything I had in my prime. That's why I'm certain I'll regain the middleweight title.'[216]

It had been unseasonably cold in San Francisco, 'so much so that at the end of July a pregnant Edna Mae called home and had a fur piece flown to her. It was a particularly difficult pregnancy, and one day she experienced severe pain and had to be rushed to the hospital. Sugar insisted on remaining at his wife's bedside, even if it meant cancelling the fight. Eventually, however, she convinced him to leave and go on with the bout. Sugar salvaged the victory, but Edna Mae's pregnancy could not be saved. "We did not let him know until after the fight that we'd lost the baby," she wrote in her memoir. It wasn't the first baby she had lost, nor would it be the last.'[217]

Edna Mae did make it to ringside at the Cow Palace to see Robinson come home a winner against Castellani. After the fight, Jim Gilmartin found her standing outside Ray's dressing room. 'Mrs Robinson gushed to this reporter, "He proved himself a champion tonight. He still has a terrific heart. He is the greatest. He's worked awfully hard and there's nothing on his mind other than winning back the title." Was she worried when Robinson was decked by Castellani's smashing left hook in the sixth round? "Worried? Why I acted just like a typical female. I screamed and jumped and hollered to my baby, 'You can do it.' My Sugar has always won with brains, not brawn. He did it again tonight. I believe he'll make that title."'[218]

A few weeks later at Greenwood Lake, Sugar Ray was making a believer out of veteran sportswriter Harry Grayson. 'Off his performance against Tiger Jones, Ray Robinson did not belong in the ring. Off his effort against Rocky Castellani, Sugar Ray

---

216 Nat Fleischer *The Ring* October 1955

217 Herb Boyd with Ray Robinson II *Pound for Pound* 2005

218 Jim Gilmartin *Daily Independent Journal* San Rafael California 23 July 1955

Robinson did not belong in the same battle pit with the Bobo Olson who came to Yankee Stadium to be knocked out by Archie Moore. But of the form Robinson is showing at Greenwood Lake, the notion is that the Harlem landlord now not only belongs in the same enclosure with Olson at the Chicago Stadium on 9 December, but he also is the best-looking 3-1 underdog we've seen since the last big upset in the beak-busting business. That is, Robinson is a good long shot against the post-Moore Olson, who in addition to his marital difficulties was anything but a ball of fire against Jimmy Martinez and Joey Giambria. In both of the latter fights, Olson was considerably heavier than 160 pounds, which he must make in defence of the middleweight championship. Robinson has no such problem.

'"Against Jones, Castellani and those guys, I had to club fight. I must have looked something awful, but I couldn't do anything else. I had no legs. Now I run five miles every day and don't labour. My legs take running easier. I get up on my toes in the ring and move. I'm just starting to find as much of myself as there is left." Robinson is making three sparring partners come to him, as he expects Olson to do. He picked off and sidestepped punches, countered with damaging flurries. Sugar Ray is talking like the old Robinson. He was asked if he had learned anything watching Moore flatten Olson. "Me, learn from Moore?" Ray Robinson sputtered. "Heck, man, you mean what Moore learned from me?"'[219]

From Chicago, Charles Chamberlain wrote, 'Middleweight champion Bobo Olson, who has sampled Sugar Ray Robinson's punches twice before, thinks he can handle any blitz tactics the former king might try in seeking an early KO victory in their title scrap Friday night. "I was a green kid and Robinson was a great fighter back in 1950 when he got me in the 12th round," Olson said as he entered the final week of drills for defence of his crown in Chicago Stadium. "But even then, my style bothered him for ten rounds. And when we met again two years later, I really gave him

219 Harry Grayson *Mount Vernon Register News* 3 December 1955

trouble before he took a split 15-round decision. We both know each other's styles and what to expect in this third fight. I look for Ray to try to knock me out early. Although reports are that he is in wonderful condition, the man still is 34 and must realise that he can't stand up under the pressure I'll give him through 15 rounds. I only hope that he tries to blitz me from the start. If he comes in to me, that will suit me fine. I know I'll go after him. I'll come in punching. It's the only style I know. Robinson has to come in and try to hurt me early. That's the fight as I see it."'[220]

And that was the fight as seen by every one of the 12,441 fans who had paid $139,725 to come into the vast Chicago Stadium off the cold city streets on that December night in 1955. It didn't last long but the dynamic ending at the 2.51 mark of round two was worth the price of admission. They saw boxing history being made by the fighter the experts were saying was all through, washed up, hung out to dry at the age of 34. Sugar Ray Robinson became the first ring champion to come back out of retirement and take the world title, only the second middleweight champion to regain the title twice, and the first to win it three times.

'My best chance is to win on a knockout, and I'll take that chance because I'm determined to win,' Ray told sportswriter Jack Cuddy a few days before the fight. What did he mean by gambling on punch alone to beat Olson? "I mean I won't try to outbox him. I'll go in to knock him out as soon as possible," he said. "I have the punch to do it. And I know the combination of blows that will take him out."'[221]

'That's exactly what happened,' reported *The Ring* magazine. 'Olson, 27 years old, showed determination to fight in close. He crowded Robinson in an effort to overpower his 35-[sic] year-old challenger at close quarters. He did the leading but found in his adversary an opponent who was primed for such tactics. Ray, with graceful counter punching, kept meeting the bull-like drives with

---

220 Charles Chamberlain *Daily Times Herald* Carroll Ohio 5 December 1955

221 Jack Cuddy *Mason City Globe Gazette* Iowa 24 November 1955

neatly placed left shots to the head but when hard pressed leaped into a clinch as a protective measure. Ray, on his toes and sharp with his left, looked like the old Ray during the short time the bout lasted, the flash knockout hitting the champ and the spectators like a thunderbolt, so unexpectedly did it come. The fight really ended with the first solid blow landed by either. It started with a right to the jaw that staggered the champion. Then, like a flash, came a left hook and seconds later followed a right hook to the jaw that put Bobo flat on his back. His sensational triumph rates one of the great feats of all time in fistic history. In rewriting that old adage, "they never come back," Ray was magnificent. His timing in the opening round, in which he boxed cleverly and displayed confidence in his every move, was a reminder of the man at his best, the Sugar Ray to whom we have so often referred as the best pound-for-pound fighter in many years. He turned back the clock in one savage attack that lasted only seconds, but the barrage was long enough to rock his adversary to sleep and bring up a new title holder.'[222]

'The end of the fight, of course, was the most spectacular part of the whole thing,' reported Joseph C. Nichols for the *New York Times*. 'In the second round, Olson showed his determination to fight in close. He grappled with Ray as often as he could, but Robinson met the moves by loosely dangling his arms at his sides and looking at the clock that indicated the time of the round. Exchanges of this nature occurred two or three times before Robinson felt the situation was in his favour. Olson had just been pushed out of a crowding attempt by Sugar Ray and the defending champion sought to punch his own gloves together in a sort of habitual gesture. But Robinson didn't let him finish. Looping a long right, Robinson found the target and Olson sagged, bound for the floor. To aid Bobo in his downward flight, Ray delivered a left hook to the head, but the punch was a mere brush. Olson landed on his back, and the question in the minds of the fans was whether

222 Nat Fleischer *The Ring* February 1956

or not Olson could get up. Bobo, at the count of six, made a motion with his head and it appeared that he might arise. But this little gesture was too much for him, and he remained on the canvas as the count proceeded to the decisive end. He is still Sugar Ray.'[223]

Recalling the fight in his autobiography, Robinson said, 'When the bell rang, Olson came out strong. But I was on time from the beginning. I dominated the first round. In the second, he was digging a few good punches into my belly when I let go a left hook that stunned him. His eyes were dazed and when his gloves dropped, I realised I had a chance to finish him. The crowd realised it too and their roar exploded around me. I was so excited, my arms were trembling with emotion. I was about to reclaim *my* title and in those split seconds, my mind worked the way it had been taught to work. Many years earlier, Jack Blackburn had told me how to finish a man. "Don't lose your head, Chappie," he had said. "When a man's in trouble, that's the time to hold your head. That man will still be there."

'I respected his advice because he had tutored Joe Louis, and Joe was the best finisher ever. If he got a man in trouble, forget it. After my lesson from Jack Blackburn, I had developed into a good finisher, and now, when I needed it most, at the age of 34 and with Bobo Olson wobbling in front of me, his advice was controlling my mind, and through it, my muscles. Without rushing, I ripped a right uppercut at Olson and followed with a left hook. And suddenly, he was on his back. At eight he made a move to get up, but he rolled over and he was counted out. My joy at regaining my title hadn't even been dimmed by the Internal Revenue Service. Their agents had put a lien on my earnings for $81,000 in unpaid taxes. My tax troubles had begun, but I didn't care. I was the champ again.'[224]

---

223 Joseph C. Nichols *New York Times* 10 December 1955

224 Sugar Ray Robinson with Dave Anderson *Sugar Ray* 1969

Sugar Ray and his famous flamingo pink Cadillac

An early photo of Ray and mentor George Gainford

LaMotta knocks Robinson through the ropes in handing him his first pro defeat in Detroit February 1943

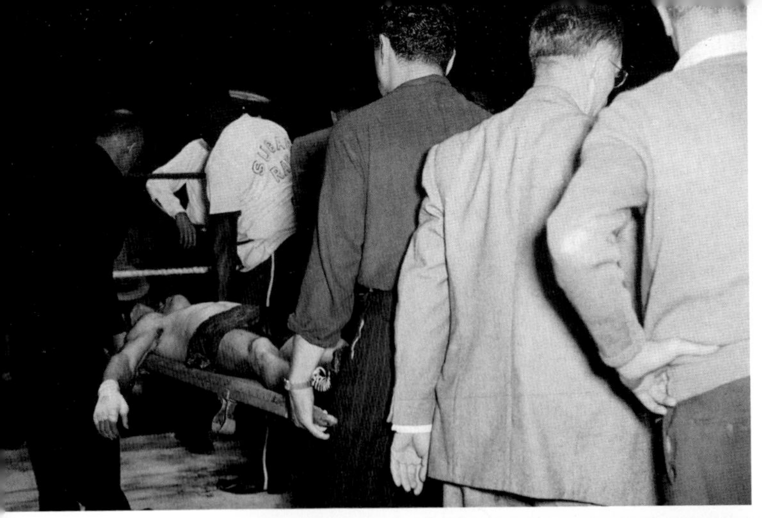

Knockout victim Jimmy Doyle is carried from the ring, Cleveland 24 June 1947 as Robinson retains welterweight title. Doyle died the next day

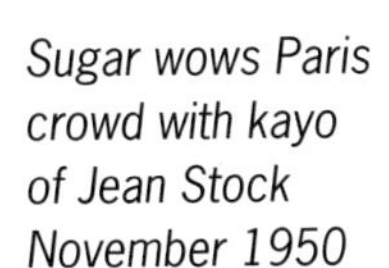

Sugar wows Paris crowd with kayo of Jean Stock November 1950

Jake LaMotta losing his middleweight title to Robinson 14 February 1951

Shock defeat by Randy Turpin in London 10 July 1951, decision 15 rounds

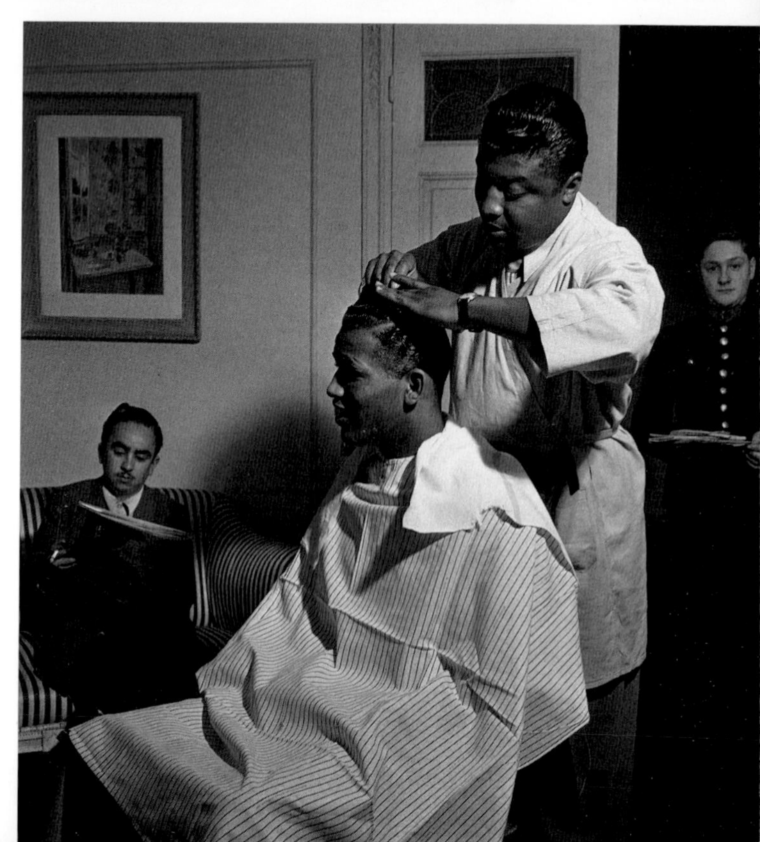

Ray's personal barber Roger Simon tending to his boss in Paris as Jimmy Karoubi, Ray's 36-inch 'bodyguard' looks on

Sugar regains title from Randy Turpin in New York 17 September 1951

Ray collapses with heat exhaustion when beating Joey Maxim in light-heavyweight title fight New York 25 June 1952

Sugar enters show business after defeat by Maxim June 1952

The song and dance man in New York November 1952

Loses middleweight title in tough 15-rounder with Carmen Basilio, New York 23 September 1957

CBS TV visits Ray and Edna Mae for Person to Person broadcast 26 October 1957

Ray takes middleweight title back from Basilio in 15 rounds in Chicago March 1958

Showman Sugar dances with Gene Kelly for NBC TV in December 1958

Robinson retires after 25 years, Madison Square Garden arrange farewell party December 1965, is chaired by former champs/victims Olson, Turpin, Fullmer, Basilio

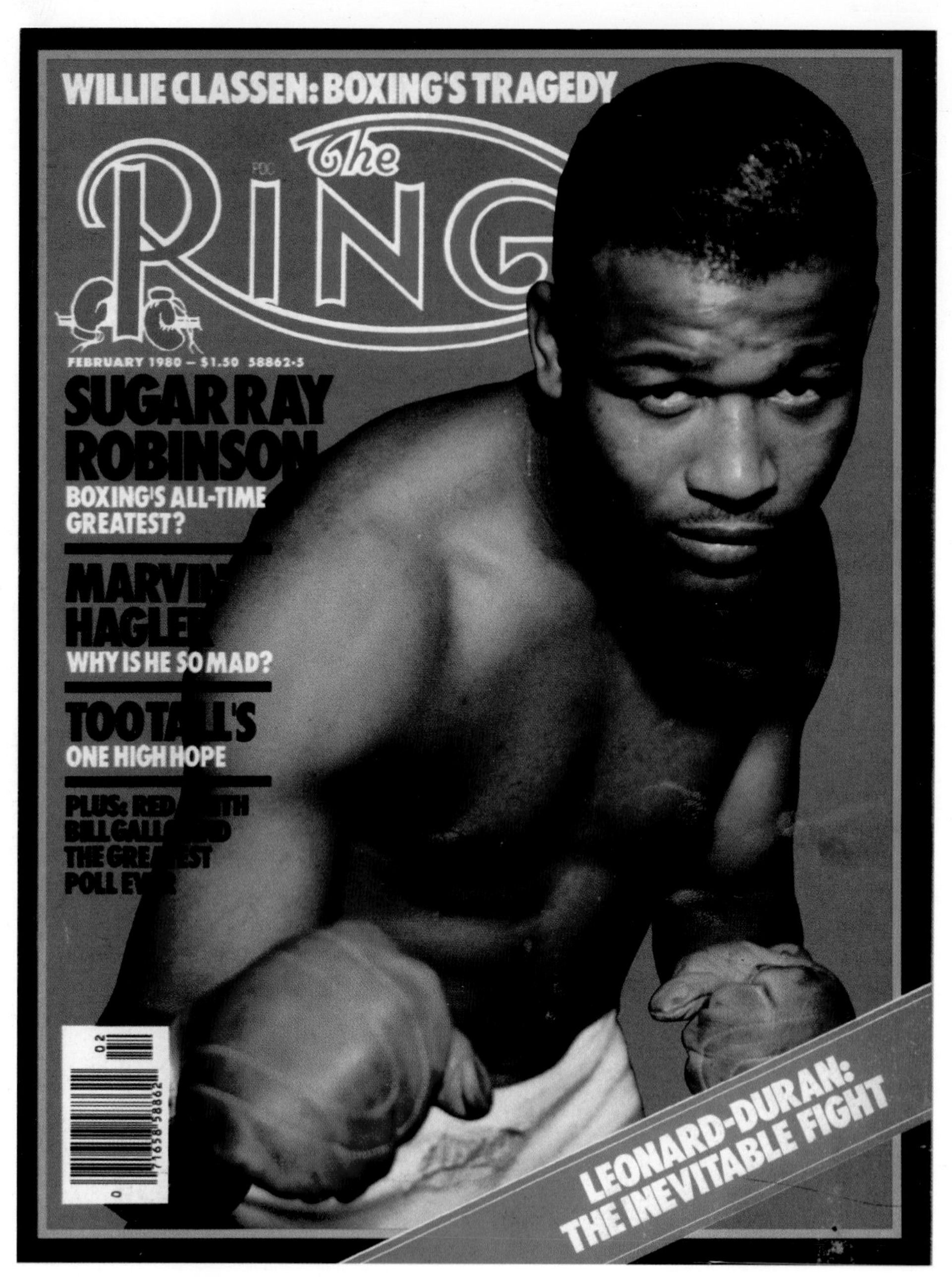

Ray on one of many Ring *covers in 1980*

16

SUGAR RAY OWNS BOBO

LEO LEAVITT promoted fights in Honolulu for 16 years before Abe Saperstein lured him into being the press agent for his Harlem Globetrotters. 'His most cherished story,' wrote Jack Bluth of the *San Mateo Times*, 'is the one he tells about how he discovered Carl (Bobo) Olson. Actually, Bobo came to Leo. He wanted to be a pro boxer at the ripe age of 15. Leo looked at the barefoot boy in shabby clothes and told him to get lost. "But he wouldn't. I was booking fights from the States and I couldn't be bothered. Bobo would go to the gym and make cracks about my best boys while they worked out. I figured I'd get rid of him by throwing him in with a good boy. He'd get belted and that would be it. Instead, he became a top attraction. I turned him over to Sid Flaherty, a sergeant in the Army at Schofield Barracks. He knew nothing about boxing until then. When he went back to California, he had a $20,000 bank roll."

'Leavitt said that Bobo has only one trouble now. He has a "master." That would be Sugar Ray Robinson. "There's a man Bobo will never beat," Leo declared. "I'll tell you why. Sooner or later, every athlete meets a man he can't beat. But it's all in the head. Bobo has it in his head that Sugar Ray is his master, that he can't beat him." Leo points to their second bout as a classic example. "Robinson had no right winning that fight. He just got back from Paris, still Bobo couldn't beat him – and he never will.'"[225] You have to give the boy credit for trying. From Santa Monica, California, United Press reported, 'Carl (Bobo) Olson today was confident he would regain his middleweight crown from Sugar Ray Robinson in their 15-round title fight at Los Angeles on 18 May. "Robinson is an old man and can't go 15 rounds," the former champ told reporters when he arrived at his Ocean Park Arena training camp yesterday. "I was overconfident, careless, and distracted by family troubles when Robinson knocked me out last year. I will not be foolish again." The 27-year-old San Francisco boxer said he would play it cagey and not attempt a knockout, but go the distance. He appeared to be in great shape. He weighed, he said, around 166–167 pounds, which his trainer, Freddy Bianchi, said was ideal for this stage of preparation.'[226]

In March, columnist Jimmy Breslin wrote from New York, 'Sometime in the middle of next month, Ray Robinson will move to Gilmore Springs, California, to start the final phase of his training for his fourth meeting with Bobo Olson in Los Angeles on 18 May. When Sugar Ray moves from his Greenwood Lake camp to the desert, it should be one of the largest expeditions to head west since the days they made movies about. Robinson will have 16 people in his entourage. Based on past performances, the middleweight champion's party averages three and a half pieces of luggage per man. The movement, however, will be much bigger this time. Robinson is even carting his own training ring to the Golden State.

'"We are now involved in the logistics of transportation," Ernie Braca, one of his five managers, says. "Robinson has been in camp for the past month. I assume this is proof enough that the fight – regardless of cockeyed rumours – will come off as scheduled. For our purposes, the fight has to take place now." Braca was referring to the Johnny Saxton-Carmen Basilio verdict. That one hit the Robinson camp like a sledgehammer. Negotiations had been under

225 Jack Bluth *San Mateo Times* California 30 March 1956

226 *Daily Independent Journal* San Rafael California 12 April 1956

way to stage a Basilio-Robinson bout at Yankee Stadium 28 June. "How do you like that? It could only happen to me. Basilio won that fight," moaned Robinson. With that, all thoughts of side-stepping Carl Olson to get the big Basilio money went out the window. The middleweight champion is guaranteed $75,000 for meeting Olson and he can't get it any place else.'[227]

As December 1955 began to slip off the calendar, Sugar Ray Robinson looked forward to spending Christmas as the recently crowned middleweight champion for the third time.

'Way off in the distant future, say September at Yankee Stadium, a Sugar Ray Robinson-Carmen Basilio match is "hanging in the sky," reported Associated Press. "We're looking toward a Basilio match outdoors," said Ernie Braca, Robinson's co-manager, last night as he discussed the future of the three-time middleweight champ. "We've got lots of plans. Maybe Charles Humez in Paris in the spring. Most of all, we're looking to Basilio. That's the only big outdoor match around. Both sides are warm to the idea." Harry Markson, managing director of the International Boxing Club, said any talk of such a match was "pretty far off in the future". Basilio has a pretty tough fight coming up when he defends his welterweight title against Johnny Saxton. That's no cinch for him.'[228]

Sportswriter Barney Nagler called Johnny Saxton 'a bug-eyed kid out of Harlem, a nervous lad who was psychically unfit for boxing'. After a troubled childhood, he found himself in amateur boxing, winning 31 of 33 bouts, two National AAU championships and a Golden Gloves title. He turned pro under Bill Miller, who introduced him to Blinky Palermo. No puncher, Johnny was a cautious stylist with a busy jab and good footwork, and he ran off 40 unbeaten bouts. Palermo, a Philadelphia mobster, was a bosom pal of underworld boss Frankie Carbo, a former Murder Inc. gunman. They managed Saxton into a fight with welterweight

227 Jimmy Breslin *Ogden Standard Examiner* Utah 27 March 1956

228 *Syracuse Herald Journal* New York 29 December 1955

champ Kid Gavilan and he took the title with a dubious decision. Tony DeMarco hammered him loose from the title only to be turned into an ex-champ in two brutal battles with Carmen Basilio. In March 1956, Blinky and his pal Frankie got Saxton a crack at the title and he was champion again, thanks to a decision that caused Jesse Abramson to write in the *New York Herald Tribune*, 'Do you know of a worse decision in a championship fight? The Saxton win over Gavilan in Philadelphia was bad, but nothing to compare with this.'

Next day, Johnny told newsmen, 'Now I would like a chance at the winner between Sugar Ray Robinson and Bobo Olson.'

Veteran scribe Oscar Fraley wrote from Greenwood Lake, 'Sugar Ray Robinson, the man who shattered the axiom "they never come back," heads west on Tuesday confident that he has the legs and the head to keep the middleweight championship of the world. Sugar Ray doesn't look the 35 years he claims to be, and certainly not the 37 which he is listed at in the record books. But no matter which age you pick, he figures he's a smarter fighter now than he ever was.'[229]

When Robinson and Olson climbed into the ring at Wrigley Field on a warm night in May 1956, before a crowd of 20,083, the experts were saying Robinson must put Bobo away early or Olson's younger years and stamina will make a difference in the last five or six rounds and he could well give Robinson a sound whipping. Las Vegas gambling people had quoted Sugar Ray as a 7-5 favourite with not too much interest evident in the actual betting. The general feeling was that Robinson, at 35 long past his prime, and Olson, a three-time loser already to Robinson, were too much of a cash risk.

Ringside, Wrigley Field, Los Angeles, Bill Miller reporting for *Ring* magazine – 'So long as his opponent is Carl (Bobo) Olson, it won't be necessary for 35-year-old Ray Robinson to prove whether or not he can hold his stylish form over the full championship

229 Oscar Fraley *Mexia Daily News* Texas 23 April 1956

15-round distance. Robinson definitely "owns" Olson. Ray's score against the Hawaiian-born Californian is now 4-for-4, which is pretty fair hitting in anybody's league. Ray's most recent triumph, here in the home of Los Angeles' baseball Angels, should convince one and all, particularly Olson himself, that there is no need prolonging the one-sided series.

'Robinson, at the peak of his brilliant form, was never more deliberate, accurate or devastating. A jolting right to the body brought Olson's guard down just long enough for Ray to whip over a blasting left hook to the chin. That was the payoff. Olson crashed to the canvas on his back, rolled over a couple of times, and made a feeble effort to rise as referee "Mushy" Callahan counted him out at 2.51 of the fourth. It was the 90th knockout victory for Robinson in 145 fights of a professional career that began in 1940. Financially, the bout was a tremendous success. It set a new California record for boxing receipts. The gross gate of $228,500 was augmented by an additional $100,000 from television.

'Out of the net, Robinson and Olson each received nearly $90,000. But there was little personal satisfaction for either rival. Olson's purse had been attached by his estranged wife, Dolores, and the Internal Revenue Department was present to slap a claim for $87,000 on Robinson for unpaid taxes.'[230]

All Olson could say, still dazed in his dressing room, was, 'How could it happen so fast? That guy has got a jinx on me, I guess.'

He should have listened to Leo Leavitt! '"Bobo is a real fighter," said Leavitt, who has handled two flyweight champions, Small Montana and Little Dado. "But with Sugar Ray, it's all up here," Leo reiterated, pointing to his head, "it's all up here."'[231]

From New York, 'Middleweight champion Sugar Ray Robinson was reported as having made a deal with Uncle Sam on the payment of back taxes. Truman Gibson, secretary of the IBC, who was present when Robinson met with government officials,

230 Bill Miller *The Ring* July 1956

231 Jack Bluth *San Mateo Times* 30 March 1956

said the middleweight champion paid Uncle Sam a substantial part of his $90,708 purse for knocking out Bobo Olson and said he will make up the difference later on.'[232]

A few months after the Olson fight, the IBC matched Robinson with Gene Fullmer, from West Jordan, Utah, over 15 rounds for the title at Madison Square Garden on 12 December.

'His folks decided before he was born he was to be a boy and a fighter,' said Fullmer's manager Marv Jenson, who raised mink on his ranch when he wasn't raising young fighters. 'His mother named him Gene after former heavyweight champion Gene Tunney, and he started fighting in exhibitions when he was eight years old.' Now 25, Fullmer had a 37-3 pro record and was rated number one contender for Ray's title.

Sugar Ray started training at Greenwood Lake and he was a little worried this would be a tough one, against a two-fisted, rock-jawed slugger whose engine had no reverse gear. He was in your face three minutes of every round and he liked to pound the body. He had no stamina problems; manager Jenson wound him up before putting him in the ring and he was still going at the final bell. That's what was worrying Sugar Ray. The champ, ten years older at 35, hadn't fought in six months and his last two fights before that saw him knock out Bobo Olson twice, in two and four rounds. Could he still go 15 rounds and come out the other end a winner? It was time to find out.

New Haven, Connecticut, was a coastal city on Long Island Sound, the home of Ivy League Yale University, as good a place as any to learn something about yourself. That Saturday night in November 1956, some 2,000 local citizens paid their way into the arena to see the veteran middleweight champion of the world travel ten rounds with Bob Provizzi, a 25-year-old kid from Freeland, Pennsylvania who was 2-4 in his last six bouts. Bob was a poster boy for Slim Jim bowties but he wasn't wearing one when he answered the bell for round one.

---

232 *Indianapolis Recorder* 9 June 1956

'World middleweight champion Ray Robinson outpointed hustling Bob Provizzi in a ten-rounder here tonight,' reported Associated Press. 'Robinson knocked his opponent down twice in the final round. They were the only times in this non-title bout that Provizzi was on the floor, both for short counts, but the 36-year-old champ staggered his young foe on at least four other occasions. Oddly enough, referee Max Muravnick gave Provizzi the tenth round and also the fifth. Robinson, 165, won the others, most of them easily. Robinson appeared to be off in his timing frequently in his first ring appearance since successfully defending his title against Bobo Olson last May, but he managed to paste the 162-pound Provizzi enough to keep his foe off balance. The champ finished in good shape and was given a 48-38 edge in points.'[233]

'Ray probably convinced himself that his legs will stand up for 15 rounds if he has to go that many with rugged Gene Fullmer in their title fight 12 December. Robinson surely would not endanger his end of $250,000 or more from the gate plus television, for $425 except 1) he was sure he couldn't get hurt and 2) he needed the workout. But until he left that New Haven ring untired and unmarked, he had some of the International Boxing Club officials on the verge of a hemorrhage. They were scared to death that he might suffer a cut that would cause postponement of the title fight.'[234]

A few days after the New Haven fight, Robinson met Gene Fullmer in New York, but it was reasonably civilised and nobody got punched in the nose. 'The New York State Athletic Commission permitted Sugar Ray Robinson and Gene Fullmer to sign official contracts Thursday under which challenger Fullmer will receive only 12½ per cent of the net gate for their middleweight title fight on 12 December. Contracts for the Madison Square Garden 15-rounder disclosed that Fullmer will receive nothing from the $100,000 TV-radio fee, although

233 *Lowell Sun* Mass. 12 November 1956

234 Pat Robinson *Santa Fe New Mexican* 20 November 1956

champion Robinson will get $60,000 from it, in addition to his 47½ per cent of the net gate.

'Marv Jenson, Fullmer's manager, made no protest to the commission at the signing ceremony, but he told reporters, "Since Gene gets nothing from television-radio, he is actually getting only about seven or eight per cent of the total net proceeds – probably the lowest percentage ever given any challenger for a title bout." Commission chairman Julius Helfand told the press, "There's nothing the commission can do about percentages arrived at by negotiations among fighters, managers and promoters." Robinson, 35, and Fullmer, 25, chatted like old pals during the signing ceremony before a large battery of cameras – press, movie and television – at commission headquarters. Each fighter passed a commission physical examination. Robinson was asked if he had any qualms about spotting Fullmer 11 years in youth. The champ replied with a grin, "I never heard of anyone winning a fight with a birth certificate."'[235]

The boys were scheduled to go at each other in the Garden on 12 December but Sugar Ray came down with a virus and Jim Norris announced that the fight would be staged on 2 January 1957.

Typical of the press reaction in New York was a headline, 'Delays A Habit With Ray.' Bill Corum wrapped it up in his column and he didn't pull his punches. 'Ray Robinson was and probably is the greatest fighter I ever saw. As a puncher, a dancer, a boxer. And as a con man. A man who knows the corners and the crevices and who curiously and deviously plots those corners. Otherwise, why did he duck out of his fight with Gene Fullmer, scheduled for next Wednesday night in the Garden? As a performer, he has been perfect. As a dancer, he earned a lot of dough in Paris. As a gentleman with any regard for those in his trade, he lacks a lot. Robinson has run out of about 20 fights. Not run out, exactly, but requested postponements that harried the other guy and almost broke the promoter. Robinson may have had the raw throat they

235 *Anderson Herald Bulletin* Indiana 16 November 1956

found yesterday; may have had the hottest fever since Dante. A fellow just calls to say Robinson pleaded with Dr Schiff and Dr Holloman, medicos who examined him and found him not able to fight Fullmer come Wednesday. They say that Ray almost cried that he wants the fight to go on and that he needed the dough for his family for Christmas.

'Christmas is a funny thing: A lot of guys need money for it. I do. And by fighting Fullmer next Wednesday, Robinson would have made Christmas for himself and a lot of others. Don't forget, Ray, that there'd been extra ticket takers, ushers, doormen, bartenders, waiters, even special policemen on duty if you were going through with the big print in your contract. And they all wouldn't have to miss that extra Christmas money.'[236]

In December 1950, respected writer W. C. (Bill) Heinz was asked to do an article for the *Saturday Evening Post* which they entitled, 'Why Don't They Like Ray Robinson?'

'Robinson's press has been generally bad, never enthusiastic,' wrote Heinz. 'Five years ago, he was receiving so little support in his quest for a shot at the welterweight title that he hired a personal press representative, Pete Vaccare, then publisher of a small boxing weekly. "When Robinson first talked to me about it," Vaccare says, "he said, 'The papers are always knocking me. I don't know why.' When I went around the newspapermen and told them I was representing Robinson, they looked at me like I was crazy." Robinson and Vaccare have been almost totally unsuccessful in getting the sportswriters – and thus the sports readers – solidly behind Robinson. They have been unable to still the charges that Robinson has been guilty on many occasions of running out on promoters for whom he had agreed to fight.

'"About the runouts," Robinson has said many times, "they can't produce one contract signed by me that I didn't honour."'[237]

236 Bill Corum *Sarasota News* Florida 5 December 1956

237 W. C. Heinz *Saturday Evening Post* 9 December 1950

As 1957 dawned, Sugar Ray Robinson was preparing to honour his contract with promoter Jim Norris and defend his middleweight championship of the world against Gene Fullmer in Madison Square Garden on Wednesday, 2 January.

'We were scheduled for 12 December at the Garden, but I developed a virus. The new date was 2 January 1957, but I was having trouble sleeping. "How about some sleeping pills? I asked Dr Nardiello. "No," he said. "I don't want you to get used to them, but I'll give you a few tranquilisers. By bedtime, you'll be so relaxed you'll go right to sleep."

'I was so relaxed, I went to sleep in there with Fullmer. The tranquilisers had lulled me. That night, I was in the ring but *Ray Robinson* wasn't. Fullmer's style bothered me, too. He had a barroom brawler's style, which I hadn't expected because Mormons don't drink.'[238]

Gene Fullmer's style had bothered 37 of his 40 professional opponents and 20 of them didn't make it to the final bell. Manager Marv Jenson told Associated Press, 'Fullmer will be aggressive for three minutes of every round. He's going to keep the pressure on all the way. We are figuring at 15 rounds at top speed. If it stops earlier, so much the better. It's no secret we'll concentrate on a body attack. We won't box him – you don't box a master. We're going in there to work those 35 years off Robinson.'[239]

'In this contest of age versus youth, 25-year-old Fullmer is favoured at 8-5 to wrest the 160-pound championship from Sugar Ray, who admits he has lost some of the speed that once lifted him to the plateau of all-time ring greats. Muscular, bull-necked Gene is favoured because he is a rugged young comer meeting a fading champion. Gene became challenger on 25 May by outpointing Charles Humez of France, middleweight champion of Europe. He is always moving, like Rocky Marciano – always applying the pressure, although he lacks Marciano's punch.'[240]

238 Sugar Ray Robinson with Dave Anderson *Sugar Ray* 1969

239 *Biloxi Daily Herald* Mississippi 13 November 1956

240 Jack Cuddy *Independent Press Telegram* California 30 December 1956

The experts were looking to Fullmer to climb all over the ageing Sugar Ray Robinson and win the middleweight title. The odds were against Robinson. Even the scientists were against the defending champion.

'The speed and power of the punching of middleweight champion Ray Robinson and challenger Gene Fullmer were tested electronically by a combination of devices specially created for the task by the Lavoie Laboratories of Morganville, New Jersey. Stephen D. Lavoie, an outstanding engineer in the field of radar and electronics who had a brief pro boxing career, picks the winner on the basis of the tests. His analysis was published in newspapers across America on the day of the fight. The results of the tests made 18 December with Fullmer and 19 December with Robinson are, of course, not entirely conclusive on the outcome of the fight. But scientifically and electronically speaking, with human factors taken into consideration, the "punchoscope" tells to a great extent not only an interesting story but also a fairly true one. Electronically, Gene Fullmer will be the new middleweight champion of the world!'[241]

Three days before the fight, columnist Jimmy Breslin was talking to Robinson at Greenwood Lake. 'Ray Robinson looks at it the other way. While everybody is busy pointing out that at 36 [sic] he can't possibly go more than eight or nine rounds against Gene Fullmer at Madison Square Garden on 2 January, old Sugar Ray asks about something else. "Do you have a guarantee Fullmer is going to be around for long?" he asks. "I've gone 15 rounds plenty of times and I can do it right now. But has Fullmer? And will he be able to? Why don't you start thinking about things like that instead of worrying about me?"

'This is an edgy middleweight champion who holds the floor at his Long Pond Inn training camp each day. Rankled by stories about the postponements he caused, plus other opinions hinting he is too ancient to handle a challenger who is 11 years younger, the

241 Stephen D. Lavoie *San Rafael Independent* California 2 January 1957

proud-to-a-fault Harlem Sugar Man snaps back at interviewers. The fighter usually is the last to find out that he is through. The best of them learn it the hard way – by being cuffed around by a kid. But Sugar Ray Robinson feels, you see, that he is what many have tabbed him – the greatest fighter, pound for pound, of any era. And that he can beat age, too.

'Young Gene Fullmer could knock that idea out of his head.'[242]

That is just about what Gene Fullmer was thinking when he told a reporter, 'I'm confident I'll win the title from Ray Robinson when we meet in New York's Madison Square Garden.

'Please don't get the idea that I'm cocky. I've studied Robinson's style from motion pictures and TV fights and have my heart set on either stopping Sugar Ray early or winning the decision over 15 rounds. I'm in the finest condition of my career, ready to go the distance if I have to. I'm not underestimating Robinson's ability, he's one of the greatest of all time, but I feel that youth will be in my corner plus my ability.'[243]

When fight day rolled around, IBC promoter Jim Norris was expecting a gate of $150,000 from a crowd of 14,000. But according to sportswriter Bob Considine, 'it was like old times around the Garden tonight. The venerated abattoir has held as few as 3,000 people for fights since the evil red eye of TV took over. But Wednesday night, with the New York television area blacked out and all burlesque houses closed, the fight drew a standing room crowd of 18,134 and $194,645, plus $100,000 for TV and radio rights. People who hadn't been around since the days of Mike and Joe Jacobs, and Jimmy Johnston, showed up for this one – as if ordained to pay becoming last respects to Robinson, a champion in different weight divisions as amateur and pro since 1939. Robinson took 47½ per cent of the Garden gate and 60 per cent of the razor company's subsidy, while Fullmer fought for only cakes (he doesn't drink coffee).'[244]

---

242 Jimmy Breslin *Helena Independent Record* Montana 30 December 1956

243 Al Warden *Ogden Standard Examiner* Utah 17 October 1956

244 Bob Considine *Pacific Stars and Stripes* 4 January 1957

That Wednesday night, before Gene Fullmer walked out of his dressing room to make his fight with middleweight champion Sugar Ray Robinson, he had a visitor. It was Harold G. (Hack) Miller, sports editor of the *Deseret News*, a newspaper published in Salt Lake City and Utah's oldest continuously published daily, founded in 1850. Miller presented Gene with the longest telegram in Madison Square Garden history, a message 36 feet and two inches long containing the names of 1,152 well-wishers from the Inter-Mountain region of the west.

Heading the names were those of his wife Dolores, baby daughter Kaye and Governor J. Bracken Lee of Utah. This was a fight he just had to win. He did.

The fading Robinson lost on a unanimous decision after 15 rounds. He was floored for six in the seventh round, cut and soundly whacked to the body throughout. Ray was gashed over the left eye in the seventh and it was widened in the 14th.

Reporting from ringside for Associated Press, Murray Rose wrote, 'Gene Fullmer, freshly crowned middleweight champion, warned Sugar Ray Robinson today that he'll be "twice as mean" and gunning for a knockout the next time he fights Robinson. "I fought for nothing this time," said the unmarked 25-year-old Mormon from West Jordan, Utah. "The next fight – if Robinson wants it – I'll be out there for the big money and to keep the title. I wanted to go for the kayo in this one but Marv [manager Marv Jenson] said I had the fight wrapped up in the late rounds and not to open up."

'Referee Ruby Goldstein voted for Fullmer by eight rounds to five with two even. Judge Frank Forbes had Gene ahead 10-5, while judge Harold Barnes had it a shade closer, 9-6. Fullmer, a thick-necked, brawny mine worker with a zest for fighting, got off to a fast start in the first three rounds, swept the sixth, seventh, eighth and tenth rounds, and clinched the first boxing title for Utah with a rousing surge in the 13th and 14th rounds.'[245]

---

245 Murray Rose *Mount Vernon Register* Illinois 3 January 1957

'It was the 15th round. Out of his corner came Sugar Ray Robinson with three minutes to go as middleweight champion of the world. Blood trickled from a deep, inch-long cut over his left eye. This was a beaten fighter but a champion, too. He proved it during those last few seconds. Against him now, charging toward him once more, was a young man of 25, the bull-necked, heavy muscled, powerful Gene Fullmer, a welder's apprentice and, very likely, with more talent for welding than for boxing. Fullmer ended his charge by crashing a right into Robinson's body. Robinson sagged back, as he had done so many times before.

'Suddenly, the crowd screamed. Few fans love Sugar Ray outside the ring but when he is working at his trade, it is impossible not to respect him. He is a brave and skilful man. So the crowd howled. For champion Sugar once more had cut loose with one of his fabulous flurries, a blinding-fast combination to Fullmer's tough head. It did seem that Sugar Ray's coldly furious combinations might work. His only chance was a knockout. He could not do it, of course, least of all after 14 rounds. Fullmer gave ground briefly, then he lunged back. Robinson caught Fullmer with a smashing right to the head, followed it with another and followed that with a right to the body. The fight came to a close with Robinson, by some miracle of longevity, still fighting on his toes instead of in an old man's flat-footed stance. The boxing bromide has it that a fighter's legs abandon him first and his punch goes last. In the case of Sugar Ray Robinson, the reverse may well be true.'[246]

'I even let him get me against the ropes, something I seldom did,' recalled Robinson. 'When your back is on the ropes, it feels like it's being touched with lighted matches – rope burns, they're called. One of the ropes even broke and I almost fell out of the ring.

'It wasn't my night. Fullmer got the 15-round decision, but at least I got $140,000 and the IRS agents let me keep it. I finally

---

246 Martin Kane *Sports Illustrated* January 1957

had some walking-around money but I was walking around as an ex-champ. Fullmer had my title.'[247]

'Of Ray's purse of $140,000, $50,000 was personally his. After expenses, it would be more than enough to set aside for a few weeks of fun with his new lover from California, a woman whose presence would threaten his marriage. Edna Mae was wise to Sugar's new affair. "I don't know if she knew that she wasn't the only one that I shared him with," she asserted, "but somehow those women seldom rocked the boat."' [248]

247 Sugar Ray Robinson with Dave Anderson *Sugar Ray* 1969

248 Herb Boyd with RayRobinson II *Pound for Pound* 2005

17
THAT PUNCH!

THE KENNECOTT Copper Mine is an open pit mining operation located in Salt Lake County, Utah, the largest man-made excavation in the world measuring two and a half miles wide and thought to have produced more copper than any other mine in history, 19 million tonnes. In January 1957, one of its employees brought more honour to the Mormon State. Gene Fullmer, a two-fisted 25-year-old apprentice welder at the Kennecott mine, made the long haul to New York City and gave the legendary Sugar Ray Robinson a bumpy ride over the 15-round distance to come out with Ray's world middleweight boxing championship.

'They took Fullmer's victory big here in West Jordan, Utah,' reported Associated Press. 'Perhaps taking it biggest of all was his wife, Dolores, 25, who says she "shouted so hard the baby started to cry," when the decision came over on television. "I was just so happy at the decision, I burst into tears," Mrs Fullmer said. She usually accompanies Gene when he leaves town for a fight, but this time she had to stay home to care for five-month-old Kaye, their baby girl.

'In West Jordan, the spontaneous celebration was like nothing seen since the end of World War II. Within minutes after the fight, many of the 2,100 townspeople were in the streets. A caravan estimated at 100 cars formed and toured West Jordan and nearby Salt Lake City suburbs of South Jordan and Midvale.

Many cars in the caravan ended their impromptu parade in front of Fullmer's home, where they cheered Dolores and members of her family who had joined her to watch the fight on television. After talking to Gene via long distance, she said his first words to her this time were that "he didn't have a mark on him and he really felt good". "I asked Gene if he could hear the neighbours outside and he said he could.'"[249]

As usual Robinson had a return bout written in the contract and as the new champ celebrated his upset victory in New York, the old champ was already looking ahead to the rematch.

'Sugar Ray Robinson, admitting that "at 35 you're not getting any better," prepared Wednesday for the fight of his boxing life,' wrote Oscar Fraley from Greenwood Lake. 'This is a new grimly determined Robinson who will strive to regain the middleweight crown from rugged Gene Fullmer at Chicago 1 May. This is no longer the laughing playboy once known as one of the greatest fighters, pound for pound, in ring history. Cowboy Gene, an "awkward crowder", is the kind of fighter old Sugar Ray at one time ate for breakfast. Today, he worries the one-time Harlem Dynamiter. You see it in Robinson's mien and in the relentless manner in which he trains. They wonder whether Robinson's legs are gone and certainly he is not the ringmaster of old. Yet they say at the Ramshackle Inn on the shores of Greenwood Lake he is punching harder than ever. Anybody can see the hurt pride driving him on, that, and a need for ready cash.

'Sugar Ray is in trouble with Uncle Sam, in the same way as Joe Louis. Each owes an incredible amount of back taxes and it is doubtful whether they will ever get "out". Yet more than that drives Sugar Ray as he prepares to climb into the ring against the Utah strongboy who, on youth and strength, rates a solid 1-3 favourite. It is Robinson's refusal to concede that he might be through.'[250]

249 *Madison State Journal* Wisconsin 4 January 1957

250 Oscar Fraley *Desert Sun* 10 April 1957

'The Mongoose is ready to mangle the ageing Cobra again,' wrote Jerry Liska from Chicago. 'That's the jungle talk middleweight champion Gene Fullmer's manager is speaking as the time approaches for Fullmer's rematch with Sugar Ray Robinson at the Chicago Stadium. "The best way to describe Fullmer is that he fights like a mongoose – striking, retreating, striking and winning in the end," the champion's pilot, Marv Jenson, said yesterday. As for animal lore, Jenson is much better acquainted with minks which he raises on a big scale in Utah. "We think he'll be shooting for a knockout from the opening bell. But, I'll tell you one thing, he'll find it just as hard to hurt Fullmer early as late. Gene has terrific reflexes. He senses punches coming. He ducks them, rides them, or comes inside them. And if they land, he can take them."'[251]

A couple of weeks before the fight, a reporter for Associated Press watched ex-champ Sugar Ray Robinson at his training camp. After his workout, Ray told the writer, '"I'm not the champion any more, and I sure want to be again." How much longer would he fight? "Long enough to get that title back from Fullmer and take on Carmen Basilio in a big outdoor fight in New York in the summer. That should do it." Robinson's pride has been stung by the loss to Fullmer, whom he sees as a "strong, awkward boy". "We've run the pictures of that fight over and over again and I still can't understand some of the things I did – or didn't do. That Fullmer is a nice, strong boy but all he's got is an awkward style."

'Sugar Ray is determined to regain the title and prestige. Almost daily, he runs five miles in the morning and works from ten to 15 rounds in the gym in the afternoon. In his boxing, the lithe, graceful veteran has two good sparring partners, Otis Woodward and Lee Williams, simulating Fullmer's style. It is evident from these drills that Robinson intends to open up early with a blistering barrage if the chance comes. With more than half of his training grind behind him, has he found the grind getting easier?

---

251 Jerry Liska *Ogden Standard Examiner* 21 April 1957

'"Man, it gets tougher all the time," replied Ray. "When you're young, you can work forever and love it. Now, when I get up in the morning and think of that five-mile run coming up, it sure breaks my heart. But I want that title back bad – real bad – and there's only one way to get it – by working."'[252]

Handling publicity at the Robinson camp was veteran Murray Goodman, whose column appeared in more than 700 newspapers before he joined the media department at Madison Square Garden in the late 1930s. 'It all started when I was asked to handle Robinson's publicity for the second Fullmer fight. In all my years of boxing, I had never worked with Robinson, always seemingly against him. I doubted that he would accept me as the man to glorify him. "That's great," was his astounding reply when I cornered him. "We'll get along fine." Yet I reported to Greenwood Lake with a variety of fears. Robinson lived at his own "cabin in the sky." He did his gym work and boxing at nearby Long Pond Inn. At both these spots, I got close to Robinson. I listened to him and I talked to him. I began to understand him for the first time.

'"I don't ever want to knock an opponent or make predictions on a fight," he said. "If God is with me, I hope to win. That is all I can ever say." That is part of the philosophy of the new Robinson. In the five weeks I spent with him, I have never found a man more considerate of the people around him. He never turned down any request made for pictures or interviews. In training he did as he was told, contrary to the belief that Robinson did as he pleased. One day he wanted to box four rounds. "Three is enough," declared Gainford. Three it was. He had been accused of carrying a lot of people around with him, mostly for laughs. That is not true. Every member of the Robinson entourage has a specific duty, even old Soldier Jones, who has been with Robinson since his amateur days. Jones is now old and arthritic but Robinson has kept him on the payroll all the time. "Robinson does many nice things," said Harry Wiley, his trainer. "Jones' job is to rub his legs after the

252 *Eau Claire Daily Telegram* Wisconsin 16 April 1957

workout. It's not much of a job but that's how Robinson keeps his old friend working."

'I like the new Robinson. I admire him. It is our humble opinion that Ray Robinson may have finally discovered humility.'[253]

'Mickey Walker, the renowned "Toy Bulldog" who, like Robinson, was a welter and middleweight champion, was a camp visitor. Sugar Ray slipped an arm around him. "This is one of the few people," he said, "who encouraged me and told me I could make a comeback in 1954. I had been out of the ring nearly two years, and he gave me a lot of tips on how to get ready to fight again."

'Sugar Ray supposedly retired because of money problems, but Walker believes it was because "he just felt he was better than the guys who were fighting for his old title". He won back the crown but was widely outpointed by Fullmer in January. On the strength of that victory, the young Mormon is a 15-8 favourite for the Chicago meeting.'[254]

Veteran sportswriter Oscar Fraley was still a Robinson believer. 'It's going to take one more win over the dancing dynamiter from Harlem before I'll admit he [Fullmer] is anything more than a very good club fighter. The difficulty is that I can't convince myself that Sugar Ray has gone back that far and – if I was the cynical type – without insinuating that all was not kosher, I'd say that the price is right. By this, I mean that at 3-1 or better, Ray Robinson figures to fight even better than his 37 [sic] years permit. As one old-timer along Bent Nose Boulevard observed, "Any time you can get 3-1 on Robinson, it's a good bet even if you lose."'[255]

(Newspaper reports at the time varied Robinson's age between 35 and 37. This writer, believing Ray's 1969 autobiography, written with Dave Anderson, has the Sugar Man born on 3 May 1921. That would make him 36 two days after meeting Fullmer.)

Jack Carberry, veteran sportswriter of the *Denver Post,* wrote, 'The more I read and the more I hear about the upcoming world's

253 Murray Goodman *The Ring* August 1957

254 *Sarasota News* Florida 23 April 1957

255 Oscar Fraley *Tucson Daily Citizen* Arizona 30 April 1957

middleweight championship fight between Gene Fullmer – the Utah strong boy Denver fight fans watched in a sorry ten-rounder against washed-up Ernie Durando – and Sugar Ray Robinson, the more I become convinced that the title, is once again, about to change hands. At 35, his published age today, no boxer is getting better. If that were not true, Robinson could have Fullmer for breakfast and still have time to devour any fighter around right now, with the possible exception of welterweight Carmen Basilio. And, just for the record, we believe there will be a Robinson-Basilio fight in one of the New York ball parks in late June or early July, and it will come close to drawing a million-dollar gate. Then came his defence against Fullmer and his loss of the title in a performance as strange as any the boxing world has viewed. Through 15 rounds Robinson, the man with one of the cleverest left hands anybody ever saw, the man who hooked and countered with either hand, the man rated as "the best fighting man, pound for pound, in the world", let Fullmer crowd him and club him in the clinches to take the title. The whole thing failed to make sense. Fullmer is a good boy. He is good in that he has strength. He is good in that he can take a punch. But the Denver fans who saw him against a completely washed out Durando know how he can be hit and how his bull-like charges can be avoided with a minimum of effort and little damage.'[256]

There were 14,753 people in the vast Chicago Stadium that night in May 1957, having paid from $5 to $25 for their seats. But Gene Fullmer and Ray Robinson had the best seats in the house, front and centre, up there in the brightly lit three-roped ring, and they didn't pay a dime to get in. In fact, promoter Jim Norris, boss of the International Boxing Club, was ready to pay them thousands of dollars as soon as their night's work was done. Each fighter figured to go home with a cheque for $68,990, an even split, which was more than Fullmer got for their New York fight four months earlier when champion Sugar Ray took every dollar

---

256 Al Warden *Ogden Standard Examiner* 17 April 1957

that wasn't nailed down for a whopping $140,000 pay packet. All Gene Fullmer got that night after a rugged 15 rounds in the Garden was Robinson's world middleweight championship, which was all he really wanted.

Fullmer was still grieving over that January pay split as he waited for the opening bell to get at Robinson, even though manager Marv Jenson was warning caution. The Mormon from Utah had infuriated Robinson with promises of a knockout published in the sports pages and he was sure he could do it this time. The smart money had him a 15-8 favourite with Sugar Ray a bargain bet at 3-1 and 4-1. As the old guy said, 'Any time you can get 3-1 on Robinson, it's a good bet even if you lose.'

Covering the fight for Associated Press, Jack Hand reported, 'This was a different Robinson from the inept, faded workman who clutched desperately in an effort to go 15 rounds only four months ago. When Sugar Ray tried to punch in bursts last January, Fullmer merely shook off the blows and came in stronger than ever.

'[In the rematch] Fullmer waded in with wild right-hand leads in the first round while Robinson fought back in the first clinch without holding as he had done in their first bout. Sugar Ray drew cheers from the crowd with a solid right uppercut midway in the first but Fullmer charged right back and was pounding him in his own corner at the two-minute mark. Just before the bell ended the first round, Robinson landed a hard left hook on the ever-charging Fullmer. Fullmer tried to move in close in the second, nestling his head under Robinson's chin and showing no respect for Ray's punching power.

'A Robinson right uppercut zoomed to its target yet Fullmer stormed in. In the final seconds of the round, the veteran from New York flurried briefly with both hands only to meet a Fullmer who came back punching. Sensing that Fullmer might be vulnerable, Robinson moved out of his corner fast at the beginning of the third. He was at mid-ring before Fullmer was off his stool. However, a crashing right to the ribs by Fullmer slowed him down.

Then came the low blow by the champion that drew the warning from Sikora.'[257]

'In the fourth,' wrote Red Smith, 'Robinson came out of his corner to throw a right-hand lead that only grazed its target, and then he threw in a flurry of lefts and rights but even as he punched, Fullmer chased him clear across the ring.' 'Unless Ray gets lucky,' Smith's ringside neighbour muttered, 'Fullmer's got to wear him out.'

'Then Ray got lucky. He had landed two heavy right-hand swings to Fullmer's ribs, the first of which landed with a smack that was audible in the gallery and brought cheers. They didn't seem to hurt Fullmer, though, who was rushing Robinson into a neutral corner when the left hook connected. The champion was knocked cleanly off his feet and halfway across the ring. He lay there in an attitude of rising, like a commuter saying, "No, it can't be 7.30 already," yet the fog in his eyes was an augury that he wouldn't get up. He didn't. Afterward, when the ring was thronged with people who own pieces of Robinson or wish they did, Fullmer's proprietor, Marv Jenson, stood towelling his tiger's face and lecturing him at length. Gene hung his head and listened, wearing a tiny frown of concentration like a schoolboy striving to understand.'[258]

This is what Martin Kane saw from the ringside seat *Sports Illustrated* had reserved for him.

'Later, in euphorious retrospect, the sugary Ray recalled that he had been subtly "showing him the right all night in order to set up the left." The Fullmer version is that he never saw the right, didn't notice it at any time. It does seem to be the essential truth, agreed upon by all, that Fullmer walked into a left hook. For a while thereafter, he couldn't walk at all.

'Robinson's preparatory right to Fullmer's body had the effect of bringing Fullmer's head over to the left. As the head swung

---

257 Jack Hand *Long Beach Independent* California 2 May 1957

258 Red Smith *New York Herald Tribune* 2 May 1957

back to the right in the same arc – Gene was planning to throw his underslung right and needed balance – Sugar Ray's perfect left hook caught it with precise timing and precisely on the Fullmer button. The lights went out. Hours afterwards, Fullmer was still in the dark as to what had happened. He could remember nothing. That part of the fight is hearsay so far as he is concerned.

'Fullmer went to the canvas so suddenly that the crowd was totally hushed for a moment. Then it burst with an ear-pounding roar of astonishment and admiration. For in the little interval that it took referee Frank Sikora to glide into position above Fullmer and start his count, it became clear that Gene, though drawing manfully on some wellspring of inherent courage, would not be able to rise again in ten seconds. His powerful legs pumped in the effort, but he had no more control of them than if he had been an infant squirming in his crib. He rolled and twisted. Sikora bellowed the seconds and they went relentlessly by. As they went, so went Gene Fullmer's brief hold on the title.'[259]

Robinson later called the blow 'the most perfect punch of my career.'

'"It's all over but the shouting," Honey Brewer, one of Robinson's seconds, had said just before the opening bell. "There'll be Hallelujahs for this one." It sounded like more bravado then, but Honey was right, and practically everybody else wrong. Especially Fullmer.'[260]

'Bewildered Gene Fullmer, his middleweight crown lifted, stood in his dressing room Wednesday night with open hands and asked, "What happened?" "He got you with one, Gene," said Fullmer's kid brother, Don. "He hit you twice and then came up with that left hook. That did it."

'"We warned him in the corner to fight like he had fought before; keep his hands up and crowd," manager Jenson was saying. "But he didn't do it." Fullmer said he "didn't think Robinson

---

259 Martin Kane *Sports Illustrated* 12 May 1957

260 Red Smith *New York Herald Tribune* 2 May 1957

fought differently. I just dropped my hands and that was it. I never kept count but I thought I was ahead and my plan was to wear him down."'[261]

Robinson's dressing room was a bedlam, but there were three well-dressed men standing in a corner and saying nothing. They didn't need to. They had earlier slapped a $23,000 lien on Sugar's purse which, according to Truman Gibson of the International Boxing Club, settled Robinson's back income tax difficulties. Sugar Ray, having just won the middleweight title for an unprecedented fourth time, was too happy to worry about the few dollars he owed Uncle Sam. 'I owe much to millions of persons who had faith in me and prayed for me,' he said, 'and I owe so much to Joe Louis, who has been with me all this time to give moral help and his knowledge of boxing. And I owe so much to Father Lang for his spiritual help. And I owe so much to my wife, Edna Mae, who suffered untold miseries as I prepared for this fight.'

'Robinson's wife, her hair dyed blond, was among those in the steaming, crowded dressing room, where a fight broke out near the door when a newspaper photographer tried to get through without police permission. He got in. New York State Athletic Commissioner Julius Helfand was on hand to say to Robinson, "Your fight tonight was a great one. I never heard such an ovation from a crowd. They love you, Ray." Turning to the reporters, Helfand said, "The reason I was here tonight to watch this fight was with a New York bout between Basilio and Robinson or Fullmer in mind. Basilio and Robinson should draw close to a million dollar gate."'[262]

'Jim Norris, IBC president, stated that he was now trying to clinch a title match between Robinson and welterweight champion Carmen Basilio at the Yankee Stadium, New York, in July, but Joe Glaser, one of Robinson's advisers, said that Ray was badly in need of a rest and would probably not defend his crown until September.

261 *Pacific Stars and Stripes* 3 May 1957

262 *Lowell Sun* Mass. 2 May 1957

"He has been in training for 90 days," he said, "and deserves to be able to take things easily for a spell."'[263]

That blazing left hook that robbed Gene Fullmer of the world title he held for barely four months 'marked Ray as a super fighter,' wrote Nat Loubert in *The Ring* magazine. 'Ring analysts see in Robinson one of the most remarkable one-punch fighters in the history of the ring. One punch, in the sense that he manoeuvres around and sets up his man for the situation he wants. One punch like the agency with which he disposed of Fullmer, like the medium with which he disposed of Olson in three of their four meetings, like the blow with which he took care of Steve Belloise in seven heats in 1949, and Rocky Graziano in three in 1952. Robinson has a faculty and a facility for setting the pattern for a fight, and sucking his rival in for the kill. As the 36-year-old Ray stressed in whipping Fullmer, he is a boxing wizard, a crafty, plotting ring general, and above all, a fighter with a mission and a scrapper with an intense pride. He hates to lose. In his own mind, he never has been beaten. Robinson as a personality certainly is not without flaws. Who is? But as a boxer, he commands the full respect – yes, admiration – of every man who knows anything about the variety of factors which go into the making of a great pro.'[264]

---

263 *Boxing News* 10 May 1957

264 Nat Loubert *The Ring* July 1957

18

A GOOD LITTLE 'UN BEATS A GOOD BIG 'UN

VETERAN NEW York columnist Jimmy Breslin was writing in September 1957, 'When he is not in a training camp or in the ring to make more money in one night than most people earn in a lifetime, as he will against Carmen Basilio on 23 September, you can find him standing at the curb on Seventh Avenue waiting for somebody to bring his flamingo-coloured Cadillac. People pass and nudge each other and point to the willowy, immaculately dressed Robinson and say that there is the man you read about all the time.

'It is, when you see this, as if there never was a Walker Smith who stood in front of a bakery on Russell Street, which is in a part of Detroit they call Paradise Valley, but it is far from it if you had to live there in 1930.

'"The Farm Crest" Dave Clark says, "That was its name. All the kids would stand in front of it and look in the window and be wishin' for some doughnuts. Kid'd get himself a nickel and go in and buy a mess of day-old cakes they gave you in a bag – they was probably four days old – and it was good because nobody was eating too good in those days."

'Clark is a trainer of fighters who was a light-heavyweight and he grew up in Paradise Valley and he remembers Walker Smith. "Maybe the man was born to fight like he can. But you can't tell me that. You got to know what it was like around here. Then you know why he fights good."'[265]

On another day, Jimmy Breslin was in Canastota and they were telling him how Carmen Basilio fights. '"Muck," the bartender was saying, "they come from the muck, they're tough. Look at Carmen, he comes from the muck. Hey, don't tell me he ain't tough." "He got scars on his hands," another guy at the bar said. "Like mine, from toppin' onions. You top onions all day, you can fight all night." The roughly dressed customers of this bleak little tavern on Main Street were talking of why Carmen Basilio fights with the never-quit viciousness of a mean pit dog. "He comes from muck," they say and if you see the place they tell about and watch how people there work, you know what they mean. It is an area, this muckland, of soggy black earth outside of Canastota, where the large Italian families that make up most of the town's population, raise onions.

'Until 1948, Carmen worked here with his family. He worked on his knees and he worked from six in the morning until dusk and he did this seven days a week during the growing season, which is long. The muckland gave Basilio the guts to fight this way. After it, nothing in boxing could discourage him. At the start, he was an unnoticed kid around the Main Street Gym in Syracuse. A colourless guy, they said, so he didn't make money, and once he had to shovel snow for three nights with a broken wrist so he and his wife, Kay, would be able to pay bills and eat because they had only 30 cents in the house.'[266]

The Robinson fight would set the Basilio family up for a while, if it ever came off. Ray Robinson was on his high horse, demanding a king's ransom for risking his middleweight title against the welterweight champion.

Martin Kane wrote in *Sports Illustrated*. 'For nine days, there was no certainty that the fight would be held at all. Most fighters

---

265 Jimmy Breslin *Logan Herald Journal* Utah 16 September 1957

266 Jimmy Breslin *The Altoona Mirror* PA. 18 September 1957

would have ranted and fumed. Basilio did nothing of the sort. Announcement that the fight was off – at least temporarily – came to Carmen while he was holding three kings in a poker game at his training camp in Alexandria Bay, New York.

'While the furies raged in New York, while Norris was stricken with what appeared to be food poisoning and taken to a hospital, while Julius Helfand, the boxing commission chairman, raged at Sugar Ray and threatened to take away his title, while Sugar Ray sassed Helfand, Basilio maintained the even tenor of his training schedule, fished in the St Lawrence River for bass and pike, and played a little poker. His managers, Johnny De John and Joe Netro, did the fuming. It was Robinson who got excited. It was Robinson who lost 10 days of proper training, it was Robinson who took sleeping pills.

'It was also Robinson, to be sure, who got a $255,000 theatre-television guarantee out of his tantrums to add to his 45 per cent of the big gate and whatever is derived from movie sales and radio. But Robinson's act got Basilio a $110,000 theatre-TV guarantee to go with his 20 per cent of gate, radio and movies: Basilio is not altogether unhappy about this.'[267]

Sugar Ray had added a theatrical lawyer named Marty Machat to his ever-growing entourage and Marty had sorted the contract for the fight. He also pointed out to Mr Robinson that his entourage was making more money than he was.

'Two years earlier, I had added my man Killer Johnson to the payroll,' Robinson recalled. 'He was one of the managers "of record", along with George and Ernie Braca. Also on the payroll was Joe Glaser. "You've got George and Killer splitting 33⅓ per cent," Marty pointed out. "You've got Braca getting ten per cent, and Glaser getting ten per cent. That adds up to 53⅓ per cent, more than half of your money. Add the money you give Wiley and June Clark and everybody else around you, and there's not much left for Ray Robinson. My advice is to get rid of a few. Braca and

267 Martin Kane *Sports Illustrated* 16 September 1957

Glaser don't do anything for you. All they're doing is waiting for you to pay them."

'The more I thought about it, the more that number 53⅓ annoyed me. I told Braca and Glaser I didn't need them any more. Shortly before the Basilio fight, I was served with legal papers. Braca was suing me for $169,084 for breach of contract and Glaser was suing me for about $80,000, the mortgage he had obtained on my business buildings in 1954. Several months later, we settled with Braca for about $18,000 and Glaser later foreclosed.

'"Robinson," George said, shaking his head, "you need more lawyers than sparring partners."'[268]

At his training camp at Greenwood Lake, New York, world middleweight champion Sugar Ray Robinson was talking to United Press about his fight with Carmen Basilio. 'For this fight, I had an immediate problem. Having fought on 1 May, I found myself low in weight when I reported to camp on 5 August. The trick was to sharpen myself without losing too much weight. George Gainford and Harry Wiley share the problem. We decided that we would do less boxing and concentrate on exercises calculated to speed up the hands and legs. Roadwork started with a walk, moved up to a jog, then a trot, with the distance increasing gradually. That builds stamina.

'What can be achieved in a training camp is strictly the sharpness of movements and reflexes. I'm not going to learn how to punch any harder than I do now nor can I change my style of fighting at this stage of my career. There is, perhaps, the advantage I have over Basilio. He can't change his style, either, no matter how he tries. That's his and as such seems suited to my style of fighting. All I can safely say is that God willing, I hope to win. I feel, from what I know of Carmen, that he can be beaten. Whether the fight lasts one round or 15, I expect a rugged evening. I have always been objective enough to take stock of myself and to consider how many rugged evenings a prize fighter of 36 has left in his system.'[269]

268 Sugar Ray Robinson with Dave Anderson *Sugar Ray* 1969
269 *Dunkirk Evening Observer* New York 21 August 1957

New York-born Arthur Susskind found fame as Young Otto, a lightweight with a heavy punch in the 20s, who scored 60 knockouts in winning 71 of his 87 fights between 1903 and 1923 before becoming a well-respected referee and judge around New York. He refereed Robinson in his first fight with rough, tough Fritzie Zivic. 'I said to myself then, "This kid is gonna be a great fighter."' *New York Daily News* columnist Jimmy Powers interviewed Young Otto, who had watched Sugar Ray training for the Basilio fight. '"Robinson showed me the best left I've ever seen in the ring. He bangs you so hard you get wobbly and can't see the right coming. He sets a man up beautifully, jolting him off balance and then coming in with the crusher." Otto reviewed Robinson's record, noting the men who went the limit with him, beat him or gave him more trouble than he bargained for. "You'll note it was the aggressive type every time. Basilio is that type, too, always pressing, never running away, giving no rest. Ray's pet punch is a right uppercut against crouchers who press. He'll think twice before using it on Carmen. The uppercut leaves you open for a hook to the chin, and a hook is Carmen's gun." [270]

To get ready for the fight of his life, Carmen Basilio set his training camp at Alexandria Bay, in the heart of the Thousand Islands region of upstate New York. 'It was the perfect spot for me to train because I could get my work in and then fish, which is something I love to do. Plus the people there were so friendly to not just me, but everyone connected with my training. It was great.' When the New York State Athletic Commission sent Dr Charles Heck up to Alexandria Bay to give Carmen Basilio his pre-fight physical, he was amazed at what he found. 'I have examined intercollegiate champions in track, crew, football as well as amateur and professional boxing. I can honestly say that this young man is in the finest physical condition possible. I have never seen an athlete in the condition this boy is. He's remarkable.'[271]

---

270 Jimmy Powers *The News* Newport Rhode Island 12 September 1957

271 Gary B. Youmans *The Onion Picker, Carmen Basilio and Boxing in the 1950s* 2007

'The summer vacationers had vanished, and the juke joints along the shore looked ready to be boarded up,' wrote a *Time* magazine correspondent. 'In the little village of Greenwood Lake, New York, only the Long Pond Inn showed signs of life. There, the champ's camp followers – boxing writers soaking up free drink, ex-athletes gone fat in the jowls, the kind of women who get their names tattooed on sailors – swapped yarns as they waited for Sugar Ray Robinson, middleweight champion of the world. Sugar Ray came down to his lakeside training camp trailing a drab crew – a couple of beefy sparring partners and a brace of trainers, all solemn and eager to pound the champ into proper shape for next week's bout with Carmen Basilio.

'Fresh from a financial knockout of promoter James D. Norris, the promise of $255,000 of television money and 45 per cent of the gate safely in his pocket, Ray was as cocky as ever. A blue, short-billed cap perched on his handsome head, a two-tone windbreaker zipped up against the mist from the lake, he smiled benevolently at his subjects. "After 17 years of boxing, all fights are the same," said Sugar with unlimited self-assurance. "The burden of proof is on Basilio. I've got the title, and he's got to come and get it. I'm the middleweight champion and I think I'm the best."

'"We know what Basilio's been doin'," said Sugar's soft-spoken manager, George Gainford. "Practising bobbing and weaving. We know what to do about that. Look at his face. He's been hit plenty, so why can't Robbie hit him? When the fight's over, why I'll assist Mr Basilio's manager to pick his man up off the canvas."'[272]

Monday, 23 September 1957, Yankee Stadium, New York City, a crowd of 38,072 paid $556,467 to see the battle of the champions. Robinson 160 pounds, Basilio 153½, his heaviest ever; 5ft 6½in to Robinson's 5ft 11in, the little man facing an uphill battle against the fighter they were calling the greatest pound for pound.

Sports editor Ben Borowsky set the scene for his readers of Pennsylvania's *Bristol Daily Courier*. 'On the night the Yankees

---

272 *Time* magazine 23 September 1957

clinched the American League pennant, Basilio entered the field through their dugout. Robinson came through the third base or visiting dugout. The electric moment at every outdoor championship fight is not when it's over, but when the fighters start walking through the "sea of humanity" on the field to the ring. The fighters and their aides, assisted by the police, move slowly through the crowd. Everyone in the park stands and looks. Some way, somehow, you feel the difference. Up to this point you've been watching, or not watching, some preliminary boys in the ring. Then the moment is at hand. The big boys are coming. The real pros are ready to take over. In the ring, a few former champions are introduced and the tension lets up a little. The gloves are put on. The introductions. The instructions. And then, at 10.37pm, there are only three men left in the ring.'[273]

Over to ringside, where Walter Wellesley Smith, or Red Smith, as he is known to a nation of readers of his columns in the *New York Herald Tribune,* sits at his typewriter, ready to go to work. 'Carmen Basilio entered the ring wearing a white silk robe trimmed with red over a bulky, hooded gray sweat suit. Bundled up like that, with the five o'clock shadow of maturity on his gaunt and thin-lipped visage, he looked just as big as Ray Robinson in a white-cowled robe of blue across the ring.

'Then they stripped down to business attire, and the difference was striking. In that moment before the opening bell, Basilio looked like a boy flung in against a man. But this was the toughest kid that ever yanked an onion out of the mucky fields of Canastota, New York. Taking the hardest, cleanest blows his marvellously gifted enemy could offer, spilling his own blood in small, steady trickles from eye and nose, Basilio went plodding forward, onward, chasing the middleweight champion through 15 rounds.'[274]

'They came out very carefully to the centre of the ring and Robinson flicked a right to the forehead which did no damage,'

---

273 Ben Borowsky *Bristol Daily Courier* PA. 24 September 1957

274 Red Smith *New York Herald Tribune* 24 September 1957

wrote Jack Cuddy for United Press. 'Robinson drove a hard right to Basilio's jaw and drove him into the ropes. But Basilio came back without showing any damage, and forced Robinson into a clinch with a barrage of rights and lefts to the body. Basilio landed a left to the body and came in with a hard right, rocking Robinson into a clinch. Basilio, aiming at Robinson's body, landed a hard right to the stomach , and then on his way in landed a left to Ray's chin. But Robinson came back with a short right that caught Basilio on the jaw as the round ended. I gave the round to Robinson.' [275]

'In the second round,' wrote Gary B. Youmans in his Basilio biography, 'Robinson again started fast, hitting Basilio with two quick jabs to the face before Basilio hooked a left to the body, followed by a hard right to the jaw; another hard hook to Robinson's ribs hurt the champion, forcing him to back up. Robinson continued to slide to his right, his jab peppering Basilio's face as he tried to set up his big right hand. The resilient challenger pressed him, ducking in close, where he blasted Robinson with hard blows to the body. The two fighters traded punches back and forth [for] the remainder of the round. Sugar Ray had demonstrated through two tough rounds that he had the better boxing skills, but Basilio had shown his tremendous grit and determination. Something had to give. Robinson was pounding him, but Basilio wouldn't go away. He just kept coming back for more.'[276]

Round three with Jack Cuddy, 'Robinson was short with a left to the jaw, Basilio drove a right to Robinson's stomach and Ray wrestled his opponent into the ropes. Robinson with a left to the chin, Basilio came back with a body attack. They sparred in the middle of the ring and Basilio caught Robinson with a hard right to the jaw, forcing Ray to hold on. Basilio drove Robinson against the ropes with another hard right to the jaw but Ray came back with body blows and then landed a hard right to the head of Basilio. They were testing each other out as the round ended. I

---

275 Jack Cuddy *Press Telegram* Los Angeles 24 September 1957

276 Gary B. Youmans *The Onion Picker, Carmen Basilio and Boxing in the 1950s* 2007

gave this round to Robinson. Into round four and Robinson short with a left lead as Basilio came in with a left to the body. Basilio started bleeding from the brow as Robinson drove a hard right to his head. Blood was flowing freely from the cut as Ray tried to land a knockout punch. He drove Basilio into the ropes with a left to the body and a hard right hook to the jaw. But Basilio came off the ropes and started a counter attack to the body, which forced Robinson to retreat. Robinson came in with a short left to Basilio's jaw and landed a hard right to the body, forcing Basilio into a clinch. Robinson drove Basilio back into the ropes with a left to the jaw and a right to the body. Another glanced off Basilio's jaw, which put him into the ropes again. Robinson was short with a looping right as the round ended. I gave this round to Robinson.'[277]

In the fourth, Basilio suffered a vicious cut over the left eye. It dripped blood the rest of the way. By the sixth, it was obvious that Sugar Ray's attempt for a knockout in the early rounds had failed. Basilio was too tough even to be floored, although he had tasted Robinson's Sunday punch. Now it was a question of whether Ray's legs would stand up to the pressure that Basilio was bound to put on.

Basilio, the ever-pressing ex-Marine from Chittenango, would recall in the sixth round, when Robinson hooked one arm on the ropes, he refused to be sucked in. 'I know he was trying to draw me in. You know, Ray was talking to me during the fight but in all the excitement I forgot what he said. I know when we were being given our instructions, he looked at my sweat pants that I wore from the dressing room. "Don't worry," I told him. "I'm going to take them off."'[278]

Seventh round and Basilio was getting into his stride, forcing the action like a mini-Marciano. Jack Cuddy saw it like this. 'Robinson was short with a left jab as they sparred in the centre of the ring. Robinson took a right to the body but drove Carmen

---

277 Jack Cuddy *Press Telegram* Los Angeles 24 September 1957

278 *Lima News* Ohio 24 September 1957

back with a left to the jaw. Robinson landed a left to the body but took a right to the head that forced Ray into a clinch. It was only the second time in the fight the referee was forced to separate the fighters. Basilio landed a hard left to the jaw which drove Sugar Ray into the ropes and he clinched again. Robinson staggered Basilio with a left to the jaw. Basilo came right back with a right to the head, and Robinson was short with his famous left hook. Basilio drove Robinson into a corner and landed a left and right to the body. Basilio landed a hard right to the jaw but Robinson came back with a right to the chin as Carmen continued to force the fighting. The round ended as they were sparring cautiously in the middle of the ring. I gave this round to Basilio.'[279]

'It was a delaying action fight, with Robinson relying on his nimble feet to carry him out of danger,' wrote Whitney Martin for Associated Press. 'When he did find an opening for his heavy artillery, he would pour over a barrage of punches. But nothing happened, except that the bloody mask forever in front of him became bloodier. Basilio was a man of purpose, and nothing was going to swerve him. When Robinson, after a warning for a rule infraction, held out his hands in a conciliatory gesture, the little man in front of him would slap down on them disdainfully. He came to fight and the niceties could wait.'[280]

'Basilio pressed the fight through most of its duration,' reported INS staff writer Bob Considine, 'and though at times this was akin to the sight of a man walking into a hamburger grinder, it impressed the judges and sometimes unnerved Robinson. Basilio's left eye had been broken earlier. Now it was smeared with a thick yellow grease which Robinson's corner frequently complained about. Not even the coating of ambergris, or whatever it was, could stop the blood between rounds, however, and now Basilio presented himself like a man reporting into a field hospital after a bad barrage. In the rare clinches Robinson leaned on Basilio,

279 Jack Cuddy *Press Telegram* Los Angeles 24 September 1957

280 Whitney Martin *Wichita Falls Times* 24 September 1957

further to weary him. But the fertile wells of strength in Basilio were far from dry. He shook himself like an angry terrier and took after Ray with fresh determination, hitting Robinson with a righthand punch that bloodied Ray's nose and sent a spray of stale sweat fanning out over the ring.'[281]

For United Press, Oscar Fraley described round 11. 'They stood there, toe to toe, one a sleek black panther and the other a whipcord little man made out of barbed wire, and they hammered each other with a mad abandon. You can talk about the night Luis Angel Firpo knocked Jack Dempsey out of the ring. But I'll take that 11th round as Basilio opened with a left to the chin, followed it up with another and hurled Robinson against the ropes. But when Robinson, the blood streaming from his nose, surged off the ropes and buried a vicious right hand in Basilio's body, they were pounding out a saga of strength and courage which will live as long as men like this brutal sport. Give me a tale about how a bitter, vengeful Joe Louis sprang out of his corner and lowered the curtain of darkness on the Black Uhlan from Germany, the sorrowful figure which was Max Schmeling.

'But when Robinson sprang forward like a cougar, slashing a series of hard lefts and rights to the chin and then shifting to the body to double the hurting Carmen into a pitiful knot, this was leather-mitten history in the making. When Basilio came out of that pit of pain and lashed back with a savagery which sent Robinson back on his heels, the crowd in Yankee Stadium rose *en masse* and howled its accolade of greatness. As Basilio reached out of nowhere, fighting on heart alone, to win that 11th round Monday night, this was one of the toughest little fighting men you'll ever see. He was out on his feet but he marched up alongside such greats of gameness as Billy Petrolle, Tony Canzoneri and Tony Zale.'[282]

---

281 Bob Considine *Salt Lake Tribune* Utah 24 September 1957

282 Oscar Fraley *Amarillo Globe Times* Texas 24 September 1957

'That seemed to be it for Robinson,' reported Murray Rose, 'His legs appeared ready to fold under him. But in the 12th he found a hidden reservoir of strength. He took command again with his stabbing left jabs and in the 13th he staggered his blood-smeared rival with a left hook to the jaw seconds before the bell. In the 14th, Ray doubled Carmen over with a stunning right hand to the pit of the stomach but again Basilio, never stopped in his career, refused to fold. His cheeks swollen, blood dripping from the cut over his left eye and his nose, Carmen drove doggedly on in the 15th to win that crucial final round with his aggressive tactics and body banging.

'It was a see-saw fight which could have gone either way. Judge Artie Aidala had it 9-5-1 for Basilio (only five rounds for Robinson with one even); judge Bill Recht made it 8-6-1 for Basilio while referee Al Berl cast the dissenting vote for Robinson, 9-6. The Associated Press scorecard had it even 6-6-3. "I have no squawks," said Robinson of the decision, adding, "I don't know whether I'll ever fight again."'[283]

---

283 Murray Rose *Mount Vernon Register News* Illinois 24 September 1957

19

SUGAR RAY – SUPER CHAMP

TUESDAY, 24 September 1971. Waking up this morning, Sugar Ray Robinson was not a happy man. Two things bugged him – he was broke, and he was no longer middleweight champion of the world. Looking over the sports pages of the morning papers, with headlines proclaiming Carmen Basilio as the new champion after his bruising battle with Robinson the night before in Yankee Stadium, two news items caught his eye.

'OVER $500,000 FOR SUGAR – Middleweight champion Sugar Ray Robinson earned more than $500,000 in losing his title to Carmen Basilio last night.' In the next column he read, 'MORE BAD NEWS FOR SUGAR RAY – The US Bureau of Internal Revenue made Sugar Ray Robinson a double loser last night by filing "a notice of levy" of $514,310 against him. The tax action was primarily an "anticipatory lien" against his expected 1957 income.'[284]

It was a no-brainer – Robinson would fight again. He would have to. A couple of days later, Associated Press reported, 'Was Sugar Ray Robinson serious when he said he was thinking of hanging up his gloves for good? No, according to most expert opinion. Robinson threatened to retire after Carmen Basilio lifted his middleweight title Monday night, but most insiders agreed he

284 *Lowell Sun* Mass. 24 September 1957

would try to regain the crown. They point out that Sugar Ray is a man of tremendous pride, and he dearly wanted to beat Basilio and retire as the champion. Now, having lost the title three times, he wants to give it one more try. If he can beat Basilio in a return, he'll call it quits. He's 36, and can't go on forever.'[285]

'He'll do it for money, perhaps,' wrote columnist Jimmy Breslin, 'but it is to be doubted if money ever could pay for the physical torture that would go into 15 rounds of fighting with Basilio. The Robinson ego – that's different. He can forget the ugly little right hands Carmen sank into his midsection the first time. He can forget clutching his middle and nearly collapsing while going back to his dressing room. He can forget that he had trouble dressing himself. What matters is people don't call him champ. The money he owes – all that can be treated casually. He didn't pay once, there's no reason why he'd pay again. But he needs the fame. Needs it badly.'[286]

Promoter Jim Norris needed the rematch badly, among other things. His International Boxing Club had been reeling on its heels since June, when a federal judge, Sylvester J. Ryan, ordered the dissolution of the IBC, which had dominated pro boxing since 1949. Judge Ryan also ordered Norris and Arthur Wirtz to sever their connection with Madison Square Garden, giving them five years to sell their interest in the Garden, which amounted to about 39 per cent of the total stock. From 1 July, they must resign within 30 days as officers and directors and they would be limited to promoting two championship fights a year for the next five years.

Now, three months later, newspapers carried reports that Norris was still fighting. 'Dispelling any uncertainty, promoter Jim Norris stated definitely that an appeal of the monopoly decision against the International Boxing Club will be taken soon to the United States Supreme Court. That move, doubtlessly, will permit the IBC to stage a return Carmen Basilio-Sugar Ray Robinson

285 *Mount Vernon Register News* Illinois 26 September 1957

286 Jimmy Breslin *Altoona Mirror* Pennsylvania 7 October 1957

middleweight title fight next year. Sugar Ray hinted Wednesday he would try to recapture the crown. It was while Norris was discussing the possibilities of a return Basilio-Robinson match that he disclosed the appeal. His disclosure was made at St Claire's Hospital, his quarters for nearly a month because of a heart condition.'[287]

'The high tribunal will not sit again until October and such an appeal might not be heard before a year hence. Meanwhile, Norris and Wirtz might be able to carry on.'[288]

Big Jim could have done without the news that the New York fight between Basilio and Robinson had lost about $100,000 for the IBC, the loss, incidentally, the biggest the club had taken in its eight-year existence.

As a welterweight in the Forties, Sugar Ray Robinson was a knockout sensation, tabbed by sportswriters the uncrowned champion of the division. He had some frustrating experiences with Mike Jacobs, then the czar of boxing, who for years worked to keep Robinson from winning the welterweight title.

In the 1950s, Robinson no longer had to worry about 'Uncle Mike'. His nemesis was 'Uncle Sam' and the men in grey suits, agents of the Internal Revenue Service, who usually got to the promoter before Sugar Ray did. He knocked out Olson in their fourth and final bout but Uncle Sam took nearly $90,000 out of his purse of $105,000. Things got better in his fight with Gene Fullmer, although he lost the title again. Fullmer got the 15-round decision, but at least Ray got $140,000.

He was on the roller coaster again when Carmen Basilio lifted his title with a split decision in their September fight in 1957. The men in suits were there and when the bell rang to start the fight, one of the agents served notice on the International Boxing Club to hold all of Robinson's money, which when totalled added up to over $500,000. A tax lawyer eventually negotiated the release

287 *Corona Daily Independent* California 27 September 1957

288 *Sarasota News* Florida 24 June 1957

of $100,000 to Ray but the case was passed on to the Treasury Building in Washington. He went with his attorney, Marty Machat, had a meeting with the tax men, who thanked them, then walked out. 'We wait,' Marty told Ray. 'We go home and wait. Maybe for years.' Ray didn't like the sound of that and he started scheming for a way to beat Uncle Sam. He found a way.

Eddie Jaffe, a Broadway press agent, was working for Sugar Ray Robinson when Robinson was scheduled to fight a rematch with Carmen Basilio. On the Sunday before the fight, Ray told Jim Norris, who headed the IBC, that he wouldn't fight unless he got all his money, $300,000 in cash. When Norris said it was Sunday, so how was he supposed to get the money, Ray told him, he was big man, and to get a bank to open. Which is what Norris did. So $300,000 in bills was put in canvas sacks that Ray gave to his lawyer, Marty Machat, and Jaffe, who were sharing a room. The night before Ray fought Carmen, they stacked his purse under the beds and went to sleep.

Ray had a return bout contract with Carmen Basilio in which each would share 30 per cent of everything, with the fight finally signed for the Chicago Stadium on 28 March 1958. In February, the fighters went into camp to get ready for the big one. Nobody had beaten Robinson twice and he couldn't see the Chittenango onion picker turning the trick. 'Before leaving Syracuse, Carmen told United Press he would not only beat Robinson again but he would stop him. He was angry about Ray's claim of having Basilio "on the way out five times" in their first fight. 'Well, let me tell you," said Carmen. "Mr Robinson never hurt me. And he was so foggy himself through most of the fight, I hit him with punches a boxer of his reputation is not supposed to get hit with, so often, in fact, it became monotonous to me."'[289]

Sugar Ray had been in camp at Greenwood Lake a couple of weeks when an Associated Press bulletin reported 'snow and sub-normal temperatures put a crimp into the sports program

289 *Pacific Stars and Stripes* 4 March 1958

along the Atlantic Coast over the weekend. Bowie, Maryland race track operated under adverse conditions Saturday but called off its Monday card after drifting snow had marooned several hundred fans when they were unable to move their automobiles. The National Basketball Association game in Boston between the New York Knicks and the Celtics was postponed. Wind and cold forced postponement of four Florida regattas. The tri-state speed skating championships at Grossinger, N.Y. were called off after one day. Several of the fighters were unable to reach Eastern Parkway Arena in Brooklyn because of the snow storm. The bouts were postponed until 1 March. Sugar Ray Robinson, who always travels with a retinue, put his party to work today to dig him out. His automobiles were snowbound at the cottage two miles from the gym where he is working out for a title rematch with Carmen Basilio. The former middleweight champion passed out shovels to George Gainford, his closest boxing associate, two sparring partners, two trainers and a masseur. They dug out the cars.'[290]

Meanwhile, middleweight champion Carmen Basilio was soaking up the sunshine on a Miami Beach golf course, where he played nine holes with New York Yankees baseball star Mickey Mantle. Mickey won the match, though they weren't keeping score. He politely turned down the offer of a few rounds with the champ, but good luck in Chicago! Basilio had set up his camp in Miami, yet a couple of weeks later he was 'looking sluggish in three rounds of sparring practice as temperatures rose to the low 70s. "This warm weather didn't agree with him," said Joe Netro, co-manager who is helping to groom Basilio for his 25 March title defence against Sugar Ray Robinson. "The cool weather was fine but now a change to warmer climate hasn't helped." Basilio's sparring partner, Archie Whitfield, said the champ landed more blows Sunday than Saturday but the punches weren't so hard.'[291]

---

290 *Valley Morning Star* Harlingen Texas 16 February 1958

291 *European Stars and Stripes* 25 March 1958

'At Greenwood Lake, Sugar Ray impressed 150 observers with the sharpness of his left jabs and countering rights during three rounds of sparring. The ex-champion's tactics against three sparmates, who imitated Basilio's pressing style, hinted that Sugar will try to keep Basilio at long range during their 15-rounder at Chicago on 25 March. Sparmate Otis Woodward, fighting out of a crouch as Basilio does, was knocked off balance repeatedly in a three-round drill. Robinson shifted his feet, poked the crouching Woodward off balance and then leaped in with a body attack.'[292]

From Jimmy Breslin's column – 'Is there a chance, people were asked, that Robinson will postpone the show? Jim Roberts of the New York branch of Jim Norris' operations was playing cards with Basilio at Alexandria Bay, N.Y. one afternoon last summer when a phone call announced Robinson had decided to take a walk. "Impossible," Roberts now says. "What's the matter with you? This guy is pretty good at counting you know. The last time, he cost himself something like $100,000. The minute he started the row that made us postpone the thing everybody stopped buying tickets. *En masse.* And they never started again. He has been bearing down in training, too. Go up to the lake and take a look for yourself. He's going to go all the way. The way he figures, he is going to win the title back and then fight Basilio back outdoors in June for all the money in North America."'[293]

Well, Mr Roberts, Sugar Ray really wanted this one, and he had a valid reason to keep his clothes on and go back to the hotel. He came down with a virus and 'everybody around me had been pleading with me to postpone the fight,' he recalled. 'The virus had lingered in me for about a week. Dr Nardiello was with me, and so were Dr John Holloman and Dr Robert Bennett. Each of them advised me to request a postponement. Even his friend Father Lang, a Franciscan priest, advised against going through

292 *Eau Claire Leader* 8 March 1958

293 Jimmy Breslin *Ogden Standard Examiner* 10 March 1958

with the fight. "If you're not well," he said, "you're endangering your health."

"Father," I said, "God will give me more strength than the virus will take away." When the commission doctors arrived for the weigh-in at noon in the stadium ring, one of them took his temperature. It was a 103. "You can't fight with that," he said. Ray pleaded but the doctor said he would have to report to Lou Radzienda, the commission chairman, who told Ray there was no way he could fight. More pleading and they agreed that Dr Nardiello would take his temperature at five o'clock and report to the commission. Robinson weighed in at 159¾ to Basilio's 153, and then he was off to bed at the Conrad Hilton.

'Shortly before five, Dr Nardiello took my temperature. "It's down a little," he said, "[It's] 101." "Doc, I'm all right," I said, "you've been with me all these years, you've got to go along with me." He picked up the phone and dialled the commission office, where Lou Radzienda was waiting for the call. "He'll be all right," Doc lied for me. To be sure, he gave me two injections. Penicillin for the virus, B-12 for strength.'[294]

One thing Ray had going for him this time was that he was fighting in his lucky ring, the Chicago Stadium. In 12 fights there, Ray lost only one, a decision to Tiger Jones. With the title on the line, he beat Jake LaMotta, defended against former champ Rocky Graziano and regained it from Bobo Olson and Gene Fullmer. And now he was ready to take it from Carmen Basilio.

When he climbed into the ring that March night in 1958, ex-champ Sugar Ray was a 7-5 underdog with the bookies. A crowd of 17,976 had paid a gross gate of $351,955, and they saw one of the greatest middleweight title battles in ring annals.

At ringside for the *New York Times,* Joseph C. Nichols reported, 'Basilio was the first one to "rough it up" and drew a warning in the first round for hitting on the break. In this session, Robinson tried to box, but Basilio bulled his way inside and he outpunched

294 Sugar Ray Robinson with Dave Anderson *Sugar Ray* 1969

Ray. They were so intense at their task that they slashed away at each other after the bell. This action infuriated a Robinson handler, who tried to climb into Basilio's corner, but the stadium staff restrained him. Robinson brought his boxing ability into play in the second round and speared Carmen with a variety of sharp punches. They didn't seem to have much effect as the onion farmer, as Basilio is known, moved ahead with his determined aim to strike the body. Robinson, though, succeeded in avoiding his punishment.'[295]

'In the early rounds,' wrote Jack Cuddy for United Press, 'Robinson took the offensive, but Basilio's counter charges in the first and second sessions gave him an edge. Sugar Ray came on strong in the third and brought blood to Carmen's nose. Basilio rallied to take the fourth with combinations to the body and head. Then Ray came back and buckled Carmen's knees in the fifth with hooks and uppercuts. In the sixth, Ray closed Carmen's left eye with a right uppercut.'[296]

'After the eye closed,' observed George McGuane for the *Lowell Sun,* 'the left side of the face enlarged. Carmen was a terrible sight to behold as he peeked out of his only good blinker and he looked more like a fabled "Cyclops" – those creatures of mythology with only one eye in the centre of their heads. Up to the fourth round, when the damaging blow landed, we had the fight even. But when the eye started to close in the sixth, it was evident the fight was all over for Basilio even though he fought like a Spartan. It's hard enough to fight Robinson with two eyes, but without height, weight or reach advantage and with only one eye, the odds suddenly became too lopsided. From the way the fight was going until the lights went out for Carmen, it was our humble opinion he was on his way to a victory. He was sharp and strong. He was alternating body punches and hard rights to Robinson's head brilliantly.'[297]

---

295 Joseph C. Nichols *New York Times* 26 March 1958

296 Jack Cuddy *Ogden Standard Examiner* 26 March 1958

297 George McGuane *Lowell Sun* Mass. 26 March 1958

For International News Service, Bob Considine wrote, 'Ray closed the poor man's left eye tighter than quarter past three in the sixth round. From that point on, the brave bull named Basilio fought from memory and touch. Whenever he could, he'd feel his way in through Robinson's blinding jabs and occasionally rocking rights like a blind man crossing Times Square at high noon without [the] benefit of a seeing-eye dog. Once in close he got in some good licks. But the remnants of Robinson's great talent prevailed. He backed off, stabbed, stuck, piled up points, turned Basilio's face into what looked like a head-on collision.'[298]

'The significance of the closing eye was recognised instantly in Basilio's corner,' reported Martin Kane of *Sports Illustrated*. 'It touched off a tense drama of decision quite as stirring as the drama in the ring, though not as visible. A closed eye can be opened, but by methods that are unsanitary, ugly and dangerous to eye and brain. Good cut men know how and many have steeled themselves to it at one time or another. For this operation, Carmen's trainer, Angelo Dundee, one of the finest of cornermen, carried a sterile razor blade in his kit on the night of 25 March. He debated the question in his own quick mind, and he might indeed have used the blade, with the permission of Basilio's co-managers, Joe Netro and Johnny De John, except that these three are men who cherish their fighter more than as a source of wealth.

'So between the fifth and sixth rounds, there came the fateful moment of decision. There was a brief weighing of the risks, including a practical realisation that lancing the eye might start a flow of blood that would stop the fight. They decided in favour of Basilio's ultimate welfare, win or lose. Only ice packs were used. The eye was now fully closed, having had some acceleration from a Robinson uppercut in the fourth round. So champion Basilio was permitted to come out for the sixth round with an eye so closed and swollen and so clearly useless that the crowd of 18,000 in the

298 Bob Considine *Ogden Standard Examiner* 26 March 1958

stadium gasped in horror. With two-thirds of the fight to go, it was a cruel handicap.'[299]

'Basilio presented a sad picture in the seventh when his eye was shut tight,' recorded Nichols. 'Robinson looked away at him as if a quick victory was to be his. But Carmen absorbed all the punishment and occasionally lashed out with left hooks to the head and body that indicated he was still dangerous. After Robinson built up a slight margin in the eighth, Basilio staged a fine rally in the ninth and tenth. He dealt out considerable damage with his crashing left hooks to the body. Robinson changed his style after that and boxed instead of trading. Through each of the last five rounds, Sugar Ray had at least one good shot at Carmen's jaw and some of these punches had enough impact to floor anyone except the iron-jawed Basilio. In the 15th round Basilio moved in and butted Robinson, for which he was warned by the referee. They shook hands and then Robinson tore after Basilio with a studied right-hand attack, punishing Carmen quite a lot, but failing to floor him.'[300]

'Hard as Basilio tried, gallantly though he came back from furious barrages of blows, and close as he managed to make even his losing rounds, he still fell further and further behind so that finally the only amazing thing about the fight was the scorecard of referee Frank Sikora, the top Illinois official. While the two judges scored the fight on the Illinois five-point must system with eight-point advantages for Robinson, Sikora scored it 69-66 in Basilio's favour, prompting more than one ringsider to say that while Basilio had one eye shut, Sikora must have had both his closed!'[301]

'In a contest that didn't quite measure up to the standard set in their New York bout,' Nat Fleischer reported, 'but which furnished the crowded Chicago arena with plenty of excitement, Sugar Ray showed why he is called a ring marvel by succeeding in doing what never before had been accomplished – winning the middleweight

299 Martin Kane *Sports Illustrated* 7 April 1958

300 Joseph C. Nichols *New York Times* 26 March 1958

301 Keith Howard *Boxing News* London 4 April 1958

title for the fifth time. His record performance is not likely to be repeated in many years. In his 17th year as a professional, fighting his 150th battle, and spotting his opponent seven years in age, Sugar Ray achieved his goal. The contest between the masterful boxer, one of the greatest of all time, and the plodding, aggressive, tear-in battler from Chittenango, New York will take its place in ring history with the great middleweight bouts of the past.'[302]

'Robinson held his press conference in pyjamas, in bed, two hours after he had won the championship. He had to be carried, virtually, from the scene, and he had to be undressed, practically, by the six men who toted him, head down, out of the Chicago Stadium and to his hotel quarters. Robinson never rides in elevators. He gets hotel rooms on lower levels, so he can walk. Tuesday night, his half dozen escorts put him on the elevator to get him to his room. His voice, when he answered questions, was so low it was almost undistinguishable. He was glassy eyed. He wasn't marked, on the exterior. A little swelling about the nose and brows. "I've gotta get some sleep," he said. "I've gotta close my eyes." George Gainford and a policeman shoved the horde from the room.

'Basilio was marked badly. His left eye was closed. It was cut. His nose was swollen. Obviously he had been punished. But he left the stadium under his own power. "I'd love a rematch," he said. "Robinson's punches never hurt me. It all comes down to the bad eye."'[303]

There was good news, however, when Basilio was examined at Chicago's Wesley Memorial Hospital. 'Dr Richard A. Perritt, eye specialist, complimented the co-managers and trainer Dundee on their restraint a few days after the fight, when surgical examination disclosed that neither the eyeball nor the retina had been injured. "If Dundee had lanced the lid," Dr. Perritt said, "he could have risked infection of veins leading to the brain, with cerebral thrombosis and permanent eye damage as possible results."

---

302 Nat Fleischer *The Ring* May 1958

303 *Pacific Stars and Stripes* 28 March 1958

"'We are being criticised for not cutting the eye," co-manager De John said, "but the doctor says we did the best thing when we did not cut. And like Angelo says, 'If it's something I can't handle, I won't handle it.' So it was best we didn't cut.'"[304]

When Basilio took the title off Robinson in September 1957, *The Ring* magazine named him Fighter of the Year and it was also their Fight of the Year. The boys got the double when their return fight was named Fight of the Year for 1958.

They never fought again.

304 Martin Kane *Sports Illustrated* 7 April 1958

20

SUGAR RAY – NOT SO SWEET

AS A prizefighter, Sugar Ray Robinson was on top of everyone's list. Ring pundits called him the greatest boxer of all time, pound for pound. Uncrowned lightweight champion, undefeated welterweight champion, middleweight champion for an unprecedented five times.

Outside the ring, however, there was a sour side to the sweet Sugarman. As a husband, and as a father, Robinson was something less than a champion. Regarding his history of philandering while married to the lovely Edna Mae, Sugar offered the following. 'From childhood, I was born to obey the Ten Commandments and I have – except for the one about adultery, and I'm not proud of having broken it.'[305]

'There had been so many dalliances, Edna Mae confessed, that after a while she became inured, feeling that they came with the territory, were simply a hazard of his celebrity. "There were so many of them and just one me," she said. "He always changed them. Of course, they had fun and enjoyed the good times and none of the bad, but somehow Sugar always tired of them and came home."

'Even Ray Junior witnessed his father's indiscretions. "My father would take me with him to various places where he hung

305 Sugar Ray Robinson with Dave Anderson *Sugar Ray* 1969

out," he remembered. "When he wasn't in training, he spent a lot of time with other civic leaders and businessmen such as Joseph Wells, Ed Smalls, who owned Small's Paradise, Red Randolph, owner of the Shalimar, just across the street from Dad's businesses, and underworld types like Bumpy Johnson. Sometimes he would drop me off with Bundini [Brown] at the Apollo or leave me in the lobby of the Theresa Hotel when Charlie Rangel was the desk clerk, while he went out and checked his 'traps', his various female partners."'[306]

'Paternity claims would surface during Robinson's career. Barbara Trevigne brought a paternity suit against Robinson claiming that he was the father of her six-year-old son. A court found in favour of Robinson even though he admitted he had been intimate with the woman.'[307]

Sugar Ray was not only cheating on Edna Mae, he was beating on Edna Mae. 'She often commented on his violent temper and how for the least little annoyance he would slap her. The abuse, which started as a slap here and there and escalated to violent punches, would continue – along with his infidelities – throughout their marriage. When Edna Mae miscarried at the time of the Rocky Castellani fight, which he won, she did not let him know until after the fight that she'd lost the baby.

'"I think one of the reasons my mother had so many miscarriages was because of the abuse she suffered from my father," Ray Junior said. "I can recall him hitting her on several occasions, often for no reason at all."'[308]

In April 1959, Ray's sister Marie, who had married Clyde Brewer, one of Ray's trainers, was diagnosed with cancer. The doctor told the family that she had only months to live. Ray sent for his father, who was living in Detroit, and he stayed with his son and Edna Mae. One morning, the champion started slapping his wife around and his father was forced to intervene before

---

306 Herb Boyd with Ray Robinson II *Pound for Pound* 2005

307 Kenneth Shropshire *Being Sugar Ray* 2007

308 Herb Boyd with Ray Robinson II *Pound for Pound* 2005

things got serious. While Ray was wrestling with his father, Edna Mae ran downstairs and phoned the local police precinct. Within minutes, two cops arrived, shocked to see it was 'Sugar Ray, the champ.' They all talked things over, Ray denied hitting his wife, gave the cops a tour of the house and drinks all round, which the officers of the law accepted. Edna Mae was asked not to press charges, and the boys in blue departed, happily clutching autographed photos of the champ. The mark of Ray's hand was still on Ednae Mae's face.

Ray's abusive behaviour continued until his bouts with Edna Mae began to resemble his sparring bouts in the gym. He was letting his punches go one day and she almost passed out when Ray Junior yelled at him to stop. When he did stop, to comfort the boy, Edna Mae ran into the kitchen and called for help. Ray's mother arrived in time to stop a further attack and Edna Mae grabbed the boy and hurried to a neighbour's house.

'Once Sugar left, his mother went to see about Edna Mae. She cringed at the sight of her daughter-in-law's face. Dr Arthur Logan was summoned, and he took one look at her battered face and rushed her to the hospital for treatment and X-rays. She was diagnosed with two concussions. After almost 20 years of marriage, infidelity after infidelity, years of abuse, and separation, she said, "I decided to get a divorce."'[309]

Writing in an issue of *Sport* magazine, Porter Wittich quoted William Shakespeare, 'saying, Nothing is good or bad, but thinking makes it so. If that's the case, Sugar Ray Robinson is the goodest-baddest man that ever lived. Attempting to study Robinson from every angle in order to find out what the man is really like, the magazine holds Sugar up to six mirrors, and the resulting reflection is a classic paradox. Sugar Ray is "the most charming rogue who ever held the middleweight championship of the world ... remote and completely unaware of anybody else's presence."

309 Herb Boyd with Ray Robinson II *Pound for Pound* 2005

'"...has the big smile, the soothing words and the jaunty demeanour of a quiz-show emcee." "...an ungrateful and treacherous heart lurks behind his suave front." "... Sugar Ray's charm is like a left hook." "He is the greatest fighter of his weight who ever lived."

'And maybe Robinson is probably best summed up by one of the public interviewed by *Sport,* "I hate his guts, but I go to see him every chance I get. They don't make 'em like that any more."

'Even among the Negro public, there is an ambivalent feeling about Robinson,' said *Sport.* "Jackie Robinson was an individualist, too," says a Negro, "but he was always helping other people fight their battles, too. When Sugar Ray fights a battle – even if it's about a racial slur to him – he's fighting only his battle. Once he has straightened everything out for himself, he's satisfied. Let the other Negroes fight their own battles." And so it goes with the public, the press, the promoters, the fighters, the managers, the friends – everywhere you turn, you're met by a different view of Sugar Ray.'[310]

In 1946, following the death from cancer of his close friend and fellow writer Damon Runyon, columnist and broadcaster Walter Winchell appealed to his radio audience for contributions to fight the disease. The response led Winchell to establish the Damon Runyon Cancer Memorial Fund. He led the charity – with the support of celebrities including Marlene Dietrich, Bob Hope, Milton Berle, Marilyn Monroe and Joe DiMaggio – until his own death from cancer in 1972.

In June 1950, just after Robinson had beaten Robert Villemain to become middleweight champion as recognised by the State of Pennsylvania (they had stripped LaMotta for failing to defend the title), 'One of my boyhood buddies had died of cancer,' recalled Sugar Ray in his autobiography. 'Spider Valentine, the skinny little guy I had helped up after I knocked him down in the 1939 Golden Gloves. I had to do something for Spider. I phoned Walter

310 Porter Wittich *Joplin Globe* Missouri 1 July 1958

Winchell, who was the chairman of the Damon Runyon Cancer Fund. I offered to donate my purse from a fight to the fund in memory of Spider.'

'"You'd really do that, Sugar Ray?" Winchell said. 'Yes, sir,' I replied. "My whole purse. But if it'll make you feel better, you can give me a dollar." "I always thought you were a tough man with a buck," he said. 'It depends what the buck is for, and I want to do this for cancer research.'[311]

The fight, for Ray's welterweight title, would take place on 9 August in Jersey City, with Charlie Fusari in the other corner. This was the fight for which Ray famously did, or didn't, make the 147-pound limit. With ounces to spare, the commission sanctioned the fight that would be Ray's last at welterweight. With a host of Winchell's Broadway pals at ringside, Robinson boxed Fusari 15 rounds. He got the decision and the fund got something like $100,000, including nearly $50,000 from Ray's purse. Sugar Ray did get a dollar! His beloved sister Marie would die of cancer in April 1959, aged 41.

'Winchell enlisted celebrities from Hollywood and Broadway – and Sugar Ray Robinson, who was another type of celebrity. "Winchell really wanted Sugar Ray for the fund," remembered Jess Rand, a young publicist at the time, who knew both Winchell and Runyon. For many, the two might well have seemed mismatched: Winchell so loud and ego driven, Robinson quiet and smooth.

But they got along, and Sugar Ray's name and nightclub appeared regularly in Winchell's column. Robinson had no intention of letting Winchell down in the fundraising efforts. The fighter would arrive in a city days before his bout, spend time raising money for the fund, whip his opponent more often than not and then, before leaving town, present a local hospital with a cheque for cancer research. Four months after Runyon's death, Winchell himself gave the American Cancer Society a $250,000 cheque. In

311 Wil Haygood *Sweet Thunder: The Life and Times of Sugar Ray Robinson* 2009

time, a board was formed on behalf of the fund; Winchell became its treasurer.[312]

'Sugar grew increasingly preoccupied with cancer and its causes and would support its elimination through various fundraising campaigns throughout his life. On 21 May 1951, Sugar arrived in Paris to fight Kid Marcel. Later, with the Marcel fight behind him, Sugar caused quite a stir at a reception when he kissed the wife of the president of France, twice on each cheek. At first, the action stunned the upper crust who'd witnessed Sugar's goodwill gesture. But they, like the first lady, Madame Vincent Auriol, quickly warmed to the occasion, and applauded after the champion placed a cheque for $10,000 from the Damon Runyon Memorial Fund in her hand. Despite his surprising loss to Randy Turpin, Sugar and his horde were loudly cheered upon their return to the States on the French liner *Liberte*. Hundreds turned out for ceremonies at City Hall and in Harlem to give him a hero's welcome. Sugar's speech was followed by remarks from Walter Winchell, who praised him for his numerous contributions to the Runyon cancer campaign, to which he had donated nearly $47,000 in proceeds from various bouts. At City Hall, the mayor presented him with a scroll citing him as one "whose interest in the welfare of his fellow human beings, as manifested in his varied activities as ambassador at large for the Damon Runyon Memorial Fund for Cancer Research, had secured the heartfelt appreciation of the people of the City of New York." Sugar stood next to his mother, while Edna Mae stood next to the mayor as they listened to music provided by the police department band and a serenade by the Police Athletic League Glee Club.'[313] As the guy said, 'Everywhere you turn, you're met by a different view of Sugar Ray.'

---

312 Sugar Ray Robinson with Dave Anderson *Sugar Ray* 1969

313 Herb Boyd with Ray Robinson II *Pound for Pound* 2005

21

PENDER DOES THE DOUBLE

IN THE summer of 1959, the wonderful world of Sugar Ray Robinson began to unravel. With his marriage now as rocky as ever, the death of his sister Marie from cancer was a knockout blow, and the National Boxing Association (NBA) had vacated the middleweight championship after Sugar refused to fight Carmen Basilio in a rubber match for which he had been offered a guaranteed half a million dollars. Insisting on more money, he declined the offer, and the next time he looked, the offer had disappeared. To rub salt in the wounds, Basilio and Gene Fullmer signed for a bout to determine the NBA champion. In a gruelling fight, the bigger, younger Fullmer stopped Basilio inside 14 rounds and when Robinson proposed a bout, he found the Mormon not interested. Neither was Basilio.

Sugar Ray was still the middleweight champ, but only in New York State and the state of Massachusetts. At least New York was still a good card to hold; the New England state was hardly an ace. Yet it was from the Boston suburb of Brookline that Robinson would find his next opponent. Boston promoter Sam Silverman offered a $70,000 guarantee to Sugar to defend his portion of the title against a guy named Paul Pender. 'Paul who?' Ray asked when George Gainford informed him of his next job.

Paul Pender was not even a household name in his own household. A thin, bent-nosed Irishman who was rated no better than sixth in the NBA ratings, he had a 35-5-2 record in ten years as a pro. But he had quit four times with damaged hands and had been stopped twice. A former fireman in Brookline, he was no four-alarm riot in the ring. He didn't even like boxing, according to an interview he gave to the *Boston Herald* while he was in training for the Robinson fight.

'Why should boxing as it is conducted today be allowed to continue?' he said. 'Recent investigations – I know they are true because I've kept my eyes open in this business – proved boxing is rotten clear through, infested by gangsters and thieves. The public has lost all confidence. I have too.' He suggested as a cure-all, a five-year suspension of professional boxing during which time the undesirable elements could be weeded out. 'After that period, pro boxing would start all over under the supervision of a tough board of control established by each state, responsible to the attorney general,' he suggested. Paul hastened to add, however, that the abolition of his profession should be held up until he gets his cheque for the Robinson fight.

'Pender spoke very highly of his own manager [Johnny Buckley Sr], "who treated me fairly and didn't try to rob me."'[314] Veteran Buckley had already handled two world champs in heavyweight Jack Sharkey and Lou Brouillard, welterweight and NBA middleweight champion. He figured he had another in Paul Pender.

Pender's remarks did not sit well with the Massachusetts Boxing Commission and he was quickly summoned to explain his allegations. Chairman Hermann Greenberg said, 'that if he presents evidence of wrongdoing in Massachusetts, the attorney general will be called in.' But when Pender stood before the commission, he told a different story, saying, 'A sports writer had written the article to make it sensational.' He added he had agreed with the writer's suggestion that a five-year abolishment of boxing would be a remedy for its ills. 'I felt I was talking off the cuff,'

314 *Bennington Evening Banner* Vermont 23 December 1959

Pender said. 'I never anticipated the story. The whole idea was misconstrued.'[315]

While Paul Pender was in the papers saying all the wrong things, Sugar Ray was in the papers doing the right things. In Boston a few days before the fight, Ray was working out in a shop window, at least the first-floor display window of Raymond's Department Store on downtown Washington Street, watched by at least a thousand good citizens of Beantown, and also helping the March of Dimes charity campaign.

Before leaving New York, after his final workout at Harry Wiley's uptown gym, Robinson said, 'I expect to surprise a lot of people who figure I'm washed up. Let me tell you this. I'm in 100 per cent better condition right now than when I won back the title from Carmen Basilio.'

With the title bout set for 22 January, Sam Silverman put his two headliners on a preview show at the Boston Garden, Pender coasting to a decision over Gene Hamilton while Sugar Ray followed him into the ring to shed some rust against Bob Young, the New England light-heavyweight champion. Ray figured to get a few rounds under his belt, but Mr Young forgot his manners and smacked Ray a hard one in round one. Bob didn't see the end of round two. The United Press reported, 'Robinson, 39 years old according to the *Ring Record Book*, confesses to only 38. But he looked like a 20-year-old as he handily outclassed Young. Ray floored Young for a six-count with a left hook, seconds after the second round began. He put Young down once more for a no-count and once for a seven count, before landing a long left to the side of Young's head for the clincher. It was bout number 151 for Ray. He has lost only six times in two decades of fighting and was stopped only once.'[316]

'I've had my hands busted seven times,' the guy was saying, 'the right four times, the left three. I'm no longer a kid. All I

315 *Monroe News Star* Louisiana 30 December 1959

316 *Sarasota Herald Tribune* Florida 15 December 1959

want is to take home a bundle and call it quits. The other guys can have the glory.'[317] This was Paul Pender, the guy who was going to fight Sugar Ray Robinson, all-time super champion. This was January 1960 and maybe Sugar Ray was no longer the guy they were writing about when reviewing the fight at the Boston Garden, where promoter Sam Silverman was hoping for a crowd of 12,000 and receipts of $125,000. With a television blackout of a 100-mile radius, there would be a $100,000 TV-radio fee to sweeten the pot. As champion, Ray was getting most of the sugar – 42½ per cent of the net gate and 75 per cent of the net TV-radio money. His total purse was expected to exceed $120,000. Pender, who was getting 20 per cent of the gate and 12½ percent of the net TV-radio fund, was expected to wind up with at least $35,000. His largest previous purse was $6,000, losing to Joe Rindone. Things were looking better already.

'Robinson seemed to be trying to end the fight in a hurry as he went after Pender in the first round,' reported Associated Press. 'However the local boy was blocking his hooks to the head and jabbing before falling into a clinch. A right to the body by Robinson almost crumbled Pender. Sugar Ray continued to apply pressure in the second but his rights were beginning to sail over Pender's head. Robinson drove home a left hook just as the bell rang and the crowd booed.

'In the third, Pender's defence became more effective as he blocked off Robinson's hooks.

'Pender took over in the fourth and fifth, jabbing and cuffing Robinson on the back of the head as they went into a clinch. A Pender right shook up Robinson just before the bell. But Robinson resumed his body attack in the sixth, ineffective as it seemed to be, and Pender began to grab more and more. There were boos in the eighth and ninth as both slowed down to a walk.'[318]

---

317 Nat Loubert *The Ring* April 1960

318 *Winnipeg Tribune* 23 January 1960

'Cautiously jabbing and moving away from Robinson in the early stages Friday night,' wrote Bob Hoobing, 'Pender made Sugar miss long right hands labelled kayo, then became more forceful in the late stages. He landed effectively on Robinson's head while protecting his own. Robinson landed his most solid blows to Pender's body. Pender, bleeding from a cut under the left eyebrow from the seventh round on, had six stitches to close the wound. While the 10,608 Boston Garden fans knew Pender in his moments of triumph, many a member of the national television audience wanted to know who was this brash upstart who unseated the ageless Sugar Ray. Pender, who says he'd love a crack at Fullmer but must take care of his obligations with Robinson first, studied the man he beat for ten years.

'"He's lived with Robinson all that time," said trainer Al Lacey. "I don't mean as a roommate, but in his mind he's gone over and over Robinson's every move. He's admired his style and now after such careful study he knows Robinson better than anyone in the game."'[319]

'Judge Joe Santoro, whose vote was announced first, called it 147-138 in favour of Pender. Then referee Joe Zupastas' ballot for Robinson, 146-142, was announced. Judge John Norton's call of 148-142 in favour of Pender drew cheers for the new champion. An Associated Press ringside poll found the writers favouring the loser 15-12. Robinson, hampered by inactivity, missed his big punches and failed to score with his combinations of old. After the final bell, the two fighters exchanged a few words in the ring. Pender, in his dressing room, said he told Robinson, "Sugar, you were getting tired on me." According to Pender, Robinson replied, "Well, I'm getting old."'[320]

'Paul Pender, the ex-fireman and boxing critic who won Sugar Ray Robinson's chunk of the world middleweight crown Friday night on an amazing upset decision, said today he is willing to

---

319 Bob Hoobing *Colorado Springs Gazette* 23 January 1960

320 Jack Hand *Cumberland News* Maryland 23 January 1960

give Ray a return shot at the title on 1 April, if the fight is held in Boston. Robinson, who claims the 90-day contract gives him the right to pick the site, insists that the bout be staged in New York. Although Robinson appeared off form, after 22 months of comparative inactivity, the once-great fighter from New York claimed Friday night's 15-rounder was just what he needed to sharpen him for an April fight. On at least two occasions, he had the speedy 29-year-old Brookline boxer in serious trouble, but he lacked the stamina and accuracy to finish Pender.'[321]

'By the time we got into the ring at the Boston Garden,' recalled Robinson, 'Pender had put together ten consecutive victories. To my surprise, he made it 11. Joe Zapustas scored eight rounds for me, only four for Pender, with three even. The judges voted for Pender. One of them somehow gave him 11 rounds for flicking his jab at me and running away. I had to admire Pender's ability to run. For the first time, I was in with a man who had better legs than I had, but he used them to run instead of fight. "Robbery!" roared George in the dressing room. "It's worse than the Brinks robbery." "Forget it, George," I told him. "I've won a lot of split decisions over the years."'[322]

Nat Loubert of *The Ring* was in Ray's dressing room after the fight and he wanted to know about the future. '"I have a 90-days return clause contract which I will be ready to take up and I'm certain Pender will honour it. There's a clause giving me the right to choose the date and place and I assure you it won't be in Boston. We will have our return early in May in New York, in Madison Square Garden, and the sooner the better." George Gainford, in a bitter attack against the judges who voted for Pender, aptly said, "You know Sugar has loaned out his title before. He'll regain it, that's my firm conviction."

'Johnny Buckley, manager of Pender, when informed of Robinson's statement, declared, "We had to go to extremes to

---

321 Jack Cuddy *Morgantown Dominion News* 23 January 1960

322 Sugar Ray Robinson with Dave Anderson *Sugar Ray* 1969

get this fight and now we are sitting in the driver's seat and we will do the dictating, no matter what the contract says. We will give Ray a return but it will take place in the Boston Garden, not in New York."'[323]

'Right now,' Robinson was telling Sam Lacy of the *Baltimore Afro-American,* 'I intend to seek the rematch I'm entitled to under the contract. But tomorrow, my mind may be changed. I could decide to go through with the challenge to Gene Fullmer. I could close for a fight with Archie Moore. Then again, I just may sack it all. I have a lot of decisions to make. I just laid off too long, I guess. The kid was bent on staying with me and I ran out of gas. It was one of those things you have to live with in my business.'[324]

The rematch was scheduled for 29 April back in the Boston ring and Sugar Ray knew he needed work. Big George signed him for a ten-round bout with Tony Baldoni in Baltimore on 2 April, but if Ray was looking for a stiff workout he was looking the wrong way. The Wilkes-Barre Italian was now living in Baltimore, had been a fighter since 1948, but had only won three fights over the last four years. He fought only three bouts in 1959, losing two by knockout. As one reporter noted, Sugar Ray probably got a stiffer workout fighting his way into the local Coliseum.

Before he took on Baldoni, he was forced to battle his way through a surging mob that stormed the place a full hour and a half before time for the feature event. The main go went on at 10.32pm but long before the principals left their dressing rooms, a police detail had to be set up outside to control the would-be customers. By 9.15pm, cops and firemen were sifting out the holders of tickets and turning away all who had not already bought ducats. Inside, there was utter confusion. Ringside patrons dealt frustration to a harried usher corps by plopping into the first available seats. Summed up, Baltimore's first 'big-time' fight in

323 Nat Loubert *The Ring* April 1960

324 Sam Lacy *Baltimore Afro-American* 26 January 1960

eight years was sheer chaos. From the Monroe Street curb line to ring centre and back.

The fight was no fight. 'Baldoni was clearly overmatched, a stationary target for Robinson's left jab, and was hurt each time Sugar Ray threw his right. The Harlem Dandy, in fact, tossed only two right hands. The first, to the kidney, dropped Tony to his knee for an eight count. The second laid him flat on his back for a count that could have gone to 28. Referee Benny Goldstein ended maters at 1.40 of round one. That's all, folks.

'"This is murder," the former middleweight king moaned as he greeted reporters. "I wanted so much to get in some good, hard work tonight. I need it. I need a working fight. How else can I get ready for 29 April? I was told this fellow was tough. It made me think he'd give me the work I need. Instead, I wind up scared he won't get up. I suppose the only thing I can do now is go back in the gym, work like hell, and hope for the best. But you just can't get the kind of action you need in the gym."'[325]

A few weeks later, the sports pages were running headlines like:

'SUGAR RAY ROBINSON IN DISAPPEARING ACT' – 'RAY ROBINSON FAILS TO SHOW FOR FIGHT.' SUGAR RAY ROBINSON: BIG FIST, LITTLE CONSCIENCE.'

In Baltimore's *Afro-American* newspaper, Sam Lacy wrote, 'I have said here many times in the past that, in my opinion, Sugar Ray Robinson was the greatest athlete in a given field I had had the pleasure of observing in my long tour of the sports beat. I also have said here many times that he can be one of the most disgusting figures one is compelled to meet in this business when he wants to be, which is more often than not. I was further convinced of how right I was on the latter score by his performance at the Maryland Athletic Commission hearing last week.

325 *Baltimore Afro-American* 5 April 1960

'Robinson was summoned to Baltimore by a state boxing commission irked by his failure to appear for a scheduled fight with Pedro Gonzales last Monday night. He came with the air of a man annoyed by the audacity of the small-time body which presumed to think it could question his behaviour. By the time he reached the hearing room, he was in a fighting mood, or pretended he was. Robinson berated the press, lambasted the promoter and castigated the commission. He did not once claim that he or any of his cronies tried to reach the Baltimore promoter to say he wouldn't show. His manager, Gainford, asserted he wanted to call the promoter long distance "but I had no phone number". Hogwash! The whole Robinson crowd knows it could have telephoned *Baltimore Afro-American (newspaper)* and the contact would have been made, happily and without hesitation.

'That would have spared some fans the disappointment of going to the stadium expecting to see him, but fans aren't important to Robinson apparently, no more important than small-time boxing commissions and little-league promoters.' [326]

'At one point in the hearing, Robinson almost came to blows with promoter Al Flora. They squared off and were about to exchange punches when friends pulled them apart. Sugar Ray had just yelled at Flora, who was on the witness stand, "You're a damned liar!" Then, turning away, Robinson had said, "For two cents, I'd bust him one." The decision of the commission was that the licence of Ray Robinson to box within the state of Maryland is hereby suspended.'[327]

There were fears that the suspension would block the Pender-Robinson rematch, now scheduled for 10 June, but the Massachusetts commission stated that Maryland was a member of the National Boxing Association and Massachusetts was not. The NBA's middleweight champion was Gene Fullmer, not Pender, and the NBA had refused to honour a suspension

326 Sam Lacy *Baltimore Afro-American* 28 May 1960

327 *Aiken Standard and Review* South Carolina 20 May 1960

of Fullmer in Boston. Also, the Pender-Robinson rematch was signed many months before Robinson's commitment at Baltimore. The local fight had already been postponed once, from 29 April, and changes had been made to TV and radio coverage. A second postponement would be a major financial blow to boxing in Boston. The fight would go ahead, on 10 June, for Pender's two-state version of the world middleweight championship. Ray got his return bout in the Garden, but this Garden was in Boston, not in his beloved New York City. And there were two restraining orders tying up the entire gate receipts, something Robinson was used to by now. Only this time it wasn't Uncle Sam and his revenue agents.

One restraining order resulted from a suit by Nunzio Camiollo, who was seeking 20 per cent of the net gate profits as an alleged 20 per cent partner in Silverman's promoting organisation. The other order was issued at the behest of the Charles Centre Boxing Club of Baltimore and asked only $9,000 for Robinson's failure to go through with a scheduled tune-up fight at Baltimore on 16 May. Robinson, Silverman and the Massachusetts Boxing Commission were defendants in that suit.

Watching the fight on a television set in the lobby of a hotel in Oakland, California, some 3,000-odd miles away, would be Sugar Ray's 21-year-old son, Ronnie. The son of the illustrious Sugar Ray currently was in Oakland as a member of the New York Chiefs, a roller derby team. Alan Ward, sports editor of the *Oakland Tribune,* chatted with the slender young man. 'Ronnie – his official given name is Ronald – has no boxing background, hasn't the slightest desire to be a part of boxing, becomes jittery when watching dad fight and hopes Sugar will regain his championship.

'"Naturally," said personable young Ronnie Robinson, "I'm prejudiced. He's my father." Jerry Lokay, drum beater for the roller derby, sat with Ronnie at the luncheon and between bites sang the praises of the youngster. "The derby didn't sign the kid because he was Sugar Ray's son. Names aren't important in our sport. Ronnie is fast. His reflexes are quick. He is a natural sprinter, a point getter. He can block, too, surprising in a 140-pounder. He has a fine future with us if he hangs on. I imagine he will."

'Even if he had had an inclination to box, Ronnie explained Sugar Ray would have discouraged it. "Pop said one boxer in the family was enough. I admire Mr Pender, although I've never met him. He is a fine boxer. It would be nice were my father to become champion again."'[328]

The morning after their first fight, Sugar Ray told reporters, 'I thought I won. Next time I'll make sure of it by knocking him out.' Sadly, it was the Sugarman himself who looked ready for the ten count when the rematch got under way in Boston. 'Although Pender had to be content with another split verdict, he beat the nearly washed-up Sugar Ray far more impressively this time,' reported Jack Cuddy for United Press. 'It seemed from the sixth to the 14th round that Robinson would be knocked out instead of merely outpointed. Sugar Ray appeared completely helpless in the clinches – and they were in clinches through the fight.

'Pender pulled and hauled and clubbed the back of Sugar Ray's head and his body with short rights in every round and the once-great Robinson, 39 or 40, wilted until it seemed he might collapse from exhaustion. Thus it was that Robinson suffered for the first time the loss of a rematch.

'Pender won the decision when judge James Carrig favoured him 149-138 and judge John Savko agreed, 147-142. But referee Jimmy McCarron had Robinson ahead 146-144. McCarron explained later to reporters that he had taken "some points" away from Pender because of his "rabbit punching" to the back of Robinson's head.'[329]

'A crowd of 8,422 paid a gross gate of $67,656, much lower than had been anticipated. After the contest Robinson, as usual the perfect sportsman, had no excuses. Obviously very disappointed at the outcome, he declared, "I wasn't rusty. I just didn't have

328 Alan Ward *Oakland Tribune* California 10 June 1960

329 Jack Cuddy *Provo Herald* Utah 12 June 1960

enough to win. I thought I had him going in the fifth when I caught him with a right to the jaw, but couldn't follow up quickly enough." Robinson seemed near exhaustion, and once missed with a wild right swing that sent him sagging over the top rope, seemingly too weary to extricate himself. It was humiliating, and the crowd were hushed, realising that they might be watching Ray for the last time."[330]

In the lobby of a hotel in Oakland, California after watching the fight on television, a subdued 21-year-old Ronnie Robinson quietly hoped he was watching his father for the last time in a boxing ring.

330 *Boxing News* London 14 June 1960

22

THE LAST CHANCE SALOON

A COUPLE of weeks after the Pender fight, Ronnie Robinson was on his way to Honolulu with the New York Chiefs, eagerly looking forward to the visit. He was disappointed to read in his newspaper that Sugar Ray was now angling for a fight with NBA champion Gene Fullmer in what would be their third meeting. Ray, the comeback king, would be aiming to win the title for the sixth time, at the age of 39.

Fullmer had just stopped Carmen Basilio for the second time and manager Marv Jenson was looking at a handful of offers for his champion. Wealthy mink rancher Joe Dupler, president of the Intermountain Boxing Club, offered Fullmer a guarantee 'of more than a $100,000' to meet Robinson in Salt Lake City. There already was an offer of $100,000 on the table for Fullmer to defend his title against Joey Giambra in San Francisco. Gene told reporters he would be willing to fight Robinson, anywhere but New York City. Jenson said that if the Fullmer-Robinson fight came off, the terms would have to be on a champion-challenger basis, a 40 per cent cut for Fullmer and 20 per cent for Robinson.

The fight was signed for 8 October with Cal Eaton, George Parnassus, and Norm Rothschild, promoting at the Sports Arena in Los Angeles, hoping for a crowd of 17,000 and gate receipts of $125,000. Robinson set up camp at Gilman Hot Springs, where his somewhat reduced entourage settled in. Edna Mae wasn't there but his mother was, along with George, Harry Wiley, June Clark, Honey Brewer and his new girlfriend, Millie Bruce, the girl he had met when in Los Angeles on showbusiness. Columnist Bob Kelley would write in the *Long Beach Press Telegram*, 'At training camp Sunday, Ray wowed many of the Southland sportswriters. After seeing that members of his "official party" had carefully collected four bits to park and 90 cents to get in to watch him train, Robinson stepped into the ring. Every time he landed a punch, Sugar's well-trained sparring mate let out a grunt, a groan. The fans loved it, the sportswriters loved it. Robinson played his little show to the hilt. Robinson candidly admits he isn't boxing many rounds in preparation for Fullmer. When you ask him why he isn't over-working, Sugar has an answer for that, too. "If I am going to beat Fullmer, it will be with my brain."

'Maybe Robbie figures he has only so much left in the old legs. All I know is that he's one of the most glamorous athletes of our time. It will be a pity to see him leave the scene, after Fullmer licks him. But don't bet on it.'[331]

If Fullmer was going to lick Sugar Ray, he would have to wait two months for the chance. A few days before the fight, the NBA champion suffered a torn calf muscle in a sparring bout. He was examined by two doctors while two of Robinson's physicians looked on, much to the annoyance of Fullmer's manager, Jenson. A new date was set for the fight, 3 December. 'I was so upset with the news that I felt like the whole world fell down on me,' said Robinson. 'Believe me, I was in top condition for this one. I feel I know Sugar Ray Robinson the best, so I know in my heart I was ready to prove that I was still a champion – not a has-been.'[332]

So it was back to the drawing board. When Ray resumed training at Gilman Hot Springs, it was Willie Orner's old place that had just been purchased by lightweight contender Cisco Andrade. A week before the fight, George Gainford, the veteran New York boxing figure who was known as 'The Emperor' and

331 Bob Kelley *Press Telegram* Long Beach California 1 October 1960

332 *Newport Daily News* Rhode Island 4 October 1960

who had been with Ray since he was a skinny teenager in Harlem, was telling reporters, 'Just a few more sparring drills and Ray will be ready.' The former champion was still attracting big crowds to his workouts and the experts agreed that he looked as sharp as he did when he was getting ready for Bobo Olson in 1956.

From Los Angeles: 'Ray Robinson will have to knock out Gene Fullmer within five rounds if he is to capture the NBA version of the world middleweight championship. That was the consensus today as the two battlers took matters easy and speculation continued over their 15-round fight to be nationally televised Saturday night in the Sports Arena. Close observers of Robinson in his boxing drills at Gilman Hot Springs, 70 miles east of here, feel that the 39-year-old New York veteran still packs a lethal left hook. There is some doubt about what was once the most feared left-right combination in the business, and the once-fine right-hand punch. The only knockout in Fullmer's career was registered by Robinson in five rounds in 1957. "No, it was not a lucky punch," the victim recalled. "It was well timed, well executed," Fullmer, 29, from West Jordan, Utah, smiled. "I don't say he can't do it again because he can, but I'll be a little more alert and cautious, knowing what he can do."[333]

Wondering if Sugar Ray still could do it, a crowd of 13,465 paid a gross gate of $122,584 at the box office that Saturday in December 1960, and they got good value for their dollars. They saw a gruelling 15-round contest and for most of those 15 rounds they saw the Robinson of old, not an old Robinson. They saw a Robinson who impressed referee Tommy Hart so much that he awarded Ray the fight by 11-4. Judge Lee Grossman called it for Fullmer by 9-5. The scoring of judge George Latka, 8-8, meant Fullmer retained his title with the drawn decision.

'Ray Robinson, the miracle man of boxing, almost made it,' Nat Fleischer recorded in his magazine *The Ring* in February 1961. 'In a terrific battle, in which heavy hitting, mauling, wild

333 *Brainerd Daily Dispatch* Minnesota 2 December 1960

bull rushes and bruises were quite prominent, the man who held the world middleweight title five times missed by an eyelash adding the National Boxing Association championship to his wonderful achievements. So far as Sugar Ray and the majority of the spectators were concerned, Robinson succeeded in reaching his goal but the record book will not show it. How such wide a variance could be tabbed by three experts is something that few who witnessed the bout in the vast arena, or saw it on the national television hook-up, could understand. I scored it nine rounds to six and 11 points to seven for Ray.

'As for Ray, he gave his finest performance in the past four years, one which definitely should have been good enough to have earned him the honours had the officials all been on the ball. At least that was the consensus not only of the majority of the spectators but of the ringside reporters who, by a margin of more than three to one, had Sugar Ray on top. Never in his long career of two decades had Sugar Ray trained so faithfully and come into the ring so well prepared for the task ahead of him. Though his punches lacked the steam of old and his ring cleverness was short of the beauty of the past, he still exhibited sufficient ring savvy to offset the bull rushes and the pawing punches of his powerfully built opponent.'

'Robinson had his man shaken in the fourth and 11th rounds from blistering all-out attacks that belied his age, and finished strongly, something that critics said just couldn't happen. In comparison, Fullmer was crude and didn't take advantage of being ten years younger. Gene had no style. He normally relies a lot on his stamina, but even this was evident only in patches. He failed to do what he was most expected to do, that is crowd his man and weaken him with body punches.

'Fullmer's best round was the ninth. He came forward throwing lefts and rights to head and body that made Sugar Ray back up. Then good combination punching doubled up Robinson in the tenth. That was the signal for the critics to nod wisely and say to each other, "This must be the end of Robinson. He'll fade now." And that's where Ray fooled 'em. He came back with a terrific rally in the 11th and had Fullmer wobbling to his corner. If Ray had clinched that last round, then he must have clinched the title.'[334]

'Fullmer had remembered the left hook I had nailed him with in Chicago,' recalled Ray, 'and that's all he seemed to be concerned about. Throughout the 15 rounds, he had his right forearm high, protecting his jaw from my left hook. I was disgusted with the decision, but my 20 per cent came to nearly $50,000.'[335]

Gene Fullmer remembered more than the Chicago left hook. 'Once, when my manager and I tried to call him for a fight, he asked, "Gene Fullmer? Who's he?" Fullmer and his manager, Marv Jenson, said they're giving the same answer to Robinson. "Gene's next fight," Jenson was saying, "could be either Archie Moore here for the light-heavyweight championship or Hank Casey in San Francisco, we don't know which yet. But as for Ray Robinson, we're through with him."'[336]

Three months later, though, Robinson was fighting Fullmer again, this time in Las Vegas at the Convention Center, again for the NBA title that many thought Ray deserved to win in their Los Angeles fight, which ended in a controversial draw. For Sugar Ray, this could be the last throw of the dice in the gambling city in the Nevada desert, yet there was little betting on the fight.

'Fullmer has been the 8-5 favourite since the fight was announced. Even those who hollered that Robinson was robbed in the title draw in December are not putting much money on the challenger. On the other hand, there are not too many willing to bet on Fullmer, on the basis of his showings against Robinson, Joe Giardello and Spider Webb. The main reason for this is the fact that Robinson has shown so little in his workouts here. He has done little roadwork, boxed very little and concentrated on hamming it up with the movie, radio and TV personalities in this resort city. Fullmer hasn't shown too much himself. But he's nine or ten years Robinson's junior, and he's stronger, better conditioned and the champ.

---

334 *Boxing News* London December 1960

335 Sugar Ray Robinson with Dave Anderson *Sugar Ray* 1969

336 *Salt Lake Tribune* Salt Lake City 4 March 1961

'The NBA champion is strong and determined to make up for his ordinary showing in Los Angeles. Fullmer has said many times he intends to call this fight his own way. This is the first time the champion has outvoted manager Marv Jenson since the May 1957 fight in Chicago when Robinson regained the title. Then Fullmer went out after a kayo and found one, unexpectedly. This offers probably the only room for conjecture in the fight.'[337]

'Sugar Ray Robinson, a once-very-sweet fighter who was once a very-sour entertainer, is in training to fight a tin-ear guy name of Gene Fullmer,' wrote sports editor George Ross in the *Oakland Tribune.* 'But Sugar Ray's heart may not be in it. He'd still rather be a song-and-dance man. This all came out in Las Vegas, where the training is going on and where the fight will be held Saturday between halves of the evening keno game. A gentleman in charge of Robinson publicity – a fighter who travels with his own golf pro surely can't go without his own sports writer – lays it out candidly. "Sugar Ray still insists that he never wanted to be a fighter as a youngster. His first and lasting interest is in dancing. It's a career he has pursued sporadically during the past ten years."

'Well, I'm all for the arts, but if it's Ray Robinson, I wish he'd have stuck to fighting. While he was working at it full time, there wasn't a guy in the business had any business being in with him. Now he's 40 – his personal sports writer says 39 but who believes sports writers – an age when both dancing and fighting are pastimes for kids. This man has been fighting – between dances – for 21 years. What keeps Sugar going? Money. Eight years ago, he was in Las Vegas to pick up $25,000 as a song-and-dance man at the Sahara Hotel. This took two weeks. Saturday night he'll get into the ring with Fullmer for the fourth time, work maybe an hour and pick up maybe $100,000.'[338]

'The Gene Fullmer-Sugar Ray Robinson fight for the NBA middleweight title will be staged tonight as scheduled – but in

337 John Mooney *Salt Lake Tribune* Salt Lake City Utah 4 March 1961

338 George Ross *Oakland Tribune* California 1 March 1961

an 18ft ring instead of a 16-footer as a result of Robinson's threat to pull out of the bout unless the change was made. Sugar Ray, who during his 20-year ring career has floored almost as many promoters as opponents by his withdrawals, announced Friday night he would pack his equipment and leave for New York today if the promoters insisted upon making him fight the bull-necked Fullmer in a "telephone booth." Robinson's demand threatened to send the $300,000 fight down the drain. Robinson's ultimatum burst like an artillery shell in the press room at the Riviera Hotel and caused many quick conferences among co-promoters Norman Rothschild, Jack Doyle and Mel Greb, as well as among members of the Nevada State Commission.'[339]

The size of the ring was reported as anything from 16ft 7in to 18ft. Robinson sent Gainford to the arena to measure the battle pit and George reported 16ft 7in. Sugar Ray, after quoting the commission rule book calling for a 20ft ring, demanded a ring be shipped in from Los Angeles. The new ring arrived, was erected the day of the fight, and would be reported as only 17ft in *The Ring* magazine. Gainford measured it with a carpenter's steel tape and told Ray it was '20ft on the nose.'

'Some time later,' Robinson claimed in his autobiography, 'I discovered that the ring had not been 20ft after all. Al Buck of the *New York Post* had measured it himself. "It was 17ft," he told me. "Then why did George say 20?" "Because the tape was at the 20ft mark, but three feet had been sheared out of the tape and the two ends had been soldered together to fool George on purpose. When the tape was stretched out, it looked like 20ft, but it was only 17." "Only in Las Vegas," I said.'[340]

Ray was further upset when the commissioner ruled that eight-ounce gloves were used in Nevada and he couldn't box in six-ounce gloves, despite Fullmer's agreement on the gloves. What everyone did agree on was the tremendous performance put up by the veteran Sugar Ray.

339 *Scottsdale Daily Progress* Arizona 4 March 1961

340 Sugar Ray Robinson with Dave Anderson *Sugar Ray* 1969

'Gene Fullmer, NBA middleweight champion, kept his title Saturday with a rough, close-quarter mauling attack that hammered out a unanimous 15-round decision over gallant old Sugar Ray Robinson. Despite his 40 years, slender Robinson started off as if to give Fullmer the licking of his life in the first two rounds. But brawly, bull-shouldered Gene weathered these two sessions and came slamming back to stagger Sugar Ray in the third, knock him into the ropes and continue to batter him after a very weak ring bell sounded. That was the beginning of a triumph of brute force over ageing ring guile. Fullmer's explosiveness saw Sugar Ray battered into near helplessness at times and forced him to hold on until the referee could separate them. 'Fullmer had Ray hurt again in the seventh round when he buckled his knees with a left hook to the head and battled him into a corner. The crowd gave Robinson a tremendous ovation after the dramatic 15th round in which he staggered Fullmer twice with a left hook to the head and then with a right to the same target. Although Fullmer won the unanimous decision, he was much the worse for wear at the finish. He was bleeding from a gash over his left eye, which was swollen almost completely shut. He also was bleeding from the nose and his right cheek was highly puffed. Robinson suffered a slight cut at the corner of his left eye in the tenth round. Robinson suffered his ninth defeat in 156 bouts, although his performance left little doubt that the once-great Sugar Man's fancy-dancing legs are somewhat gone. He was unable to muster enough stamina, despite the use of oxygen in his corner between rounds, to sustain a damaging attack against Gene.'[341]

'Ray declared that he was defeated by the failure of the commission to give him a larger ring.' reported Nat Fleischer in *The Ring* magazine. '"I didn't have a chance to move around as I'm accustomed to and that was why Fullmer was able to corner me so often and to pin me against the ropes." Ray was the victim of a terrific shellacking in the third round. In that frame, the NBA champ went all out in an effort to clinch the verdict via the

341 Jack Cuddy *Provo Herald* Utah 4 March 1961

knockout route. It appeared he would succeed as he had Robinson pressed against the ropes, and tossed 22 consecutive lefts and rights to the midsection and head without Robinson returning one blow. Ray didn't fire a punch. After the bell had sounded, with neither the referee nor the fighters hearing it, Gene delivered six more. How Ray withstood that heavy bombardment, few could fathom. He proved in that one round that he had conditioned himself for the goal he had set, but condition wasn't sufficient to turn the tide. Thereafter, Fullmer went on to win as he had planned – by applying pressure, rushing with his head down like a bull and whaling away every time the pair came in close.'[342]

'Manager Marv Jenson, although despising Sugar Ray Robinson as a man, admitted Saturday night that he still had a lot of respect for the Sugarman's ability as a fighter. "Sugar Ray is a marvel the way he stood up under Gene's battering for 15 rounds and was still able to fight at the end," he said. "I'm very serious when I say I'm glad Gene didn't have to fight him in his prime."'[343]

In a sidebar to his column in the *Las Vegas Sun,* George King noted, 'Gene Fullmer is still the middleweight champion – and deservedly so – but Sugar Ray Robinson was the hero of the TV fight fans throughout the country who admire sheer, unadulterated guts. James Deskin, a member of the Nevada State Athletic Commission, became so exasperated over Sugar Ray's temperamental outbursts over the size of the ring and his threats to run out on the fight, he finally yelled at George Gainford, Robinson's manager, "As far as I'm concerned, you can put Robinson on a bus and send him back to New York." Deskin shouted those words around 2am Saturday morning after hours of wrangling. Adjoining seats were set aside at ringside for Rocky Marciano and Joe Louis but neither of the former heavyweight champions were on hand for the bout.'[344]

The old guys missed a helluva fight.

---

342 Nat Fleischer *The Ring* May 1961

343 Ray Schwartz *Provo Herald* Utah 5 March 1961

344 George King *Las Vegas Sun* 6 March 1961

23
STILL CHASING THE TITLE

IN THE 12-month span from September 1961 to September 1962, headlines jumping off the sports pages did not make Ray Robinson look too sweet.

MOYER HAMMERS SUGAR RAY – Underdog wins 10-round decision; SUGAR RAY LOSES TO PHIL MOYER; SUGAR RAY OUTPOINTED BY YOUNG BRITON TERRY DOWNES.

Six months after Gene Fullmer thrashed him in their last NBA title fight, Robinson climbed into the ring in his native city Detroit to go ten rounds with Wilfie Greaves, middleweight champion of Canada, in the new Convention Centre. Both Ray and Greaves staged a training programme outdoors at the suburban Northland Shopping Centre. 'I'm a ham,' Ray told the local reporters. 'I'd like to win the championship again before I quit boxing.'

His chances didn't look very good in there with the Edmonton brawler. Greaves shambled forward throwing wide lefts and rights during most of the fight as Robinson tried to straighten him up with wide uppercuts followed by combinations. Greaves seemed hesitant on several occasions to mix it up. He did catch Robinson with a wild right in the sixth and Sugar buckled and hung on. In the eighth, Greaves sank home a whistling left hook to the belly just before the bell. Robinson sank in pain, his hands clutching the midsection, along the ropes near Greaves' corner. Referee Lew Handler counted to one as the bell rang. 'Sugar put on his best flurry at the start of the ninth round, twice staggering Greaves, 16 years his junior. Robinson unleashed a series of lefts and mixed in a couple of stinging right crosses that buckled Greaves' knees. At the final bell, the former champ had a split decision victory.'[345]

Then it was back to his training camp at Greenwood Lake to get ready for Denny Moyer. 'I'm back shooting for the middleweight championship again,' chirped the irrepressible Sugar Ray as he prepared to break camp. 'I'm a prizefighter and at this stage in the game, I've got to prove it all over again. As soon as I win, everyone will be back on my side. A lot of promoters are interested in me.'

'Sugar Ray Robinson goes back into Madison Square Garden on Saturday night still blithely certain that somewhere just ahead there is another shot at the middleweight crown,' wrote UPI columnist Oscar Fraley. 'But don't sell Robinson short as he preps for Saturday's not-too demanding engagement with 22-year-old Denny Moyer of Portland. In this one, at least, he doesn't have much worry against a youngster of only 35 bouts who is neither a knockout puncher nor a punishing hitter. That's why Robinson is the 9-5 choice. They have warned him to stay away from such as body-busting Florentino Fernandez, the clouting Cuban who almost flattened Fullmer in August. For at 41, Sugar Ray doesn't have either the old speed or the power of yesteryear. Sugar Ray is, like ancient Archie Moore, an ageing leading man still playing "heavy" roles. They are the only two left from the pre-television era whose names still are magic at the box office. They are awash in the same canoe, a couple of Spencer Tracys acting like Andy Hardy.'[346]

'Sugar Ray Robinson, the 41-year-old Methuselah of the ring, outpointed baby-faced Denny Moyer of Portland, Oregon, in an action-packed ten-round bout in Madison Square Garden.

345 *Danville Bee* Virgina 26 September 1961

346 Oscar Fraley *Eureka Humboldt Standard* California 16 October 1961

Robinson, who turned professional 21 years ago when Moyer was just a year old, won the verdict of all three officials, but not the crowd of 7,800, who jeered the decision. Moyer, who weighed 157 and is 19 years Robinson's junior, made a good fight of it. He showed no awe for the five-time world middleweight champion and was perfectly willing to mix it up. There were no knockdowns and both fighters came out of the fray without a scratch. But Moyer did stagger Robinson with a right to the head in the fourth.

'Although the fans in the Garden greeted the decision with mingled cheers and boos, matchmaker Teddy Brenner disclosed, "Our television sponsors report that TV stations which carried the fight were swamped with phone calls of protest against the decision." A poll of 13 sportswriters at ringside had five favouring Moyer, four scoring for Robinson and four calling it a draw.'[347]

The November weather in Providence, Rhode Island was bad enough to keep the local citizens at home despite the appearance of former double champ Sugar Ray Robinson, at 40, fighting at the Auditorium with Philadelphia's Al Hauser. The hardcore fans who braved the elements numbered only 1,860, paying $4,504 into the box office. When Sugar fought Randy Turpin at the Polo Grounds in New York, the turnstiles clicked 61,437 times with gate receipts of $767,626. But that was ten years ago and this was now and the one-time Harlem Hepcat was fighting a guy who had lost 15 of his 22 fights. He lost this one too when he was going up and down in the sixth round and the referee ended his misery.

The rough Canadian Wilfie Greaves fancied another shot at Robinson, after dropping a split decision in Detroit, so they hooked up again at the Civic Arena in Pittsburgh. Greaves had floored Ray in their first fight in round eight. New York columnist Jimmy Breslin was ringside with former heavyweight champ Rocky Marciano for the rematch.

'An untalented middleweight named Wilfie Greaves stumbled into Robinson in the second round and chopped a right hand to

347 *Associated Press* 22 October 1961

the face,' wrote Breslin later. 'Robinson's eyes looked up at the top of his head and he fell down. He took a count of eight and got up, but he appeared weak and unsure. "Now," Marciano said, "Now he finds out." 'Robinson seemed ready to go the way of all the others who have stayed in this business too long,' noted Breslin, 'but with something you can only call courage, he refused to fold. After that, he boxed well but seemed to have no strength. By the start of the eighth round, Sugar Ray looked ready to fall apart physically. But he came out and caught Greaves with two murderous left hooks and scored a knockout 30 seconds later. It was a rare display of Robinson's old power. As he climbed out of the ring, Marciano was saying, "Didn't he look bad? He won't get any better either. Look at how the age showed. The guy's just going to wind up being carried out."'[348]

Those early months in 1962 were no time to mess with the Moyers, the fighting family from Portland, Oregon, especially if you fought as Sugar Ray Robinson. Tommy Moyer was an amateur star in the late 1930s, had a brief stint as a pro before carving out a solid business career to finish up a millionaire. His two nephews, Denny and Phil, were more than Robinson could handle. After Ray took a debateable decision from Denny in the Garden, the kid took a lop-sided decision from the Sugarman four months later. All three officials handed in a 7-3 verdict at the end of ten rounds in the Garden. Encouraged by his brother's success, Phil Moyer fought Sugar Ray in Los Angeles and punched his way to a split decision over ten rounds for the family double. Robinson was 41 years old by the time Phil got to him.

The Ring magazine headed its report – Age, Rust, Moyer … beat Sugar Ray. 'Whatever chance Ray had of winning was shattered in the ninth round when Moyer unleashed all he had and belted the former champ, almost finishing him. However, he lacked the knockout blow after he staggered Ray with a left to the jaw and drove him to the ropes. "My exorbitant income tax debt

348 Jimmy Breslin *Saturday Evening Post* 17 March 1962

to Uncle Sam makes it necessary for me to continue in the ring," said Ray. "I'll go to England to fight Downes after a broken bone in my hand mends."'[349]

Before getting into the ring with the Paddington Express, Sugar Ray made an appearance on the stage in the British television show *Sunday Night at the London Palladium.* The critics knocked his six-minute performance, for which Ray would be paid $5,600. 'Sugar Ray fell flat on television last night,' commented Elizabeth Prosser in the *Daily Herald.* 'As a singer, I mean. His crooning sounded sourly off key.' In the *Daily Mail,* Peter Black wrote, 'Sugar Ray offered the novelty of a boxer singing, not very well.' Neville Randall in the *Daily Express* wrote, 'I haven't expected much from Sugar Ray Robinson, but I had expected him to sing in tune.'[350]

At least Ray looked the part, immaculate in a dazzling sky-blue suit. What did they expect?

A week later, he was in the ring at Wembley's Empire Pool ready to go ten rounds or less with Terry Downes, the British middleweight champion who had held Paul Pender's two-state title briefly. The Londoner had learned the American style of fighting while serving in the US Marines and whose 29-8 pro record included Pender, Joey Giardello and Don Fullmer. At the end of the ten rounds at Wembley, the illustrious name of Sugar Ray Robinson would be added.

'London once again proved an unlucky spot for Sugar, who was pounded into a ten-rounds points defeat by the strong, colourful Cockney. It was sad to see such a ring great as Sugar Ray tasting the bitter pill of defeat and when the verdict was announced in favour of Downes, some spectators booed. But the boo-boys were unfair to Downes, who won all the way. Whereas we thought Terry, who at 25 is Sugar's junior by 16 years, would wait for his veteran opponent to tire, the London lad set the battle alight at the

---

349 Bill Miller *The Ring* September 1962

350 *Long Beach Independent* California 18 September 1962

opening bell and made Ol' Sugar fight. But the weary American could not stand the pace. Fifth round and as Downes followed him, out came the old bolo. This time it really hurt Downes. Terry tottered unsteadily and Robinson rushed in with another assault. A left to the head, a right to the jaw. Downes stopped both and seemed badly hurt but managed to escape. The last round was a real thriller. Robinson, sensing that only a knockout could save the day, changed his tactics completely. Carrying the fight to Downes for the first time, he mustered his last ounce of strength from his weary body and cut loose with both hands. Terry was caught napping but he fought back and during a fierce Robinson bombardment received a tremendous right to the jaw. Downes' supporters were aghast. His seconds, white with fear, yelled at him, "Move, Terry!" Downes tried to slug it out but Sugar, fighting with unexpected ferocity, blazed away with his big guns and was distinctly on top in this round, catching Downes with punch after punch on a far-too-exposed chin. Sugar had gambled everything on the last round but the gamble did not come off. He had left it too late.'[351]

'I took a fight in London with Terry Downes,' Ray recalled in his autobiography. 'He got the decision. Not long after that, Edna Mae applied for a Mexican divorce. Millie was with me, in Europe, and we got engaged in Vienna. I know she loved me, because there wasn't anything else for her to love. My flamingo Continental had been sold. My café had been closed. The symbols of my success had disappeared. Only *me* was left.'[352]

'He was still trying to recoup money owed to him from as far back as the first Basilio fight four years earlier in September 1957,' wrote Herb Boyd in his Robinson biography. 'Then, Sugar received a most miraculous windfall. The IRS sent him a cheque for $123,935.65. The full amount seized had been $313,449.82, but Sugar had used it each time he needed it as credit on his taxes and the cheque the IRS sent him was the amount left over.

351 *Boxing News* London 28 September 1962

352 Sugar Ray Robinson with Dave Anderson *Sugar Ray* 1969

'Ray Junior was in Sugar's office the day the money arrived. "I was there at the office that day and saw my dad and a few of his friends holding duffle bags full of money," he recalled. "The manager of Chase Manhattan Bank had called them to say the government had made a mistake and there was a release on his money. And he wanted Dad to come in that day and pick up all the money owed to him. It was absolutely astounding to see all those duffle bags and shopping bags full of money." But Sugar was in for a very rude awakening – and Edna Mae would be no better off. The money he received was taxable (of course, Sugar had never entertained that possibility) and Edna Mae would be informed later that she was equally responsible for the indebtedness, though she never received any more than the stipulated support money during separation. With Sugar laying plans for a European sojourn in the fall of 1962, Edna Mae booked passage to Mexico for a divorce. It was granted on 2 October 1962 and by that time Sugar was in Vienna, where he was to fight Diego Infantes.[353]

When the news filtered through to him, he and Millie got engaged at the City Hall, where he would celebrate by knocking out the Spaniard in 1.15 of round two. Main event that night saw the American world welterweight champion Emile Griffith score a 15-round decision over Detroit's Teddy Wright for the newly created junior welterweight championship (154 pounds), a title he immediately relinquished as world champions were not permitted to hold two titles at the same time. The European Boxing Union, British Boxing Board of Control and the World Boxing Association with headquarters in the United States declared they would not recognise the bout as for the junior welterweight crown.

Sugar Ray's bout was actually a scheduled eight-round semi-final, with UPI recording, 'Robinson weighed 160 pounds for the first preliminary bout in which he had participated in 22 years.

353 Herb Boyd with Ray Robinson II *Pound for Pound* 2005

Not since his first year as a professional in 1940 had he fought in anything but a main event. It was his 148th victory and 96th knockout in 164 fights.'[354] Next stop for Robinson was the Palais des Sports in Lyons, where he stopped Georges Estahoff in the sixth round. More than 7,000 spectators cheered Robinson wildly when he floored Estahoff twice with a right to the jaw and a left hook to bring the signal for retirement from the Frenchman's corner. In fact, with Estahoff suffering his 12th defeat in 17 bouts, manager Sablier indicated his boy would fight no more. Robinson and Millie rounded up their suitcases and booked a flight home.

'Meanwhile, boxing men keep wondering why Robinson continues to expose himself to punches when there is so little left of what used to be. The most obvious answer is money. Joe Glaser, Ray's former manager, disagrees. "Nobody can make me believe he's broke.

'He's still fighting because he thinks he can regain the middleweight title. Anyway, that's what he says in three letters I've had from him in Europe." Nobody should know more about Robinson's financial condition than Glaser, the theatrical agent who loaned him $112,000 when he started one of his many comebacks and later advanced him $10,000 more. Glaser, of course, is only one of many to stake Robinson, but is the only one who covered himself by taking mortgages on the string of buildings and stores in Harlem which once were Ray's nest egg. A year ago, Glaser foreclosed on the property after trying to get Sugar to pay off the debt.

'But he insists that Ray isn't as bad off as many believe. "He made too much money to be broke," Glaser says. "He was making over $50,000 a month when I got him booked as a dancer. When he quit doing his act, he was still making $5,500 a week. For the second fight against Basilio, Jim Norris offered him $100,000, but I got him $468,000. Sure, I foreclosed on his property when he

354 *Nevada State Journal* 18 October 1962

refused to pay me back. So, I've got to believe he really believes he can win back the title.'"[355]

Back from Europe, Sugar Ray was soon in harness again, meeting welterweight Ralph Dupas at the Miami Beach Convention Cener in what Robinson considered 'a very important bout for me. I don't want to be forgotten when I quit. I want to quit good.' He had said that back in 1951when he beat Randy Turpin to regain his title. An eternity, two lost fortunes, untold smashed dreams and four world championships ago. Today, at 41, Robinson was still trying to 'quit good'. It was time to quit now, according to veteran sportswriter Oscar Fraley, ringside in Miami.

'It was a mockery of a legend,' Fraley wrote for UPI. 'There was the old litheness of form, the sarcastic eye and the familiar stand-up style with the once-explosive fists cocked and ready. But this was not the man out of the storied past. He had a 12¼-pound weight advantage, he was facing a man who couldn't knock off your hat with a baseball bat, and he stole it. Joe Louis, Willie Pep and King Levinsky might have been the chief mourners at a funeral when they climbed into the ring before the bout for an introduction. And it almost was just that. Dupas swarmed all over the Sugar man, and he was the victim of one of the neatest bits of thievery since the great mail robbery. Robinson was a 2-1 underdog before 5,500 fans who were predominantly and lustily in his corner. But, as it developed, it should have been no worse than 6-5 and take your pick. Dupas treated him like a preliminary boy and Robinson fought a defensive fight. Dupas demanded, "What do you have to do to win a fight in Miami Beach? This is the third time I've been robbed here." But actually it was the money-hurting Robinson who was robbed. Beaten, he might have packed it in. He should. The Tiger from Nigeria will chew him into little pieces.'[356]

'"They've been counting me out since 1952," Ray told an AP reporter a couple of days before the Dupas fight, "and I've won

355 *Independent Press Telegram* Long Beach California 11 November 1962

356 Oscar Fraley *Brownsville Herald* Texas 31 January 1963

the middleweight championship three times since." Robinson is controlled by deep driving emotions. He is a showboat, a crowd pleaser, a peacock that struts for the applause that stirs his blood like nothing else can. "I've got so much man, man," he said. "They've got to kill this ham to stop me. You walk down the street and suddenly you are surrounded by a mob of kids. They look you up with bright young eyes and they holler, 'Sugar Ray, Sugar Ray.' Man, after that, what is there?'"[357]

What there was after that for Sugar Ray Robinson was a tough guy named Joey Giardello. Ten rounds in Philadelphia, Joey's hometown. Once again, Sugar Ray was in the last chance saloon. Drop this one to Giardello and he will surely be on the long road to nowhere. Local favourite Giardello was the third-ranking middleweight contender and he was a 7-5 choice with the bookies, going into the ring at the Convention Hall before a capacity crowd of 8,598. He brought a fine record to the ring, 121 fights with 90 wins and eight draws. Three years earlier, Joey had fought NBA champion Gene Fullmer to a blistering, foul-filled 15-round draw, and he was looking now for a shot at champ Dick Tiger. And so was Ray Robinson, the guy standing across the ring waiting for the bell. When it rang, Giardello went after Ray with both hands working, hooking to the body and the head. He brought a roar from the crowd in the fourth round when a savage left hook put the Sugarman down for a count of nine from referee Buck McTiernan, and Robinson was again in trouble in the sixth round when he was saved by the bell. The former champion suffered a nick on his left brow in round eight but by the final bell he had taken one of the worst beatings of his long career.

In his dressing room, a jubilant victor said, 'I waited ten years to get this fight with Robinson. Really, he didn't fight me now, he fought my rating, because he thought if he beat me now he could move up toward a title shot.'

---

357 *Lincoln Star* 28 January 1963

'Sugar Ray said he is "very seriously" considering retiring in the wake of his lopsided defeat by Joey Giardello. He said he will make up his mind by the end of this week. "If I do retire it will be because of business ventures which will be consummated soon."

'The former champion also disclosed that the government has held up his entire purse from Monday night's bout, estimated at $14,500 "for reasons I don't know." He said he was leaving for New York immediately to consult with his attorneys to "find out why."' Robinson was talking to Art Carter for the *Baltimore Afro-American* 6 July 1963.

'I needed a significant victory,' Ray said in his autobiography. 'I thought I might get it in a match with Joey Giardello in Philadelphia, but he got the decision. In the fall I went to Paris, where Charlie Michaelis booked me. In five fights, I didn't lose. Two of my victories were over Armand Vanucci. "I never heard of Vanucci," Lew Burston said to me on my return. "Is he any good?" "He's very big in Paris," I said. "He's a guard for the Mona Lisa at the Louvre." I hadn't impressed myself in those fights, but at 42, my mirror told me that I was in good shape. One more whirl, I convinced myself. One more whirl at my title. "Try it with me once more," I pleaded with George, "one last time." He went with me to Portland, Maine and Pittsfield, Massachusetts. The money wasn't much, maybe $700, but it kept me going on my last whirl to another title shot. "You've got the feel of the ring, Robinson," he kept telling me, "and when your chance comes, you'll be ready."'[358]

---

358 Sugar Ray Robinson with Dave Anderson *Sugar Ray* 1969

24

HAVE GLOVES, WILL TRAVEL

'THE GREAT ones never lose their style,' Dave Anderson, the *New York Times* columnist, wrote in a *True* magazine piece in 1964. 'It's this way with Sugar Ray Robinson. He's wearing white trunks and his black boxing shoes scratch across the resin-covered canvas. He could be fighting anybody, anyplace, but this night last summer in Pittsfield, Mass., he's in with somebody named Clarence Riley in a dumpy little outdoor arena named Waconah Park. Suddenly, Sugar Ray throws two quick left hooks and the small crowd comes alive. But the real boxing people haven't seen Robinson lately. It's just as well. He's a sideshow freak now. His skill is shot. Now, at Wahconah Park, at the gray wooden ticket booth, there were six people in line. Once, at Yankee Stadium, the ringside seats were $40 a pop when he fought Carmen Basilio. There were maybe 1,500 people in the old ball park and they shouted when Sugar Ray hopped up the wooden steps and climbed into the ring. Clarence Riley, a lanky, loose-muscled middleweight out of Detroit, was standing in his corner looking across at Sugar Ray almost in awe. When the bell rang, Sugar Ray turned and strutted into the middle of the ring, his slim legs moving gracefully and his white satin trunks shimmering under the overhead lights. In the sixth round, Riley was down for the third time. He was up at nine but he was wobbling. The referee put his arms around Riley and the fight was over. The people were yelling, "You're still the best, Sugar."

'Some of the crowd were waiting for Robinson as he came out of the dressing room. He signed autographs for them and then he walked into the gray wooden ticket booth to pick up his money from Sam Silverman. "About $700," Silverman said later. This fight in Pittsfield didn't even make a paragraph in the New York morning papers.'

A couple of weeks later, the Sugar Ray Robinson roadshow was in Nebraska. 'There wasn't much money for Sugar to get up front in his bout with an unknown Art Hernandez in Omaha. That nobody in boxing circles had heard of Hernandez and that the fight was taking place at the City Auditorium in Omaha and not one of the major arenas was indicative of Sugar's plight. He had fallen off the charts, and there was no point in his applying the hard negotiating tactics that had made him such a pain in the neck to the big-time promoters in New York City. Getting Hernandez to ink a contract took little cajoling; he was just as eager to get a payday as the star of the main event. But although it was a breeze to get Hernandez's name on the dotted line, it proved much tougher to line him up for one of his patented hooks, Sugar learned. They fought to a draw.'[359]

'Omaha middleweight Art Hernandez battled to a draw against veteran Sugar Ray Robinson in the ten-round main event before 3,593 fans here Monday night. Sugar Ray dropped Hernandez twice in the final round but he was up both times before the count. Hernandez and his handlers insisted both knockdowns came on low blows. Referee Bill Engel ruled the punches were low but were not intentional and did not penalise Robinson. "I thought it was a close fight, but I thought I won it," said the 23-year-old Hernandez. Robinson protested, "At 43, I'm trying to get another shot at the championship. This ain't fair."'[360]

---

359 *Pound for Pound* Herb Boyd with Ray Robinson II 2005

360 *Beatrice Daily Sun* Nebraska 28 July 1964

Two months later, Sugar Ray returned to a British ring, 11 years after blowing his middleweight title in an upset to Randy Turpin and two years after Terry Downes gave the former champion a ten-round beating in London. This time he was in Scotland, at Paisley Ice Rink, where former champion Peter Keenan had signed him to fight Mick Leahy, an Irishman from Coventry with a 52-14 record and holder of the British middleweight title.

'Robinson, by virtue of his superior boxing skill and cleaner punching, seemed to have done sufficient to earn the verdict,' reported London's *Boxing News* on 11 September 1954. 'But referee Ike Powell, of Wales, obviously thought differently and had no hesitation in indicating that Leahy was the winner.

' The decision met with a mixed reception. The superb boxing skill, which made Robinson five times middleweight champion of the world, was nowhere in evidence, and if he hopes to achieve his ambition of being champion for a sixth time he will certainly have to do better than he did against Mick Leahy.

The American press carried a UPI report from Paisley, 'Referee Ike Powell of Wales, the only ring official, gave the verdict to Leahy and the decision was immediately disputed by Robinson and his manager George Gainford. Robinson showed only flashes of the ability that once won him the world middleweight crown. Gainford, however, thought Sugar Ray produced many more telling blows. "It was a shocking verdict," Gainford said, "and I have asked the Board of Control to examine the referee's card – he must have counted wrong."'

On the same page, a report out of Philadelphia stated middleweight champion Joey Giardello has been offered $100,000 to defend his title against Sugar Ray Robinson in Tampa, Florida next February. Arnold Giovanetti, Giardello's advisor, said he was very much interested in the offer from promoter Al King but described it as premature. '"We must first defend our title against Rubin (Hurricane) Carter in Las Vegas on 23 October," Giovanetti said. "Then we will be glad to sit down and discuss this offer. We are always interested in good money." Giovanetti said a telegram from King offered Giardello $100,000 and Robinson $50,000. Giardello won a lop-sided decision over Robinson in June 1963.'[361]

Giardello had beaten Dick Tiger for the world title in his next fight after Robinson. He retained it against Hurricane Carter before losing the rematch with Tiger. Joey and Sugar Ray never met again.

When Robinson lost to Leahy, matchmaker Mickey Duff gave him another job, ten rounds with Johnny Angel of Nigeria. They would go in the main event at the opening tournament at the Anglo-American Club, Hilton Hotel, in London's Park Lane, promoted by Ivor Barnard.

That fight was scheduled for 12 October, so Robinson popped over to Paris, where Charlie Michaelis had fixed him up with Yoland Leveque, ten rounds at the Palais des Sports. This did not go well.

From Paris, AP reported, 'Sugar Ray Robinson jabbed and back-pedalled his way to a ten-round disputed decision over Yolande Leveque of France last night. The near-capacity crowd of about 5,000 whistled and booed in disapproval after the decision was announced. Robinson, 44 [43], had a stiff jab and his long ring experience to back him up. But all the zip had gone from his punch and his timing was off. A cut was opened over Robinson's left eye in the ninth round, apparently after a collision with Leveque's head, and blood flowed freely. Robinson was able to weather the round, however, and the cut did not re-open in the final round.'[362]

Back in London, looking for his first win on British soil, Sugar stopped teak-tough Johnny Angel in six rounds, referee Harry Gibbs stopping the fight to save the Nigerian further punishment. Angel protested what some thought a premature stoppage and there was slow handclapping by the crowd. 'Pity that Robinson's victory should be blotted with faint praise,' wrote *Boxing News*. 'His moves were masterly. Sugar had caned Angel with a great

---

361 *Middletown Times Herald* New York 4 September 1964

362 *San Rafael Daily Independent* California 29 September 1964

variety of blows which were becoming more accurate as the bout wore on. Age has dulled Ray's reflexes. He gets hit with punches he used to see coming. He is no longer the violent Ray. Yet he still oozes with the fighting class of a man who has become a legend. The straight jabs, the bolo punches, the successive left hooks were all there. Only the timing was missing. Yet often he cracked home a corker. On this showing, Sugar Ray is far from finished. Even at near 44, his star is still bright.'[363]

With those words putting a smile on his handsome face, Sugar Ray headed back across the Channel for a handful of bouts and a few bob for expenses. At the Palais des Sports in Nice, he took a ten-round decision over Jackie Cailleau and back in his dressing room was congratulated by Prince Rainier of Monaco, who presented Ray with a medal struck at the time of his wedding to actress Grace Kelly. A fortnight later, Ray was in with former French welterweight champion Jean-Baptiste Rolland at Caen. There were 5,000 fans in the local exhibition hall and they cheered the American as he boxed his man for nine rounds and dropped him for a nine count in the final round to take the decision. At Marseilles, he gave Jean Beltritti a boxing lesson over ten rounds before heading for the Olympic Sports Palace in Rome, where he had an engagement with Fabio Bettini.

The boys had swapped blows one year previously, at Lyon in France, where they battled to a draw. Fast forward to Rome, November 1964, and they did it again. But the crowd of 15,000 whistled and jeered through a dull contest. Robinson thrilled the crowd twice when his left hook bounced off Bettini's jaw, but Fabio was still standing when the dust settled. The referee stopped the fight in round eight after angry fans threw paper cups into the ring, telling both fighters to mix it up because the fans were booing. Ray figured it was time to go home.

In the summer of 1960, a handsome young man named Cassius Marcellus Clay visited Sugar Ray at his café in Harlem. He was

363 *Boxing News* 16 October 1964

on his way to Rome as a member of the United States Olympic team and informed Ray he was going to win the gold medal, and when he did he wanted Ray to manage him when he turned pro. Robinson was flattered by the young man's admiration but told him he couldn't manage him while he was still an active fighter himself. Clay duly won the gold medal in the light-heavyweight class, turned pro and began an unbeaten run that led to him shocking the world and Sonny Liston to become heavyweight champion. That was in 1964 and by that time Clay's mouth was making more headlines than his fists. Sugar Ray had followed the kid's career and when he took a fight in Kingston, Jamaica in March 1965, he renewed his friendship with the champ, who now called himself Muhammad Ali, 'The Greatest'.

'When there's snow in New York,' wrote Ray in his autobiography, 'it's always nice to arrange a fight somewhere in the Caribbean. When the promoter there heard me discussing my friendship with Clay, he had an idea. "Call the champ in Miami," the promoter said, "and invite him down to work in your corner as a second." It was a good stunt. He had required hernia surgery that delayed his November return with Liston and was still recuperating. When I phoned him, I told him I'd give him $1,000. He was on the next plane.'[364]

From Kingston, UPI reported, 'Five-time middleweight champion Sugar Ray Robinson scored a second round knockout over Jimmy Beecham of Miami in a scheduled ten-round fight at Jamaica's National Stadium Saturday night. Robinson, who had as his second heavyweight champion Cassius Clay, said after the fight that he was looking forward to a world title fight against current champion Joey Giardello in June. Robinson pummelled Beecham's face with jabs in the first round and weakened him with solid rights to the midsection. In the second round, Robinson snapped Beecham's head back with three stiff jabs and then decked him with an overhand right to the head. Beecham got to his feet

---

364 Sugar Ray Robinson with Dave Anderson *Sugar Ray* 1969

but was back on the deck for good moments later when Robinson connected with a left hook. The time of the knockout was two minutes and four seconds of round two.'[365]

After the fight, Ali told Sugar Ray that Elijah Muhammad had said he'd collect $700,000 for Robinson if he would embrace the Muslim faith. Ray told Ali to thank Mr Muhammad for the offer but he didn't wish to change the way he was, a Christian believer in God.

Savannah, Georgia, 3 April 1965, Sports Center, promoter Grady Bragg, main event Earl Leroy Bastings v Sugar Ray Robinson, ten rounds. The crowd numbered about 1,600 and after two minutes 34 seconds of round one, most of them were looking at their neighbour and asking, 'What the hell just happened in there?' What happened was that Robinson struck Bastings with a rather hard left hook which deposited him on the canvas. As referee Tommy Kiene counted to eight, Bastings got to one knee before collapsing back on the canvas to be counted out. That's what happened.

A few weeks later, Sugar Ray was in the downtown bullring in Tijuana, Mexico to swap punches with Mexican middleweight champion Memo Ayon. 'The dust from the dirty streets is in the air in Tijuana,' recalled Ray. 'As I sweated, I felt the grime forming on me. "Wipe my arms," I told George between rounds. "Wipe my chest and back – get this dirt off me." I was more worried about the dust on me than the fight. I wasn't having any trouble with the mailman. But when the decision was announced, Ayon had won it. It had to be the worst verdict of my career.'[366]

'Robinson appeared to pile up a clear edge in the early rounds with his superior boxing, but had some rocky moments in the latter stages of the action-packed fight. Ayon suffered a cut over the bridge of his nose in the eighth round and it bled until the finish. Ayon took a split decision, one judge voting for Robinson. The UPI reporter saw it for Sugar Ray 98-86 on the ten-point

365 *Kokomo Morning Times* Indiana 8 March 1965

366 Sugar Ray Robinson with Dave Anderson *Sugar Ray* 1969

must system. An estimated 5,000 highly partisan fans applauded the decision. Robinson, who received a $4,000 guaranteed purse, said he felt he had won the fight decisively.'[367]

'After the fight, he and Millie left town immediately, driving all night to Los Angeles. Their destination was Millie's apartment, where she lived upstairs over her uncle and aunt. But Sugar suddenly changed his mind. "We're going to Las Vegas," he told her. It was time for them to get married, he insisted. They drove to the Los Angeles International Airport and got the next flight to Las Vegas. From McCarren Field, they took a cab downtown to the marriage licence bureau.

'With the licence in hand, their next stop was the chapel near the Sands Hotel. Sugar wore his sunglasses to conceal his identity; he didn't want any publicity. On 25 May, 1965, they were married. What little honeymoon the newlyweds had coming took a back seat to Sugar's bout with Stan Harrington in Honolulu. Sugar had to enjoy the picturesque landscapes and cobalt blue ocean through puffed-up eyes. Harrington was a lot more than Sugar expected. "He busted me up over the eye with a butt, and he got the decision. I was a bloody bridegroom," he said.'[368]

'Stan Harrington of Honolulu outpunched Sugar Ray Robinson last night and won a unanimous ten-round decision before a sellout crowd at the Honolulu International Centre. Robinson bled profusely from the sixth round to the finish from cuts opened above and below the right eye. But the appreciative crowd of 8,677 gave Robinson a standing ovation at the end of the spirited bout. The referee and one judge gave the veteran Honolulu fighter a one-point margin. The other judge gave it to the 31-year-old Harrington by three. There were no knockdowns, although Harrington rocked Robinson on four occasions. The crowd, one of the largest in recent Honolulu history, paid $34,144 to see the fight.'[369]

---

367 *El Paso Herald Post* Texas 25 May 1965

368 Herb Boyd with Ray Robinson II *Pound for Pound* 2005

369 *Daily Independent* San Rafael California 2 June 1965

There are more losers than winners in Las Vegas and Sugar Ray was out of luck when going ten rounds with Ferd Hernandez at the Hacienda Hotel. The Nevada middleweight champion was only half a pound lighter than Ray but was almost 20 years younger and it showed as he shoved Robinson around in the clinches to come out with a split decision after a rugged evening. There were flashes of the former champion with left hooks and right crosses but the punches lacked the old power to hold off the burly Fernandez.

Having turned 44, the Sugar man still dreamed of getting the middleweight title back – he considered it was his anyway – and there was hope of a fight with number one contender Joey Archer. Archer didn't figure to be too much for the old champ as he was a pure boxer and they said he had no punch. In winning 45 of his 49 fights, Joey scored only eight knockouts.

In the meantime, Robinson popped back to Honolulu to avenge the defeat by Stan Harrington but the local racked up the double to take another decision after ten rounds. Ray emerged with a cut by the left eye and was outboxed and outslugged almost throughout the fight. Was the Archer fight a non-starter now that Sugar Ray had lost for the fifth time in his 14th fight of the year? Well, never say never. There was always Don Elbaum …

25
TWENTY-FIVE YEARS – THE LAST MILE

'BACK IN the seventies, people were getting blown up all the time around here,' wrote Dan Coughlin in the *Elyria Chronicle-Telegram*. 'It was a very popular way to settle disputes. Cleveland was called the dynamite capital of the world. So when somebody wanted to do away with Don Elbaum, Danny Greene was offered the job.

'"I knew Danny because he came to my fight shows. He always bought a bunch of tickets," said Elbaum, who promoted fight shows at the old Cleveland Arena. "Back in those days," he said, referring to his Cleveland career, "there was no in between. People who liked me loved me. But some people hated me." All of that explains why somebody wanted Elbaum blown up and asked Danny Greene to do it.

'"Danny said he would blow up my car but not with me in it. He said he would blow it up as a warning," said Elbaum, who treasures that kind of loyalty. "I was in my motel room when I heard a loud 'boom' outside. A minute later, the phone rang. 'Mr Elbaum, are you driving a Cadillac and was it parked outside?' said the lady at the front desk."'[370]

---

370 Dan Coughlin *Elyria Chronicle-Telegram* Cleveland 15 March 2008

So Don Elbaum lived to fight another day. George Gainford called Elbaum on one of those days, in late 1965. Sugar Ray Robinson was nearing the end of a glorious career and wanted one more crack at the world middleweight championship. 'Ray needs to re-establish his credentials before he gets another title shot,' Gainford pressed. 'Who in the top ten do you think he can beat?' Elbaum suggested Joey Archer, with the winner to fight then-champion Joey Giardello. But first he wanted to build Robinson up with a few easy wins. He signed Robinson to fight Peter Schmidt over ten rounds at Johnstown, Pennsylvania on 1 October 1965. 'You've got more of a hometown feeling in a Steubenville and a Warren, Ohio,' Elbaum said. 'It isn't like a big city, where you just make the rounds. People are hungry for it.'

A born hustler, Elbaum had his show cards all over Johnstown advertising 'The Two Greatest Fighters of All Time', Sugar Ray Robinson and Willie Pep. Ray had beaten Willie when they were both skinny amateur kids umpteen years earlier, two skinny amateur kids headed for boxing immortality. Willie Pep became one of the greatest featherweights in boxing history and Robinson, he became Sugar Ray.

'Some 4,000 fans crowded into the Johnstown War Memorial to watch the fights. In the main event of the evening, Sugar Ray Robinson took a hard-fought unanimous decision over Canadian welterweight champion Peter Schmidt. The fight was a good scrap from the second round when Schmidt seemed to find the range. He was downed twice by Robinson, the second time by a terrific left from the former champion's glove in the eighth round. Sugar Ray showed flashes of his former greatness throughout the match. He obviously paced himself with light flurries at his opponent as he displayed an example of his ring skill. Former featherweight champion Willie Pep gave a classic display of boxing before copping a technical knockout over Willie Littles in 1.06 of the third round of their bout.'[371]

---

371 *Uniontown Morning Herald* Pennsylvania 2 October 1065

'"If you look good against Schmidt," Elbaum said, "it might lead to something big, Archer in Pittsburgh." Joey Archer was a leading challenger, a flat-nosed Irishman from the Bronx, a good boxer but no punch. With a win over Archer, I'd be in line for a title shot. When I arrived in Johnstown, I thought it was the grayest place I'd ever been in. All those steel mills, gray. The smoke, gray. The river, gray. The sky, gray. Even the leaves on the trees looked gray. But not to Elbaum. He'd been waiting all his life to promote a card with me on it. He was a little round-faced guy with curly black hair and sunglasses.'[372]

'We have this big press conference,' Elbaum said, 'We do this great speech about how it was 25 years to the day and everything. Then I told Ray, "We've got one more surprise, Ray." We turned out the lights and four girls came out with this tremendous cake. I've got my hands behind my back and say, "Ray, we've also got a very special present for you. We want to present you with the gloves you used 25 years ago in your debut." Robinson had tears in his eyes. It was something incredible. We asked him to put them on and pose for pictures. He agreed. Then, he stopped. He stared at the gloves. Then he looked at me and shook his head. "I can't do it," he told me. "It's too emotional." "Come on, Ray," we prodded him. He still refused. Then I saw what he saw. They were two right-handed gloves!'[373]

In the dressing room after the fight, Ray was visited by Archie Litman, the Pittsburgh promoter who wanted him to meet Joey Archer in Pittsburgh on 10 November. Elbaum chirped up, 'Don't forget I'm putting you in Steubenville on the 20th of this month with Rudolph Bent. You won't have any trouble with him.'

Rudolph had other ideas as he told the press the day he arrived in Steubenville. 'They seem to have forgotten about me,' he said. 'They are all talking about Ray Robinson and Joey Archer. What happens when I beat Robinson? I said when, not if, then I want

372 Sugar Ray Robinson with Dave Anderson *Sugar Ray* 1969

373 Dave Bontempo *The Ring* magazine December 1984

to fight Archer in Pittsburgh. I knocked out Peter Schmidt and Robinson could only beat him by decision. The last fight I had, I boxed Gomeo Brennan, who had never been down in over 70 fights. I floored him three times. What do you think I'll do to Robinson when I hit him?'[374]

Sugar Ray Robinson, still a master craftsman after 26 years of fighting, was awarded a technical knockout over Rudolph Bent of Kingston, Jamaica at 2.20 of the third round of a scheduled ten-round bout at the Steubenville Community Arena. A crowd of 2,500 saw the classy Robinson deck his willing opponent twice in the first round and once in the second before referee Jack Stauffer intervened in the third round after a hard right to the jaw sent Bent sprawling into a corner. Robinson, Gainford and their wives and trainer Al Smith left Steubenville early today for New York to take in the Joey Giardello-Dick Tiger title bout.

They would see the tough Nigerian Tiger claw his title back from Joey at Atlantic City with a 15-round decision. Sugar Ray fancied his chances against Tiger, telling reporters, 'I figured I would have had less trouble with Tiger than I would have with Joey. Tiger was a straight-ahead plodder, perfect for me. The matador and the bull all over again. When I arrived in Pittsburgh for the Archer fight, all the sportswriters had the same question, "Why was I fighting?" "To win the title again,' I'd say. "The beautiful end of a beautiful story." A couple of nights before the fight, I was in my room at the Carlton House when the phone rang. George answered it, and his eyebrows shot up and he looked at me. "Joe Glaser," I heard George say. "It's been a long time, Joe." When I took the phone, Joe's scratchy voice was saying to me, "Ray, promise me now, if you don't win this fight, you'll quit. Promise me, Ray. I'm coming out to see the fight, but you've got to promise me that if you lose, you'll quit. I'll find some things for you to do – nightclubs, television. Promise me, Ray." I didn't have to promise him. I knew that if I didn't get past Archer, it wouldn't

374 *Weirton Daily Times* West Virginia 20 October 1965

make any sense to go back to Tijuana or Johnstown or any of the other towns where I could always get a few hundred dollars.[375]

'Joe Glaser, sitting in his busy booking office on Fifth Avenue, remarked, "I like the guy, you know. He's got that personality. It's impossible not to like him when he comes around. But then you get stuck with him and you can't get any money out of him. Why, only back in September George Gainford called me. He said they were in bad trouble. They had a fight coming up in Detroit – the first time he boxed Greaves – and they needed $800 to finish training and get out to the fight. I called Madison Square Garden and asked Teddy Brenner, the Garden matchmaker, why they weren't helping out Robinson. He said he couldn't, he had advanced Robinson too much money already. So I said, 'All right, I'll go for the 800.' But I made sure I got it back."'[376]

The end came on a Wednesday night at the Civic Arena in Pittsburgh, on 10 November 1965. 'Tonight in Pittsburgh, this ghost out of the past faces Joey Archer, young, fast, skilful, who is next in line for a shot at Dick Tiger's world middleweight title,' wrote Jesse Abramson in the *New York Herald Tribune*. 'As humble now as he once was arrogant and commanded 45 per cent and gave promoters ulcers, Robinson will earn maybe $5,000. This is his life, fighting anywhere he can find a willing promoter who can dig up an opponent and hope enough fight fans will want to take a look at Sugar Ray before he nestles into the record books. Why?

'"Not for the money," said Robinson before departing Wiley's Gym for Pittsburgh, where he'll finish training and help boost the box office. "I want to win the middleweight title just once more and then I'll quit for good. Look, I've never been a failure yet. Four times I've been right, coming back to win the title when people said 'Why doesn't he quit, he's through.' Archer is the top contender. I know I can beat him. I will beat Archer, then I'll

375 Sugar Ray Robinson with Dave Anderson *Sugar Ray* 1969

376 Jimmy Breslin *Saturday Evening Post* 17 March 1962

fight Tiger. The Dapper Club in Pittsburgh will guarantee Tiger $75,000 to fight me.'"[377]

A pipe dream? Well, this night, the reality was ten rounds with Joey Archer, a fight he had to win. It wouldn't be easy. The 27-year-old Irishman from the Bronx had lost only one fight in a 45-bout career, reversed that defeat, and was already being called the uncrowned middleweight champion after defeating two of the toughest guys in the division, Hurricane Carter and Dick Tiger.

'His handsome, square face, set off by high cheekbones and solid chin, bear the unmistakeable stamp of an athlete. But it is the nose that spells out the profession of Joey Archer. Once it must have been long and slim, adding a look of intelligence to his strong, clean-cut features. Today it is a smashed-in shadow of its former self, a jarring reminder that this will-o-the-wisp has known and survived the pounding of padded leather. Joey has learned from the lips and hands of Whitey Bimstein and Freddie Brown, a pair of taskmasters who are rated with the top trainers in the nation. As much as anyone, they can take the credit for transforming a tough Irish kid into a boxer who is now only one fight away from the middleweight championship of the world.'[378]

Joey Archer, the boxer from the Bronx, the guy they said couldn't punch his way out of a paper bag, decked Sugar Ray Robinson in the fourth round and rocked him repeatedly in winning a unanimous decision over ten rounds that kept a crowd of 9,023 on the edge of their seats. This had to be the end of the former champ's quest for a sixth shot at the middleweight title, the one he had come to think of as his own. He had won it five times.

A 2-1 underdog in the betting, Sugar turned everything on in the third round, the old combinations flashing but, sadly, not flattening the other guy. He fought himself out in that round and his punches had little power the rest of the way. Archer surprised by flooring Robinson with a right to the jaw in round four and

---

377 Jesse Abramson *New York Herald Tribune* 11 November 1965

378 Lee Greene *Championship Boxing Annual 1965*

the veteran had to scrape himself off the canvas at the count of nine from referee Buck McTiernan. In the sixth, Ray found a hard right hand from somewhere and hit Archer in the head with it, following up with flurries of lefts and rights. It was a strong round for the old guy. In the final round, Archer chased Robinson from pillar to post and was a deserved winner of a unanimous decision. McTiernan saw Joey a winner 48-41, judge Ernie Sesto called it 49-40 with George Lupinacci 50-39 for Archer.

'Early in the fourth,' wrote Martin Kane for *Sports Illustrated*, 'after Archer had hooked him twice and landed some light jabs, Sugar missed with a big right hand. A look of concern came over his face. Archer was jabbing and moving, and Robinson was missing with rights and lefts. Then, suddenly, Archer landed a left to the head and followed it immediately with a long right. Sugar Ray went down on the seat of his white silk trunks, rolled to his side and, dazed, took a nine count resting on one knee. Now Sugar and everyone knew that his fight plan had failed, and so had his grand plan.

'The rest of the fight was nothing but the last steps down for a gallant Robinson. He all but hit the canvas again in the sixth and once again in the seventh, looked better in the eighth and slugged it out with Archer in the ninth. In the last minute of the tenth round, men at ringside were standing and pleading, "Don't hit him again, Joey! That's enough!"

'It had been a long and glorious trail for Sugar Ray Robinson, who just may have been the best fighter ever. Next afternoon at the airport, waiting for a plane to take him back to New York, Sugar Ray smiled, hunched his black leather, hip-length coat about his shoulders and said that retirement was the only course open to him now. "But we have this offer of a return bout with Archer," one of his followers protested. "Aw, what would be the point?" Robinson said.'[379]

---

379 Martin Kane *Sports Illustrated* 22 November 1965

New York writer and columnist Pete Hamill recalled Ray's finale. 'His last fight was in Pittsburgh one bad night in 1965. He was boxing a good Irish middleweight named Joey Archer. On his best night, Archer could not break a potato chip with a punch, but he was a skilful boxer with a lot of courage, and Robinson was then over 40 and long past his prime. In the fourth round, Archer knocked Robinson down. The old champion got up slowly, dusting off his white trunks, looking humiliated. A few seats away from me was Miles Davis, the great trumpet player, who used to work out with Robinson at Harry Wiley's gym in Harlem. Miles is a tough, laconic man, but as he rose, looking into the ring at his stricken friend, tears moved down his cheek. Later, we were all in the dressing room, and Robinson looked tired and old. He had lost a ten-round decision. His left hand was jammed in an ice bucket. And Miles started whispering, in his deep croaking voice, that it was over, that it was time to pack it in. Robinson nodded agreement. Slowly, he got up off the rubbing table. "I never wanted to hurt anybody," he said to me. "If you write it up, put that in. I never wanted to hurt anyone." Sugar Ray had never looked sweeter.'[380]

Back at the hotel, they were in the room, Big George, Sugar Ray and Millie, and George was talking, as usual.

'"That return with Archer," he was saying, "you ought to consider that, Robinson. That could draw big again." Good old George, always trying for another payday. But instead of getting angry, I shooed him out of the room,' said Robinson. 'I wanted to talk to Millie, more than I'd ever wanted to talk to her before. "Honey," I said when we were alone, "I'm not going to have any more fights."

'"Oh, Ray," she said, and she was crying with her head nestled in my neck, "I'm so happy you decided. I didn't want you to fight any more, but it had to be your decision."

'"And I promise," I said, "no comeback."'[381]

380 Pete Hamill *New York Post* 13 April 1989

381 Sugar Ray Robinson with Dave Anderson *Sugar Ray* 1969

'"I die inside when he fights," Millie used to say. "It's hard to see a person you love in that ring. He's a wonderful fighter, a wonderful human being. I've never known a man like him. He's something else."'[382]

He is, and always would be, Sugar Ray Robinson, even if he was no longer doing what we liked to watch him do – fight. Well, he was back in the ring at Madison Square Garden just a month after the Archer fight and a crowd of 12,146 gave him a standing ovation when he entered the ring. No, he hadn't broken his word to Millie. He wasn't going to fight anybody. He had already fought the guys gathered around him up there under the ring spotlights. Randy Turpin, Bobo Olson, Gene Fullmer and Carmen Basilio. John Condon of the Garden had arranged the whole thing, ending with the presentation by former mayor Vincent Impellitteri of a big gold trophy inscribed to 'The World's Greatest Fighter.' 'This is the first time I've ever had an experience like this,' he said. 'I don't know at this opportune time whether to be happy or sad.' More applause greeted each sentence he spoke and even Cassius Clay (who would become Muhammad Ali), seated at ringside, joined in. 'I'm not a cry baby but I'm full up inside,' continued the 44-year-old Robinson, if you go by his count, or the 45-year-old Robinson, if you go by the book. 'This is not goodbye but it is farewell to a career that has spanned a quarter century,' he said, feelingly. 'I'm not going to say goodbye. As they say in France, it's *a tout a l'heure.* I'll see you later.'

As Ray climbed down from the ring to make his way back to the dressing room, singer Gordon MacRae was singing, 'Should auld acquaintance be forgot …' People stood and cheered as he made his way towards the 50th Street exit, down the stairs, along the gloomy corridor, into Room 30.

Milton Richman, UPI sportswriter, described Room 30 as, 'precisely the kind of place you might expect a condemned man to spend his last few moments before walking to the gas chamber. It is

382 Larry L. King *Sports Illustrated* 6 September 1965

situated in the dimly lit recesses of the Garden, it has no furniture other than a couple of crude wooden benches, it is uncommonly narrow and high-ceilinged … This is the room in which Sugar Ray Robinson began and ended his farewell to boxing Friday night. "It has a lot of memories for me," he said when he walked inside. Someone asked him, any regrets? "Not one," he replied. "I'd do it all over again the same identical way. I wouldn't change a blessed thing." In less than ten minutes, he was back in his street clothes. He took one last look around room 30 and walked out.'[383]

'About two hours later, I was the guest of honour at a midnight banquet at Mamma Leone's. Mayor Lindsay was there, and so was my mayor, Vincent Impellitteri. Basilio, Fullmer, Turpin, Olson and LaMotta were there, and so was Cassius Clay. Man, I wanted to talk all night, I wanted to keep that night going forever, but soon the waiters in their red jackets began scooping up the dirty dishes. "I think," Millie said, nudging me, "that we're supposed to leave." Outside, in the winter chill of 48th Street, a few people stood with us while the parking lot attendant got our car. "You'll always be our champion," one of them called as I drove away with Millie.

'Twenty minutes later, I carried the big trophy inscribed to "The World's Greatest Fighter" into my new apartment. I had to put it on the floor. The only table in the apartment was a beige metal card table, with thin legs, in the middle of the bare wooden floor in the living room. We had our meals on it. The only other piece of furniture in the apartment was an old scratched wooden bed. For the first time in his life, "The World's Greatest Fighter" really knew what it was to need.'[384]

---

383 Milton Richman *Lebanon Daily News* Pennsylvania 11 December 1965

384 Sugar Ray Robinson with Dave Anderson *Sugar Ray* 1969

26

ALL OVER, LIKE A WEDDING

WHAT DOES an ex-champion prizefighter do when the ride is over, when the cheers and the headlines are for some other guy? He glances at the sports pages before moving on to the classified pages, looking for the heading 'Men Wanted'.

'Now that I was out of boxing,' he told his biographer Dave Anderson, 'I not only had no money, I had no way of making any. I had to borrow. I got a few thousand from Vincent Impellitteri, my mayor, who had become a judge. I got a few more thousand from some other friends. My ego had trapped me. Another man would have got a job, any job, for a hundred a week and lived on it. Not me, not Sugar Ray. I had established my style. I had to live that way. Or no way. Our apartment was costing $365 a month. I could have rented a cheaper one, facing into the shadowy courtyard, but I had to have a balcony with a view of the sunset across the Hudson River. I had a card table, an old bed, and a view.'[385]

'Sugar considered going back in the ring, which would have meant going back on his word, but he concluded that fighting exhibitions wouldn't be the same as taking on professional bouts. Gainford, who had been with Sugar throughout his boxing days, shot the idea down. And the "Emperor" was right again: It would

385 Sugar Ray Robinson with Dave Anderson *Sugar Ray* 1969

not be fitting to see this glorious gladiator hauled from the arena on his shield. With few options available to him, he went back into showbusiness. He still had his looks, those great legs and a decent singing voice. He decided to produce another album, as he had done back in the early sixties. Sugar, working in his undershirt and pants in the hot (Regent) studio, had a large clientele with him who nodded with approval at the playbacks. His biggest fan was, as usual, his sister Evelyn.

'Sugar also tried his luck in Hollywood. He picked up a few bucks from acting in a number of television dramas starring Ben Gazzara, Danny Thomas, Mickey Rooney, Tony Randall or Gary Crosby, mainly cameo roles. "When the movie *The Detective* was shot on location in New York, Frank Sinatra got me a bit part as a cop," he said. He had a much larger role with Robert Conrad in a *Mission Impossible* segment that focused on the underworld's grip on boxing, a fitting theme for the ex-champ.'[386]

Hollywood – Hardy Westervelt reporting for *The Ring* magazine. 'Once one of the real greats of boxing history, now a motions picture and stage actor, Ray Robinson has been on the stage in *The Odd Couple* with Tony Randall and Mickey Rooney in Las Vegas. This coming stage season on Broadway, thespian Robinson will star in *Mr Congressman*, produced by David Merrick. He has played a fighter in *Run for Your Life* and has an assignment to work with Liz Taylor and Richard Burton in a movie to be made in Rome. In short, Robinson emphatically is launched on an acting career after having been a professional fighter for 25 years.

'Interviewing Walker Smith-Ray Robinson has always been a delight for the reporter. To get him started is easy. To keep him talking is no arduous chore, to listen to his comments often is a sheer delight. He rarely fails to say something. Confronted with the customary openers of the professional interviewer, Robbie replied, "What I am is an egotistical ham. I love the roar of the crowd. It sends the blood running swifter." You look him over in one of

386 Herb Boyd with Ray Robinson II *Pound for Pound* 2005

those movie chairs on the Paramount lot and you know him for a character beyond the ordinary. Right now he is wearing a moustache and a wispy beard. When asked if he was a method actor, Robbie laughed. "I don't exactly know what that is. Marlon Brando once told me, 'Sugar, don't fall for that study gag. You won't be yourself, and it's yourself they want, not a duplicate of some teacher.'

"'Frank Sinatra gave me a part in his fine movie *The Detective*, which has been going over real big from coast to coast. He taught me some tricks about acting. He showed me the value of relaxing. He said, 'Ray, hold your head steady in the close-ups.' I am learning about the movies and television, about the basic musts. After a day in front of the cameras I am bushed, far more tired than I ever was after a hard, 15-round championship fight. Acting in front of the cameras is exhausting emotionally." Now he is finished with the fights for good, and on his way to continued profit as a real honest-to-goodness actor.'[387]

When he retired just after losing to Joey Maxim in a New York City heatwave in 1952, Robinson signed up with Joe Glaser as a song-and-dance man, (well, a dancer really), prompting one Broadway booking agent to observe, 'As a dancer, Ray was a good fighter.' He was better than good, Sugar Ray was a fantastic fighter, rated by some experts as the greatest pound-for-pound in the history of the game. He played this game so well, his record will take some beating, if ever.

As an amateur Ray put together 85 victories, 69 by KO – 49 in round one. As a professional, he was unbelievable. In 202 bouts, he racked up 175 victories, 109 by KO, 19 defeats, six draws, one no decision and one no contest. He was never knocked out and the only time he failed to finish the course, he was felled through sheer heat exhaustion. Robinson was unbeaten as a lightweight, undefeated champion at welterweight and an incredible five-time winner of the world middleweight championship in a 25-year pro career.

387 Hardy Westervelt *The Ring* magazine November 1968

'After watching a masterful exhibition of the Robinson technique against Kid Gavilan, an awed reporter was moved to write, "When Robinson fights, every prizefighter in the United States should pay his way in to get a boxing lesson." Boxing hadn't seen his equal since the days of George Dixon and Joe Gans. Even the great Benny Leonard couldn't hit like Robinson, the old-timers admitted.'[388]

'The placards outside Madison Square Garden for Ray's fight with Denny Moyer described Robinson as "The All-Time Great Champion of Champions." Defending the claim, the Garden's boxing director Harry Markson told *New York Post* columnist Milton Gross, "During the height of his career, Sugar Ray didn't lack a single attribute which the great fighters need. He had a left hook, a right cross, defensive skill, the will to win, ring generalship, speed of hand and foot, courage, a sense of pacing, a variety of punches, the ability to size up an opponent after a round or two, split-second reflexes, magnificent legs, and the ability to reach superior heights when the situation required it."

'Garden matchmaker Teddy Brenner added, "People are inclined to overlook that along with his great skill, Sugar Ray was the greatest one-punch hitter we've ever had. Was there ever a tougher fellow than Gene Fullmer? I don't think so. Ray got him out of there with one left hook, and that was a guy who'd seldom been off his feet before, let alone knocked out. Steve Belloise took a good punch, Sugar Costner looked like a coming champ, if you think Bobo Olson wasn't a good fighter, look at his record when he was young. Well, Ray took them all out with just one shot. Many a guy was around at the finish of a fight with Robinson just because Ray felt like sharpening up his boxing that particular evening."'[389]

'He's the best fighter of his generation,' said Arthur Daley in the *New York Times* on 19 December 1952 when Ray retired in December 1952 after the Maxim fight. 'Beyond question, the

---

388 Lee Greene *True Boxing Yearbook 1965*

389 Ted Carroll *The Ring* magazine March 1962

best all-around fighter these eyes have ever seen. As a boxing artist, Sugar Ray was unmatched in this pugilistic generation. Some 20 or 30 years from now, he will be mentioned in the same awed tones that old-timers reserve for Stanley Ketchel, Joe Gans, Benny Leonard, Terry McGovern, George Dixon and a few other titans of the past.'

'Believe it or not,' wrote *Boxing News* editor Claude Abrams in a 2005 special, 'but when Sugar Ray Robinson was still competing, the magnificent American wasn't even hailed as the greatest ever welterweight or middleweight, never mind the finest fighter the sport has ever known. But it wasn't long after Robinson finally called time on a remarkable career before boxing folk recognised the super-smooth former two-weight world champ as being in a class of his own. That reputation has gathered momentum and now, 40 years on since his final fight, it's pretty unanimous that Robinson is the most complete fighter ever to set foot in a ring. One can only marvel at his achievements: how he kept coming back to win the world middleweight title; had the audacity to challenge for – and nearly win – the light-heavyweight crown when he was effectively only a light-middle, took on the hardest men around during an era of painful bruisers and seriously classy operators; continued to box at a respectably high level to the end, losing in his final bout to the world's top contender.'

Sugar Ray Robinson was ring royalty, and if you thought that a little over the top, read on … 'One evening in 1969, Ray had a surprise for his wife. They were going to London. He had been personally invited to attend a birthday party [her 43rd] for Queen Elizabeth II. Millie was beside herself – London, Buckingham Palace! As they flew away from America, the cities were still on fire, the protests on college campuses raging about America's war in Vietnam, and there was much talk in London about the unrest on American streets and campuses.

'Prince Philip, the queen's husband, pulled Robinson aside and wanted to talk to him about the turmoil in America. Then Prince Philip suggested to Robinson that he get engaged. "Sugar," he said, "I believe you could help that." He told Robinson that youngsters looked up to him, that his popularity would make him a role model. Back at their hotel, Sugar Ray couldn't stop talking to Millie about the conversation he'd had with the prince, even if he couldn't quite figure exactly what he was going to do about it.'[390]

What he did about it was get together with a friend of Millie's who owned the house she had been living in, Wright Fillmore, and talked Mr Fillmore into working with him to start a youth foundation. 'One day, I got a telegram from London that he wanted to see me,' Fillmore told writer Bill Heinz, who was in California to interview Ray for a book. 'I wondered, with all the people he knew, why he wanted to see me. I waited and he and his wife flew in and, it being hot, we sat in the backyard. I asked him what was so important, and he said he'd always wanted to do something for youth. I said, "What do you want me to do about it, Ray? With all the people you know, you want me to put something together for children? I'm retired." He said, "No. You have just started working." I told him, "We need money and we need children. If you can get the money, I can get the children."'

Fillmore, a slim, immaculate man, bald and wearing dark glasses, told Heinz that he had worked for the Southern Pacific Railroad for 40 years as a waiter and then as an instructor, and he had been retired for seven years when Robinson and he started the foundation in 1969. 'The Southern Pacific,' he said, 'had given me a three-year course in human relations, and what we try to do here is make good citizens, not only a Sugar Ray Robinson or a Sandy Koufax.'

Before he left, Heinz said to Robinson, '"So how do you get along now?" "I've got friends," Ray said. "I borrow five grand and I pay back three. I borrow three and pay two. Then something drops in, and I pay everybody. People say to me about this foundation, 'What are you gettin'?' They can't understand doing something

390 Wil Haygood *Sweet Thunder: The Life and Times of Sugar Ray Robinson* 2009

for kids. I've always been a Christian believer in God. I was gifted with a talent that helped introduce me to people, and all that was in preparation for what I'm doin' now."'[391]

'Sugar Ray may have been apolitical, but the presidential candidacy of Robert F. Kennedy excited him. Kennedy invited him to Hickory Hill, his estate in McLean, Virginia, where they talked about the problems of urban America. Robinson would have liked Kennedy's independent streak – he had stood up to labour racketeers as US attorney general, and now he was connecting with blacks in an unusual soulful manner. But then came the assassination, and that took the breath out of so many.'[392]

'Sugar was eventually diagnosed with a number of crippling ailments, including diabetes, hypertension, arteriosclerosis and Alzheimer's disease. Each illness had its own way of ravaging his once-glorious body, robbing him of his strength, curtailing his prodigious appetite for life, even removing the memory of his greatest triumphs before thousands of cheering fans. There is no way to determine the degree to which Sugar was aware of his steady physical decline, how he dealt with the irony of his name and the debilitating diabetes, and the arteriosclerosis, which hardened vessels that used to supply the blood flowing to his magnificent legs, destroying their once-enviable elasticity. And he may have been spared any full realisation of the Alzheimer's, given its slow but steady erosion of one's faculties. Between his last appearance at Madison Square Garden in 1981 and the time he was saluted in 1988, Sugar and Millie settled into a quiet life in Los Angeles, with occasional trips to Las Vegas to attend a big fight at Caesars Palace. He also spent some time at his Foundation, mainly to meet and greet celebrities and potential donors. During these appearances, he was rarely ever to do more than wave to well-wishers, given the degenerative impact of Alzheimer's.

391 W. C. Heinz *Once They Heard the Cheers* 1979

392 Wil Haygood *Sweet Thunder: The Life and Times of Sugar Ray Robinson* 2009

'The last few months of his life found him in seclusion, save for the presence of family and close friends. When he was in public, he was impeccably dressed and always managed to summon that famous smile. Towards the final days of his life, Sugar's battle against several ailments, including diabetes and hypertension, escalated. It was as if for every lethal punch he'd delivered, he was getting back two in return. That matchless stamina of his was finally down to the last breath.'[393]

'Sugar Ray spent much of January through April in bed, a sick man. Then Millie noticed something; it had begun in April. He would fold his arms across his chest and his fists would be balled. Every night, those charcoal-coloured fists laid across his chest. She couldn't bear to open them. On the morning of 12 April, she heard some laboured breathing. She checked on him, then found herself trying to revive him. Unable to, she rushed for the phone. He was taken to the Brotman Medical Centre in Culver City. But there was nothing they could do, and 15 minutes after his arrival, the great prizefighter died. It was 10.09 in the morning. The final autopsy would show he died of heart failure. He was 67 years old.'[394]

Wednesday, 12 April 1989 – Sugar Ray Robinson died today. The man in the white coat said heart failure. Factor in Alzheimer's disease, hypertension, arteriosclerosis. You should also add in 25 years as a professional fighter, 200 fights with the best of three weight divisions. Never knocked out, but knocked down several times by men who could take your head off if they caught you right. Like the man said, go out in the rain and you will get wet! Sugar Ray didn't always wear his raincoat.

Shirley Povich, columnist for the *Washington Post*, wrote, 'There was a sadness in the news that came out of that hospital room in Los Angeles on Wednesday. They said Sugar Ray Robinson had died. He was 67 years old, beset by many illnesses.

---

393 Herb Boyd with Ray Robinson II *Pound for Pound* 2005

394 Wil Haygood *Sweet Thunder: The Life and Times of Sugar Ray Robinson* 2009

But for those with the memories, there still is a temptation to muse that had they laced a pair of boxing gloves to his fists, Sugar Ray would not have lost that last decision. It is fair to say that until he came on the scene as a street kid in 1940, winning his first pro fight with a two-round technical knockout, the likes of Sugar Ray Robinson had never been known to boxing in its two centuries of history. He still defied comparisons to the day of his death.'[395]

Dave Anderson, Pulitzer-prize-winning sportswriter for the *New York Times*, who would write Robinson's autobiography with him, recalled Sugar saying, '"I was a gladiator, and like a true gladiator, I never lost. Something just happened to keep me from winning." Not often.'[396]

'Sugar Ray was representative of the innocent 1950s, the Eisenhower 1950s, the '57 Chevy '50s,' wrote columnist Mike Imrem. 'Beginning when I was maybe five years old in 1950, I would carry on a conversation every Friday evening with the man who mopped the floor in my father's Logan Square grocery store. He was a proud black man proud of black athletes, but baseball and football players weren't his favourites, not even Jackie Robinson for breaking baseball's colour barrier. My friend appreciated boxers the most. He enjoyed Archie Moore and Jersey Joe Walcott and Ezzard Charles – but absolutely idolised Sugar Ray Robinson. In fact, as young as I was, I still remember the man with the mop as the first to call Sugar Ray "pound for pound the best fighter ever." Jackie eventually would be the Robinson with the biggest social impact. I guess his accomplishments were a beacon for blacks as the civil rights struggle intensified. Even compared to Jackie, Sugar Ray was a hero among heroes.'[397]

'He was one of the finest human beings who ever lived, even a better person than a prizefighter,' said Sid Lockitch, Robinson's business manager for 19 years. 'He was charitable, he cared very

---

395 Shirley Povich *Washington Post* 13 April 1989

396 Dave Anderson *New York Times* 13 April 1989

397 Mike Imrem *Daily Herald Suburban Chicago* 20 April 1989

deeply for children. That's why he started the youth foundation 20 years ago.[398] It was a way to help the children, keep them off the streets.' Lockitch was referring to the Sugar Ray Youth Foundation in Los Angeles.'

Pete Hamill would write in the *New York Post,* 'So last April, all over New York, people talked about Robinson. He was for a while, in the '40s and '50s, the ultimate New Yorker. Two generations tried to walk like him. Everybody envied his style, toughness and grace. Gangsters wanted his autograph. Shoe-shine boys stared at his clothes and came away with $100 bills. Women dissolved. For a lot of us, he was the first man to show us what beauty was, transforming his violent trade into something that resembled art. Now he's gone. And hearing the news that April day, people stopped all over New York, in barber shops and taxi cabs, in prisons and schools, men with gray in their hair and women who once saw him walk out of Frank's, and they remembered. They did the same in London and Mexico City, in Chicago and Miami, in Bogota and Buenos Aires and in all those bad places where men stay up late and drink too much and sing the old songs. They remember Sugar Ray Robinson. Champion of the world.'

---

398 *Logansport Pharos Tribune* Indiana 13 April 1959

EPILOGUE

THE FUNERAL took place at the West Angeles Church of God and Christ in Los Angeles. The limos were parked deep: among the 2,000 in attendance were former Governor Edmund G. Brown, Motown founder Berry Gordy, singer Lou Rawls and actresses Elizabeth Taylor and Barbara McNair. The sun was shining. The former fight champions Bobo Olson, Archie Moore and Ken Norton were easily recognised. Inside the ornate church, flowers covered the sides of the beige coffin. Children from Robinson's youth foundation wept some more. Elizabeth Taylor walked down the aisle holding Millie's hand. 'Elizabeth loved Ray,' said Mel Dick. Mel tried to find Edna Mae: he knew she was there somewhere. Then someone told him she was indeed there, sitting toward the back. She was wearing a blonde wig, trying to disguise herself.

'In the months and years to come – she died in 1995 – an elegant lady was often spotted crossing the grounds of the Evergreen Cemetery. It was Millie Robinson, flowers in hand, going to meet her prizefighter.'[399]

Robinson's father Walker Smith died in 1969, his mother Leila died in 1987, George Gainford died in 1981 and Edna Mae, suffering from Alzheimer's disease, died in 2002, still in love with Sugar Ray. 'To see him reduced to that state because of his illness, I would have felt very, very badly for him, because that was not

---

399 Wil Haygood *Sweet Thunder: The Life and Times of Sugar Ray Robinson* 2009

the Sugar I knew. I don't know who the person was who entered that magnificent body and cloaked over his mind with whatever it was that that sickness does. But I know God was good to Ray to take him out of that darkness.'[400]

---

400 *Ebony* magazine December 1989

BIBLIOGRAPHY

Anderson, Dave *Ringmasters* (London; Robson Books 1991)

Batchelor, Denzil Ed. *The Boxing Companion* (London; Eyre & Spottiswoode 1964)

Boyd, Herb with Ray Robinson II *Pound for Pound* (New York; Harper Collins 2005)

Dalby, W. Barrington *Come in Barry* (London; Cassell 1961)

Fried, Ronald K. *Corner Men* (New York; Four Walls Eight Windows 1991)

Haygood, Wil *Sweet Thunder: The Life and Times of Sugar Ray Robinson* (New York; Alfred A. Knopf 2009)

Heinz, W. C. *The Top of his Game* Ed. Bill Littlefield (New York; Literary Classics of US Inc. 2015)

Heller, Peter *In This Corner* (London; Robson Books 1975)

Jarrett, John *Dynamite Gloves* (London; Robson Books 2001)

LaMotta with Jake Joseph Carter & Peter Savage *Raging Bull* (New York; Da Capo Press 1997)

Myler, Thomas *Sugar Ray Robinson* (Dublin: Relym Publications 1996)

New York Times *The Complete Book of Boxing* (New York; Arno Press Inc. 1980)

Odd, Gilbert *Debatable Decisions* (London; Nicholson & Watson 1953)

Roberts, J. B. & Skutt, A. G. *The Boxing Register* (Ithaca, NY; McBooks Press 2011)

Robinson, Ray with Dave Anderson *Sugar Ray* (London; Putnam & Co. 1969)

Schoor, Gene *Sugar Ray Robinson* (New York; Greenberg 1951)

Shropshire, Kenneth, *Being Sugar Ray* (New York; Basic Civitas 2007)

Smith Red *The Very Best of* Ed. Daniel Okrent (New York; Literary Classics of US Inc. 2013)

Sugar, Bert Randolph *Boxing's Greatest Fighters* (Guilford, Conn.; The Lyons Press 2006)
Youmans, Gary B. *The Onion Picker* (New York; Syracuse University Press 2007)

Magazines

Boxing Illustrated
Boxing News
Boxing & Wrestling
Ring
Sports Illustrated
Time
True Boxing Yearbook

Websites

BoxRec.com
Espn.com
Newspaperarchives.com
Wikipedia

Newspapers

Albert Lea Evening Tribune
Amarillo Daily News
Aniston Star
Arizona Independent Republic
Billings Gazette
Biloxi Daily Herald
Bismark Tribune
Bluefield Daily Telegraph
Burlington Times
Charleroi Mail
Charleston Gazette
Chester Times
Coshocton Tribune
Daily Globe
Daily News Standard
El Paso Herald Post
Elyria Chronicle Telegram
Evening Independent
Findlay Morning Republican

Galveston Daily News
Hammond Times
Hayward Daily Review
Indiana Evening Gazette
Jefferson City Post Tribune
Joplin Globe
Kingston Daily Freeman
Lima News
Lincoln Nebraska State Journal
Lincoln Star
Loch Haven Express
Lowell Sun
Lubbock Morning Avalanche
Madison Wisconsin State Journal
Manitowoc Herald Times
Mansfield News Journal
Monessen Daily Independent
Montana Standard
Moorhead Daily News
Nevada State Journal
New Castle News
New York Times
Oakland Tribune
Ogden Standard Examiner
Piqua Daily Call
Reno Evening Gazette
Salt Lake Tribune
Sandusky Star Journal
San Antonio Express
San Mateo Times
Sheboygan Press
Steubenville Herald Star
Syracuse Herald
Syracuse Post Standard
Titusville Herald
Twin Falls Daily News
Tyrone Daily Herald
United Feature Syndicate Inc.
Winnipeg Free Press
Wichita Daily Times

INDEX

INDEX

INDEX